Catherine of Siena
A Sacred Covenant
of Caring for the Sick

Mary Elizabeth O'Brien, OP
Foreword by
Bro. Ignatius Perkins, OP

NEW PRIORY PRESS
EXPLORING THE DOMINICAN VISION

Cover photo: Domenico di Bartolo, *The Care and Healing of the Sick*,
1440-1441
Back cover: Fr. Lawrence Lew, O.P., *Fr. Bruno Cadore, O.P.*
Production Editor: Terry L. Jarbe

ISBN-13: 978-1-62311-042-0

Prologue

Saint Catherine of Siena has long been admired as a prophetic witness in mediating the ecclesiastical and political conflicts of her day. This book is not, however, a chronicle of Catherine's intellectual prowess. It is not a memoir designed to applaud the wisdom of a distinguished Doctor of the Church and advisor to popes and prelates. It is, rather, a love story; a story written to honor the memory of a selfless young Sister of Penance of St. Dominic who blessed the sick and the poor with her caring and her tenderness. It is the story of a courageous Dominican tertiary who ministered to the marginalized and the outcasts with a spirit of joy and of gentleness. It is the story of a gifted Mantellata nurse for whom no task of caregiving was distasteful or burdensome.

No man, woman or child was considered too unimportant, too wounded or too broken for Catherine's understanding and her compassion. The secret was that she saw in each neighbor the personification of Christ, her Beloved Spouse. Dominican Thomas Schwertner, writing in 1916, observed: "Because Catherine loved God...she would see His beauty reflected as fully and unbrokenly as possible in the mirror of every human soul"; the saint, he added: "lived to love."[1]

This book is written in an attempt to portray, in some small measure, the life of Saint Catherine of Siena, as a life "lived to love."

Preface

In an April 2003 article in *Theology Today*, Catherinian scholar
Suzanne Noffke OP posed a rhetorical question by entitling an article:
"Catherine of Siena: Justly, Doctor of the Church?" Noffke's purpose was
to present a well-researched and considered response. The professional
community of those who minister to the ill and the infirm might pose a
different yet related query: "Catherine of Siena: Justly, Patroness of
Those Who Care for the Sick?" The question derives from the fact that,
with the exception of the *Legenda* written by her confessor Blessed
Raymond of Capua, most studies of Catherine pay only minimal attention
to her ministry to the ailing. The majority of nursing histories published
in the early to mid-20th Century, however, discuss and explain
Catherine's caregiving activities as providing an exemplar for the
spiritual dimension of the profession. She is frequently identified by
nurse historians as the patroness of all who minister to the ill.

This book responds to the question of whether we can truly consider
Saint Catherine of Siena as "Patroness" of those who care for the sick. To
do so, I have collected data from a broad range of writings reflecting
Catherine's "lived experience" of healthcare ministry in the later middle-
ages. A secondary purpose is to show what the saint's spirituality can
teach today's caregivers. The study has relied on sources such as
Catherine's *Dialogue*, *Letters* and *Prayers*, the *Leggenda Maggiore* or
Legenda Major of Blessed Raymond of Capua, the *Leggenda Minore* and
the *Supplemento Alla Vita di Santa Caterina da Siena* by Fra. Tommaso
d'Antonio Caffarini, *The Miracoli of Catherine of Siena,* and twenty-seven
other biographies or hagiographies of Catherine.

Hagiography is generally understood as a literary genre that includes
writings descriptive of the life of a saint or holy person that focus
primarily on the individual's virtues or positive characteristics. The
purpose is to inspire. Hagiographers are, consequently, sometimes
criticized for ignoring or at least downplaying the faults or negative
attributes of the person whose life they portray.

Many early works on the life of Saint Catherine of Siena, notably the
Legenda of Blessed Raymond of Capua, are rightly considered to be
hagiographies. Such reverential biographical writings about religious
figures were the norm of the day in the late middle-ages and for some

centuries after that. Hagiographical material can provide valuable insights provided that we keep before us a clear understanding of the purpose, style and spirit with which it was written.

A number of excellent books explore the life and spirituality of Saint Catherine of Siena. The present work, uniquely, focuses on her ministry to the sick. Individual anecdotes describing Catherine's care of the ailing, as well as the saint's abiding compassion for all who were ill or infirm, can be found in the literature; they are, however, sometimes buried amidst a work's theological, mystical or spiritual discussions. The ultimate goal of this book is to identify, explore and analyze Catherine's caregiving activities guided by a contemporary theoretical framework, that of "A Sacred Covenant of Caring for the Sick." The work, I trust, will be of interest to a variety of persons who minister to the ill such as nurses, physicians, chaplains, therapists, social workers and pastoral care team members serving in parishes.

Chapter One explores Saint Catherine's world in 14th century Siena as the setting for her ministry; the saint's early spirituality, containing within it the seeds of her vocation to care for the poor and the sick, is also discussed. In Chapter Two, Catherine's vocation to the Dominican community of Sisters of Penance of St. Dominic (the "Mantellate") is examined, including her time of contemplative solitude and ultimate call to active ministry to the sick poor. Chapter Three identifies aspects of Catherine's personal spirituality that acted as catalysts for service to those in need. The following chapter explains briefly the methodology employed in this study of Catherine's ministry to the sick, including conceptual orientation and data sources; in the chapter key passages from Saint Catherine's *Dialogue, Letters* and *Prayers* are presented to demonstrate their relevance for twenty-first century caregivers. Chapters Five, Six, and Seven contain examples of Catherine's care of the sick as models for today's ministers to the ill. Chapter Five explores the healthcare environment of the later middle ages within which Catherine functioned, focusing on key illness and disease conditions including the *bubonic plague, leprosy* and *traumatic injuries,* the last related to the violent feuds of the era. Also identified are examples of Catherine's ministry in three key Siena hospitals: *Santa Maria della Scala, Casa della Misericordia* and *San Lazzaro.* In Chapter Six, Saint Catherine's multidimensional ministries to the sick are examined, that is, her ministries of hospital care, home healthcare, public health or Community healthcare (the plague epidemic; prison ministry) and spiritual care. The final discussion, presented in Chapter Seven, explains how Saint Catherine of Siena's 14th century ministry to the ill and infirm may be analyzed and understood in light of a 21st-century model of care for the sick.

This book reveals the breadth and the beauty of Catherine's many instances of tender and compassionate care for the sick. She served her ill neighbors in the hospital, in their homes, in the prisons and in the community. Catherine practiced holistic healthcare, including the assessment of spiritual needs and the provision of spiritual care, whenever appropriate. This work will, I hope, persuade the reader that Saint Catherine of Siena has indeed earned and truly deserves to be justly considered the "Patroness" of all who care for the sick.

Acknowledgements

Finding the words to thank all of the individuals involved in creating a book such as this is an intimidating task. Nevertheless, I must try, as it surely "took a village" to complete a study of Saint Catherine of Siena's sacred covenant of caring for the sick. First, I am immensely grateful to Father Gabriel O'Donnell OP, of the Pontifical Faculty of the Immaculate Conception, Dominican House of Studies, Washington, DC. His mentorship led me to a deeper understanding of and love for the teachings of Saint Dominic and the Dominican spirituality which guided the ministry of Saint Catherine. Next, I must thank Brother Ignatius Perkins OP, recipient of the "St. Catherine of Siena Chair in Catholic Health Care Ethics" at the Pontifical Faculty of the Immaculate Conception and "Director, Office of Health Services" for the Dominican Province of St. Joseph, who trusted my attempt to convey, in writing, an account of Saint Catherine's Dominican ministry to the sick. From the beginning of the research undergirding the work, I was blessed by the ongoing caring and support of Brother Gerard Thayer OP, Director of Facilities, Dominican House of Studies, who was unfailingly present to listen and to advise as new questions and concepts emerged.

There are a number of other mentors who assisted in a variety of ways as the story of Saint Catherine's passionate care for the ill and infirm began to take shape. Father Benedict Croell OP, Vocation Director for the Dominican Province of St. Joseph, introduced me to several contemporary sources of material on Saint Catherine's spirituality; Father Andrew Hofer OP, Master of Students at the Dominican House of Studies offered advice and prayerful support; Sister Mary Michael Fox OP shared her understanding of Saint Catherine's religious vocation; Sister Anna Grace Neenan OP reviewed meditations written to describe Catherine's spiritual philosophy of caring; and Sister Anna Wray OP and Sister John Mary Fleming OP supported the work with their concern and their prayers.

I am deeply grateful, as well, to dear friends and colleagues who gave of their precious time to review a first draft of the book manuscript: Father Mario Calabrese OP, Parochial Vicar, St. Thomas Aquinas Parish, Charlottesville, Va., Brother Ignatius Perkins OP, PhD, RN, FAAN, FNYAM, FRSM, ANEF, Brother Gerard Thayer OP, Dr. Patricia McMullen PhD, RN, J.D, CRNP, FAANP, FAAN, Dean of The Catholic University of America

ix

School of Nursing, Dr. Sue Idczak PhD, RN, CNE, Director of the Nursing Program, Siena Heights University, Adrian, MI. and Ms. Martha McNeill, MSW, MA. Special thanks go to Deacon Camillo Pasquariello for generous assistance with translation of Italian texts cited in the work.

Prayerful gratitude goes also to Joan Butler, OP, President, and the members of my Lay Dominican Chapter of "St. Catherine of Siena/Our Lady of Lourdes," who have supported me with their caring and their prayers.

I am especially appreciative of the dedication of Terry L. Jarbe, production editor at New Priory Press, who enthusiastically embraced the concept of St. Catherine's ministry to the sick and gently shepherded the manuscript to publication.

I have been gifted by the witness and prayers of the Dominican Priests and Brothers of the Priory of the Immaculate Conception and the Dominican Sisters of St. Cecilia who continually inspire me by their loving commitment to follow the spiritual path set forth by our Holy Father Dominic. Ultimately, my deepest gratitude is to God the Father, the source of my strength and the center of my life, to His Divine Son, Our Lord Jesus Christ, whose love nourishes my soul and to the Holy Spirit of wisdom and understanding without whose guidance the following pages would never have seen the light of day. To God be the glory!

Foreword

DOMINICAN FRIARS
HEALTH CARE MINISTRY OF NEW YORK

Seldom, in writings about the lives of the Saints, do we encounter such a carefully executed research study as that found in Sister Mary Elizabeth O'Brien's *Catherine of Siena: A Sacred Covenant of Caring for the Sick*. Employing a hermeneutic phenomenological approach, O'Brien traces the life and the healing ministry of Catherine of Siena, a 14th Century Dominican saint, mystic, nurse, scholar, and Doctor of the Church. What O'Brien has uncovered in her extensive research is a premier role model for bringing caring, healing and hope to people in every nation, especially the lost, the last, and the least, all masterpieces of God's creative design. Catherine of Siena's caregiving model provides a rich theological encounter with Jesus, the Healer, that is deeply imbedded in a covenantal relationship between the person who seeks care and relief of suffering and the person who promises to care and to heal.

On many occasions, and recently during his pastoral visit to the United States, our Holy Father, Pope Francis, has challenged us to embrace the *New Evangelization* and take the Face of Jesus to the peripheries of human existence. With his call to embrace the theology of accompaniment in healthcare, we are challenged to go well beyond just caring for the well and the sick by implementing strategies to prevent illness and disability. With a sense of urgency we are called to bring caring, healing and hope to our brothers and sisters who are forced to live on the fracture lines of human life; to those who remain in the shadows of our cities in deafening anonymity; and to the millions who are forced to live in morally flawed systems of oppression and suffering that dehumanize them. This seminal study, *Catherine of Siena: A sacred*

xi

covenant of Caring for the Sick, brings to the healing ministry of the Church a model for human caring, designed in the 14th Century, that calls us to accompany our suffering brothers and sisters on their journeys in seeking the healing Face of Jesus; to help them move to new and different places into the very center of the human family where dignity, freedom and human flourishing will be protected and affirmed; where the unwanted, the abandoned and the unloved will be touched through the care and compassion of others; and where caring, healing and hope are enjoyed by all persons in every nation.

It is indeed fitting on the occasion of the Eight Hundredth Anniversary of the foundation of the Order of Preachers that *Catherine of Siena: A sacred covenant of Caring for the Sick* is being published by the New Priory Press. We are captivated by the enduring and evolving themes that spoke to the urgency of caring for the sick, the unloved and the unwanted of the 14th Century, and the striking similarities of these same themes in our families, communities and societies today. As a Dominican, Catherine defended and protected human dignity and freedom, and promoted flourishing across the spectrum of human life. Her model of caring and healing, as articulated in this work, represents a spirituality that is urgently needed today as we bring the healing ministry of Christ to the peripheries of human life; to care for the unwanted, the unloved and those who are hopeless. May the application of Saint Catherine of Siena's theology of caring help transform our world and promote hope and healing for all people.

Bro. Ignatius Perkins, OP
Executive Director
Dominican Friars Health Care Ministry of New York
1 October 2015

Contents

Chapter 1. "A Heart Drawn by Love"

Chapter 2. "On Two Wings You Must Fly"

Chapter 3. "Lose Yourself on the Cross"

Chapter 4. "Ablaze with Loving Fire"

La Scala

It is dusk as the night sky gently blankets
        The Tuscan countryside;
Lighted windows welcome weary travelers
        Returning from their labors.
But Catherine stands at the doorstep,
        Poised to depart for her
                Ministry to the sick.
She is Dominican garbed in tunic and mantle;
        The symbol of her call
                To care and to serve.

Tonight the young Mantellata will leave
        The sanctuary of her cell
                To be present to the poor;
She will serve with joyful heart, comforted
        And consoled by the love
                of her Spouse;
For it was He who called Catherine forth
        From the solitude she treasured;
And for Him she will risk
        to love and to honor
                the suffering neighbor.

Catherine peers down the cobblestone streets;
        To glimpse, in the distance,
                The great hospital they
                        call La Scala;
She takes no food or money for the trip;
        Only a small Lantern to light her way
                As darkness envelops
                        The sleeping city.

Catherine will traverse the quiet wards in
        The night,
                Comforting and caring.
While others rest, the Mantellata Sister will

Tenderly embrace the pain of the
Lonely.

Catherine does not know what anguish she will
Find on meeting the sick;
But the Sister of Penance is not afraid; she is
Following the call of her Beloved
Bridegroom.
For this is His ministry and not hers;
It is with His tenderness that she must touch
and not hers;
And it is with His Blessed words and not hers
That she must console.

In her care for the least of His brothers and
sisters, the Lord Has blessed His Catherine
with a treasured gift:
The gift of nursing the ill and the infirm,
The gift of comforting the sad and
the sorrowing,
And,
in caring for them,
The precious gift of ministering to Him,
to whom alone,
the Virgin's heart belongs.

Chapter 1. "A Heart Drawn by Love"
Catherine's Promise

"The human heart is always drawn by love"
Catherine of Siena: Dialogue 26

The Promise
A child, young Catherine was,
this Bride of Christ
with heart drawn
by love.

She promised faithfulness,
her trust became
the fulfillment.

She vowed a lifetime,
her commitment became
the journey.

She desired to serve,
her hope became
the calling.

She chose to care,
her ministry became
the gift.

Catherine of Siena, 14th-century Dominican saint, mystic, scholar, and Doctor of the Church, remains to this day also the "patroness" of nurses and of all who minister to the ill and the infirm. Yet, many biographies of Catherine have paid only minimal attention to the periods of her life committed to caring for the sick. Catherinian scholars have addressed the beauty of the saint's mystical spirituality, especially her years of solitary contemplation and prayerful interaction with the Lord.[2] As pointed out by early biographer, Augusta Theodosia Drane, however, Catherine ultimately heard and responded to Christ's mandate calling her forth from contemplative prayer to the service of her neighbor. Drane poignantly observed that Catherine "in abandoning her solitude... had feared at first to lose that continual presence of her Beloved which was dearer to her than life itself. But He is pleased to abide in other sanctuaries than the solitary cell, and Catherine learnt to seek Him and find Him in His two chosen dwelling places-the Sacrament of His love and the person of the poor."[3] Augusta Drane cited Catherine's own words as written in her famous *Dialogue*: "God himself is beyond our reach, therefore the services we cannot render directly to Him, He wills we should render to our neighbor."[4]

Catherine, Drane asserted, "beheld in each poor sufferer to whom she ministered nothing less than the person of the Lord. She sought Him in the streets and the broadways of her native city, and found Him in the hospitals of the lepers, and wherever sickness had assumed its most terrible and repulsive forms."[5] Augusta Drane's perception is supported by that of another distinguished biographer, Edmund Gardner, who remarked: "Whenever men and women in Siena were suffering or in need, Catherine was always there. The sick were healed, the dying comforted when she stood by them; hardened sinners were moved to repentance at her bidding, and heard sweet assurance from her lips 'Fear not, I have taken your sins upon myself.'"[6]

The following pages represent an attempt to construct a window into Catherine's world during those periods when the saint's love of God and love of neighbor were importantly lived out in her Dominican vocation of ministry to the sick. As a model for contemporary caregivers to those suffering from physical, psychological or spiritual challenges, Saint Catherine's selfless and sacred covenant of caring provides inspiration, guidance and support.[7]

Catherine's World: The Church, Politics, and Family Life in 14th-Century Siena

We cannot begin to explore Catherine's ministry to the sick without some understanding of the world in which the saint practiced her caregiving; the world of Tuscan, Italy in the later middle ages. As with today's nurses and others who care for the ill, Catherine's life and worldview were influenced by the philosophies embraced by her family, her church and local as well as national politics. Catherine Benincasa entered the world in 1347, a time of confusion and turbulence for the

Church and for Italy's political environment. Although the country had suffered from such devastating trials as war, famine and the plague, commonly known as the "Black Death," Catherine's family members were relatively secure in their understanding of the spiritual and practical dimensions of their lives.

The Family

Let us travel back in time to the mid-14th Century, to the family home of Giacomo and Mona Lapa Benincasa, located on the Via dei Tintori, in the Fontebranda ward of the city."[8] Siena is divided into geographical districts labeled *contrade.* Catherine's neighborhood was the Contrada dell'oca.[9] In Saint Catherine's era, Siena was one of the most unruly cities in Italy, filled with discord and discontent, yet it was, paradoxically, also the home of many holy people, thus being accorded the title "Vestibule of Paradise."[10] One cannot help but ponder how the young Catherine's developing spirituality must have been influenced by the location of the Benincasa household. The house was situated in the Fontebranda Valley dominated on one side by the great Siena Cathedral, or Duomo, and on the other by the Dominican Church of San Domenico. We are told that Catherine's home was continually "overshadowed by the two churches whose bells competed noisily as they reverberated across the valley."[11] Thus, from early childhood, the saint's life was impacted by a "sense of the dominating religious presence in her city."[12]

While there were elegant homes in Siena, owned by nobles and wealthy merchants, as well as modest middle-class dwellings, there were also underdeveloped sections of the city where disadvantaged citizens lived in poverty and squalor. The story of Catherine's care of the ill and infirm will lead us to follow the saint, clad in the Dominican habit of a Sister of Penance, as she trod "the narrow streets, choked as they were in the days of the plague with the dead and dying, entering churches… prisons, and pesthouses."[13] We will also accompany Catherine in her ministry to the sick in local hospitals, especially those of the great charitable institution *Santa Maria della Scala*, the more modest facility *Casa della Miseracordia*, and *San Lazzaro*, the leper house located outside the city walls.

Catherine's father, Giacomo, a prosperous dyer of wool, was a devout and gentle man who maintained an atmosphere of respect and peace in his large household. Although the Benincasa family was financially

3

comfortable, they belonged to the working class, the *populo minuto*, of Siena. It was reported of Giacomo that even when he encountered challenges and disagreements he would never respond with anger or coarse remarks.[14] Two things were particularly repugnant to Giacomo: slander and immodest language. Catherine's mother, Mona Lapa, did not have her husband's patience, and one day, when she had spoken critically of one of Giacomo's enemies, her husband replied: "Let the man be and you will be better off. God will show him his error and He will defend us."[15]

Mona Lapa Benincasa, nevertheless, was described as "industrious," "prudent" and capable in handling her domestic responsibilities[16] as well as being possessed of "common sense" and a "modest piety."[17] She was considered to be a good Christian woman, but she practiced religion according to her own vision of propriety. Lapa trusted that raising her children in a devout family was the appropriate response to her vocation of motherhood. She did not believe that anything more would be asked of her by God.[18]

Catherine was the 24th of 25 children of Giacomo and Mona Lapa; her twin, Giovanna, died shortly after birth. Thus, the mother cherished her surviving daughter and lavished love and tenderness on the infant. Despite this maternal care, unfortunately Lapa would never truly understand the religious call and mystical devotion of her sainted daughter.[19] Although, she came to accept Catherine's Dominican vocation in time, Mona Lapa was frequently at odds with her daughter's ministries to the poor and marginalized, especially to those ill with contagious and potentially life threatening diseases such as leprosy and the plague.

Catherine was a happy child, reflected in her being assigned a pet name "Euphrosyne" (Greek for "joy"); she was also a prayerful youngster, having learned the "Hail Mary" at the age of five, a prayer which she repeated frequently during the day.[20] It was around this time that other children in the neighborhood began to gather around Catherine and imitate her devotional practices. The young ones did this secretly to avoid their parent's detection while they performed their small penances and prayed the *Pater* and *Ave* in the manner of their small leader.[21]

In an anecdote describing her burgeoning spirituality, we are told that the young Catherine, possessed by the desire to live as a solitary in the desert, set off to find a hermitage, taking with her only some bread and

4

water for the journey. One of her married sisters lived near the gates of Siena, so Catherine knew how to exit the city in search of a desert refuge. She came upon an abandoned cave not far from Siena and believed that she had arrived at the hoped for sanctuary. After several hours alone, however, as darkness descended on the city, Catherine became frightened and began to consider her parents' worry when they discovered her missing. She returned home not telling anyone of her pilgrimage.[22]

Catherine learned of the ministry of the Dominican Friars through accompanying her family to worship at the vast Gothic Church of San Domenico. In a childlike desire to become a Dominican, Catherine envisioned herself as imitating Saint Euphrosyne who disguised herself as a man in order to enter a monastery. Euphrosyne's wealthy parents sought marriage and position for their child; the young woman had, however, committed her life to Christ and viewed admission to a male monastery as the only option. In witness to her own calling, each morning Catherine travelled the cobblestone streets of Siena from the Benincasa home to the hill of Camporeggio and the Church of San Domenico where she observed the Dominican Community at prayer. So enamored was Catherine of the Dominicans that she is said to have kissed the footsteps of the Friars as they passed along the road.

The Church

A number of problems related to the Church and to both local and national politics were closely intermingled throughout Catherine's lifetime. At the time of her birth, the Papal residence had, for over half a century, been established in Avignon rather than Rome. Thus, the Church was, to a degree, under the control of the King of France. One of Catherine's later missions was to encourage Pope Gregory XI to leave France and return to his rightful place in Rome; this he did in January of 1377.[23] Ten days after Gregory's untimely death, in March of 1378, an Italian Pope, Urban VI, was elected to the Roman seat. Unfortunately, Pope Urban, although officially elected by 16 Cardinals of the Church, did not fulfill the hopes of those who had chosen him. He was described as having "a brusque, violent, suspicious and even extravagant temperament, with no regard for anyone not of his opinion, even if it were a Cardinal of the Holy Church."[24] While Urban's election could not be considered invalid, in September of 1378 a splinter group of

Cardinals convened a second conclave which elected Clement VII, who proceeded to move a competing papacy back to Avignon; this brought about the Great Western Schism which lasted from 1378 until 1418.[25]

Catherine, regrettably, did not live to see the resolution of the schism; the saint's earthly life ended in 1380 when she was only 33 years of age.[26] The confusion in Papal allegiance remained a suffering for her as well as for many Italian Catholics of the period. Dominican Father Joseph Marie Perrin remarked that the schism was "undoubtedly... the most harrowing trial the Church has ever gone through, although neither the Faith itself, nor the certitude that Christ had founded His Church on Peter, was in question. Instead, the whole issue was simply to determine who exactly was St. Peter's successor."[27] Perrin added: "As we look back over the centuries, we can see how this time of trial was to make men much more keenly aware of Catholic unity and of the spiritual cohesion necessary for the Church. But, in the 14th Century, the Christian world felt only the piercing reality of the disaster."[28]

The confusion in Church leadership, coupled with the impact of a first horrendous plague outbreak in 1348, had repercussions for both clergy and laity. There are no precise mortality statistics available as the number of deaths from the plague epidemic varied from city to city; however, friars living in communal settings were severely impacted. For example, "the number of friars in the Dominican Priory at Monpellier fell, in one year, from 140 to 7; at Florence 78 friars died, and in Siena, 50 of them succumbed to the plague."[29] Ultimately, Friar Perrin asserted, "the appalling losses suffered by the mendicant orders in the middle of the 14th Century shook the very foundations of the religious life."[30]

The complicated political and religious elan of the era and the mixed loyalties of some religious also "did not facilitate conventual life, especially the practice of fraternal charity and obedience."[31] As a result some communities "threatened with excommunication, and even with imprisonment, those religious who would meddle with politics or would appeal to outside influences to exert pressure on their superiors or ignore their commands."[32] Following the losses experienced by so many monasteries, fewer young men entered the priesthood and there was an atmosphere of disquiet within many seminaries and religious communities: "In order to exist, monasteries and religious communities everywhere had to make up their numbers hastily by curtailing their usual careful training and selection of religious."[33]

Losses also occurred in the ranks of the secular clergy.[34] A number of bishops and priests were considered less than orthodox in their attitudes and behavior and some lay people stopped attending Church altogether.[35] For other members of the laity, however, "a medieval, like a modern, man remained a Christian because he was born a Christian... his life was inseparable from that of the community to which his Church gave a variety of color, here radiant, there distressing."[36] Nevertheless, the Papal schism and the plague had taken their toll on the Church and on the country.[37] The Tuscan community was in dire need of the healing presence of Saint Catherine in her future role as a Sister of Penance of St. Dominic.

Politics

Related to the impact of the "Black Death" on Italian society, fortunes waxed and waned for many families in Catherine's city of Siena and in the surrounding countryside. The initial plague outbreak in 1348, the year following Catherine's birth, was notable in its devastation of Siena.[38] For almost a year, usual civic, social and work related activities were disrupted and three-quarters of the population perished. Victims fell dead in the streets and "natural and religious bonds seemed annihilated. Without any ecclesiastical ceremony, the abandoned dead were thrown indiscriminately into great trenches hastily dug in different parts of the city."[39]

Illness and death, and the lack of strong spiritual guidance from the Church, also provided the catalysts for disagreements and disputes among citizens, leading to feuds that were often physical in nature. As Catherinian scholar Edmund Gardner observed: "everywhere dissent and quarrels arose over questions of heritage and succession."[40] These feuds were of concern to Catherine as she grew older and became aware of the resultant traumatic injuries presented at local hospitals; thus she sought to mediate Sienese conflicts as well as those occurring in the neighboring towns. While not generally considered a politician, Saint Catherine's trips outside of Siena to such cities as Florence and Pisa were looked upon as having "specific diplomatic motivation" in assisting with the resolution of disputed issues.[41]

Two national ruling political parties in central and northern Italy, the "Guelphs," a faction supporting the Pope, and the "Ghibellines," a group favoring the Holy Roman Emperor, and the local Sienese "Party of Nine," later the "Party of Twelve," battled over the country and the papacy. Membership in local ruling political parties changed frequently in cities such as Siena adding to the insecurity of the populace.[42] Dominican Martin Gillet asserted that 14th-century Siena reflected a "political atmosphere of violence and class egoism which sought to release people from all constraints of the moral and religious order, even the most sacred."[43] Igino Giordani, a member of the Italian Focolare Movement, explained that, at the time, "political, economic and social transformations were taking place"… to the accompaniment of bitter struggles, violent hatreds, plots, desolation and ruin."[44] Thus, it was within this decidedly unstable and fluctuating church and political environment that Saint Catherine would live out her ministry to the ill and the infirm.

Catherine's Early Spirituality
Seeds of Ministry to the Sick Poor

One day while walking along Siena's Valle Piatta with her brother, Stefano, the six-year-old Catherine experienced a vision of Christ hovering above the Church of San Domenico.[45] The saint saw Our Lord, dressed in Papal robes and crowned with a shining tiara, raise His hand and make the sign of the Cross over her.[46] In Catherine's vision, Christ was accompanied by the Apostles Peter and Paul and Saint John the Evangelist. Catherine was deeply moved by the experience of seeing the Lord bless and smile at her. One biographer mused that "so mighty was that benediction from the hand of the Eternal that Catherine was rapt beyond herself, and though timid by nature, she remained standing in the open street, in the midst of the traffic of men and beasts, immovable and with uplifted eyes."[47]

When Stefano tried to hurry Catherine along the lane she replied: "If you could see what I can, you would not be so cruel and disturb me out of this lovely vision."[48] In considering the experience of the young Benincasa siblings, Third Order Dominican Claire Mary Antony visualized the scene:

> We can picture the children standing hand-in-hand beneath the olives, gazing up at the towering walls of the great church, Stefano seeing nothing, half-ashamed, half-inclined to scold; Catherine weeping

8

bitterly because when she turned away her eyes the vision had disappeared with the evanescence of a swiftly-dying rainbow.[49]

Additionally, Arrigo Levasti, remarked: "She was only a child; she hoped that Christ would appear to her again, would smile again, perhaps speak... and she wanted to pray."[50] Catherine's youthful experience had a profound impact on her future attitudes and behaviors.

Following the vision, Blessed Raymond of Capua reported that Catherine gave up the majority of her childhood games and began to immerse herself in prayer. She also began to fast from certain types of food, especially meat and wine, which was "unheard of" in a child of her age.[51] Blessed Raymond asserted that "it had become clear from Catherine's virtues, the gravity of her behavior, and her extraordinary wisdom, that under her girlish appearance, there was a fully formed woman. Her actions, indeed, had nothing childish, nothing girlish about them, but showed all the signs of a most venerable maturity."[52]

Catherine now "gave great importance to identification with the suffering of Christ."[53] In the book *Praying with Catherine of Siena*, Patricia Vinje explains that this would not be unusual for one living in the 14th Century, which embraced a "cult of suffering."[54] Through spiritual practices of suffering, medieval individuals, in the absence of martyrdom, "decided to die in small ways for God."[55] The young saint from a very early age continually sought ways of mortifying her body as a reflection of her love for Christ.

Catherine's daily Mass attendance at the Church of San Domenico resulted in her heart becoming more and more captivated by the images of the Dominican Friars in their black and white habits. She desired ardently to join in their ministry directed toward the salvation of souls. Catherine would later record, in her *Dialogue*, God's words to her in describing his beloved son, Saint Dominic: "His task was that of the word, My only-begotten Son. He was such an apostle in the world that, by spreading the truth and light of My Word, he was able to banish darkness. He was a light given to the world through Mary, in accordance with my will."[56] She also had a familiar Dominican role model in Fra Thommaso della Fonte, her adopted brother who had been raised in the Benincasa home.[57]

Catherine now began to beg her father to allow her to give some of the family's household provisions to the sick and the poor of the city. Within this early desire to give food and clothing to the needy of Siena were planted and nourished the seeds of the saint's later nursing ministry to the ailing. Blessed Raymond observed that Catherine loved the poor so much that she "could never be happy about her own home as long as the family was comfortably situated"; the saint so identified with the disadvantaged that, even as a child, she wished her small room furnished with only the barest necessities.[58] Catherine slept on a bed of hard boards, fasted, eating only salads and drinking wine diluted with water; she also introduced the practice of spending long hours in prayer into her daily routine.

The words of Sofia Cavalletti, author of *The Religious Potential of the Child*, provide some understanding of the childhood prayer reported of Saint Catherine: "It is a fact that children have an extraordinary capacity for prayer, as regards duration as well as spontaneity and dignity of expression. Theirs' is a prayer of praise and thanksgiving, which expresses the nearness and transcendence of God at the same time."[59] Cavalletti added: "Children pray with great facility; we find they are always disposed to prayer, which can be a time of special enchantment for them."[60] Additionally, nurse author Margaret Burkhardt observed that children "live in their spirits more than adults," spirituality being the "deepest core" of the child's being.[61] And, pediatric Chaplain George Handzo asserted that "Children think a lot about faith and have more ability in theological reflection than most adults give them credit for."[62] The perceptions of Sofia Cavelletti, Margaret Burkhardt, and George Handzo were all reflected in the lived experience of religion and spirituality as described for the young Catherine of Siena.

The Promise

Throughout the first year after her youthful vision, Catherine spent more and more time in silent meditation; this culminated in her commitment to a vowed life of virginity made at the age of seven. It was reported that "in an impulsive outburst she said to Christ: 'My Lord Jesus Christ, I promise Thee and give thee my virginity, that it may ever be Thine alone, and that Thou mayst ever be the guardian of my purity.'"[63] Blessed Raymond of Capua related a prayer of Catherine to the Our Lady asking her, as the mother of God's "only Son... to give me as Husband Him whom I desire with all the power of my soul, your most holy Son, our one Lord Jesus Christ; and I promise Him and you that I will never choose for myself any other husband, and will always do all I can to keep my virginity unspotted."[64]

Another biographer proposed a touching conceptualization of Catherine's promise:

> Withdrawing to a secluded place where she could speak aloud without being heard, and addressing herself directly to the Mother of God, she pronounced her vow in clear and vibrant tones: 'O most blessed and holy Virgin, you were the first among women to consecrate your virginity to the Lord by a perpetual vow, and you received from Him the singular grace of becoming the Mother of His only Son. I implore your ineffable piety not to look at my merits, not to consider my weakness, but to grant me nevertheless, the grace of receiving as my spouse Him who draws all the fibers of my heart, your Son, who is sanctity itself, our only Lord, Jesus Christ. I promise Him, as well as you, never to accept any other bridegroom and to keep for Him, to the measure of my power, my virginity perpetually intact.[65]

Friar Martin Gillet, the author of this imagined prayer, offers support for the validity of Catherine's vow with the question: "How can we doubt the testimony of a child of seven, who tells us that her vision determined her to change her life radically and take no other spouse than Jesus Christ, when she knew, having often heard it said at home, that her mother was resolved to see her married, cost what it may."[66] After the vision, Gillet concluded: "Catherine was changed, not perhaps into a woman of seventy, as Raymond emphatically states, but into a courageous and intrepid young girl whose enlightened will would never allow itself to be thwarted by any obstacle, interior or exterior."[67]

In considering wording of Catherine's promise such as that suggested by Friar Gillet, Igino Giordani offered the following interpretation:

> It may well be that the expressions used by the little girl in formulating her vow were more simple and that this rather elaborate form is the work of the theologian, her confessor, who put into Latin a confession made to him by Catherine years after the event; however, this was its substance. Little Catherine already knew the manner of the saints in this regard, and these ambitious words were not beyond her childish understanding. Indeed her sentiments could hardly be contained even in the formula given; she spoke with a soul enamored and entirely dedicated.[68]

11

While, admittedly, it may seem very difficult for one with a 21st-century mindset to accept, as realistic and valid, a lifetime vow of virginity made by a seven year old, theologian Judith Allen Shelly maintains that "stories abound of very young children who made serious and lasting commitments to God."[69]

In looking back, not only to Catherine's world of 14th-century Siena, but to her youthful spirituality as well, we are seeking to learn how the saint understood the gospel message of Jesus and how it influenced her life. We are not concerned with Catherine's past, as one biographer wrote, "but with that which is timeless or, rather, with that which is present and actual, the elements in her life and character that we can incorporate into our own."[70] Saint Catherine's personal spirituality, including the desire to commit her life to Christ, was manifested while she was still chronologically young. While understanding such a personal spirituality, on the part of an elementary school child, may seem challenging, it must be remembered that Catherine was living in the era of the later middle ages. Religiously speaking, this was a time when spiritual experiences, often accompanied by visions and ecstasies, were almost commonplace in the lives of holy people, even in the faith beliefs of the very young.

It is also important to take into account the fact that chronological age in the 14th Century cannot be compared to that of the present day. Individuals matured earlier and died earlier as well. It was considered the norm in Catherine's world for a pre-teenage female to begin making plans for marriage and a family. Adolescents, especially those who were members of large families such as the Benincasas, not only helped with housework but also assumed responsibilities in the care and raising of younger siblings. Thus, it is not so difficult to accept the fact that Catherine should begin to think about a future life, which, for her, included a virginal commitment to Christ, at such an early age.

One interpreter of medieval childhood culture identified youngsters such as Catherine Benincasa as potential saints who skipped over some of the more mundane pleasures of their companions. A future saint was described as a child who "folds his hands, kneels and raises his eyes heavenward in prayer before knowing the words of the prayer (and) keeps his distance from the mischief and games of his contemporaries."[71] An example of Catherine's childhood devotion was suggested to demonstrate the point: "When she was 5 or so, after having learned the 'Ave Maria,' she would halt at every step, when going up or down stairs, kneel, and recite a sentence from the prayer."[72] This description of one of Catherine's religious practices was, the author noted, "based on observation of the conduct of a small girl engaged in ritual repetition as is often the case with children."[73]

In exploring the internal spiritual lives of medieval children, such as Catherine, we must consider not only the societal culture of "wars, epidemics and famines," but must also view the child within the context of family life.[74] In the central and later middle-ages, communicating the Christian faith was generally done by the mother, teaching such prayers as the "Our Father" and the "Hail Mary," bringing the children to Church, introducing them to holy images and statues and instructing them in "gestures for their prayers."[75] These were activities that would have been carried out primarily by Mona Lapa Benincasa, and occasionally by her husband Giacomo.

While scholars of medieval children's spirituality admit that paternal love, in the middle-ages, might seem more measured than that of the mother, they argue that it remained strong, and that there are "many medieval examples, demonstrating the existence of the sensitive father, close to his children, sharing their joys and sorrows."[76] It was, in fact, the head of the Benincasa family, Giacomo, who not only supported Catherine's personal devotions but also facilitated her generosity to the poor in allowing his daughter to distribute household goods to those in need. Ultimately, the devotional practices of the devoutly Catholic Benincasa parents must surely have been influential in the spiritual and religious development of their youngest child.

Challenge to Spiritual Commitment

Between the ages of 7 and 12, Catherine lived her spiritual program of daily Mass, private prayer and small penances quietly without, seemingly, much notice from her large family. Her parents and siblings appeared to view Catherine's religious practices as childhood whimsy, a state which she would ultimately outgrow. It was expected that when she reached the teen-age years, Catherine would put aside these childish behaviors and devote herself to the usual interests of young women of the era.

When her daughter entered her pre-teen years, around ages 11 or 12, Mona Lapa began to exhort Catherine to enhance her personal appearance as befitting an adolescent girl preparing to seek a future

13

husband. The saint's family, unaware of her private promise of virginity, were now in the throes of seriously trying to find a suitable match.[77] Catherine demurred from any sort of marriage-planning, however, having spent many hours in prayer and meditation guided by her secret vow of virginity. This caused Mona Lapa to press the case even harder.

Knowing that Catherine loved and admired her older sister, Mona Lapa enlisted Bonaventura's help in her mission to prepare Catherine for marriage. Bonaventura tried to entice Catherine to imitate her example by accepting secular adornments of jewelry and attractive clothing.[78] Catherine, not wishing to displease her beloved mother and sister, reluctantly began wearing fashionable clothes and jewels, even bleaching her hair in the manner of Sienese women of the day.[79] For a period of time Bonaventura succeeded in presenting her younger sister as an attractive adolescent and Catherine seemed to enjoy the experience.[80]

Sadly, however, Bonaventura died in childbirth in 1362, when Catherine was only 16, leaving her sister bereft. After a period of grieving, remorse set in, and Catherine began to feel guilty for "having prayed less, for having drawn away from God, desiring the good things of the world and consenting to enjoy some of the world's pleasures."[81] She realized that the attraction to a worldly lifestyle had been only a challenge to test her resolve and her religious vow to live for and to love Christ completely. The saint now wholeheartedly resumed her daily schedule of devotions and penance resolving never again to fail in the virginal commitment of her life to her Blessed Lord. In the end the bereavement had two important results: to free Catherine "forever from the vanities of this world, to devote herself with new ardor to her Divine Spouse and to conceive a special devotion to Saint Mary Magdalene, whose contrition she desired to imitate."[82]

Frustrated by their daughter's return to her religious devotions, the Benincasa parents appealed to their adopted son, Fra Tommaso della Fonte, now a Dominican priest. Fra Tommaso, orphaned by the plague of 1348, and having been raised in the Benincasa household, seemed the perfect person to convince Catherine of the error of her ways. The family begged Fra Tommaso to dissuade her from what they considered youthful foolishness and to accede to her parents' wishes that she accept a husband of their choosing.[83] Catherine instead convinced Fra Tommaso so completely of her determination never again to abandon her vow of virginity that he was obliged to support her.[84] Tommaso believed that Mona Lapa would give up the idea of Catherine's marriage only if it became impossible; the young Dominican also "knew Catherine well enough to realize that her resolution to remain a virgin in accordance with her vow was inflexible. Consequently, he advised Catherine to take the only step that would, temporarily at least, safeguard her vow and thwart the plans of Lapa: that of cutting her hair."[85]

When Catherine appeared in a veiled cap, shorn of her beautiful hair, the family, especially Mona Lapa, began to persecute her, threatening that when her hair grew back she would be forced to marry. The formerly loving Benincasa home now became a place of torture for Catherine; she was ordered by her distraught parents to move from her private bedroom to one shared with a sibling, to cease the practice of solitary prayer and to undertake all of the menial household chores formerly carried out by a maidservant. During this period Mona Lapa remained angry and aloof because of what she perceived as her daughter's stubbornness in refusing to seek a husband.

Catherine suffered greatly over the lack of privacy for her religious devotions, but she accepted the chastisement with gentleness and patience. It was during this period of punishment that she conceived, with the guidance of the Holy Spirit, the idea of creating in her soul a "secret cell" where she could dwell alone with Christ. As she would later advise her disciples: "Make yourself a cell in your own mind from which you need never come out."[86]

In her role as the Benincasas' maid, Catherine now sought to serve God through her household tasks. She cooked, cleaned and waited on the family, seeing to their every need. She imagined her father as Christ and her mother as the Blessed Virgin; her siblings were pictured as the Lord's disciples.[87] Even though she was sometimes treated harshly, rather than complaining Catherine attempted to anticipate the desires of her family and obeyed them joyfully.[88] The kitchen became Catherine's "sanctuary" where she could retreat into her interior cell, a place from which she would not have to depart.[89]

One day, however, during Catherine's period of household discipline, Giacomo Benincasa witnessed his daughter in prayer with a white dove hovering above her head. Giacomo's report of this experience, combined with Catherine's revelation that she had made a private vow of virginity and hoped to enter the "Sisters of Penance of St. Dominic," moved the family deeply. Catherine's parents and siblings finally recognized the

15

seriousness of her religious commitment and determined no longer to oppose it.[90] Giacomo advised Catherine: "Keep your vow. Do exactly as you wish, and as the Holy Spirit teaches you."[91] He then promised: "From now on we shall leave you in peace to your holy works, and put no more obstacles in the way of your holy exercises."[92] Her father added: "Pray for us all a great deal, that we may be worthy of the promises of your Husband who in His grace singled you out from your earliest years."[93]

Now again, biographer Igino Giordani related, Catherine was allowed a small room of her own:

> She chose the narrowest and most inconvenient one. It was above the kitchen, with a little window looking over the narrow street of the Tiratoio. She furnished it to her own taste: a bench upon which in the daytime she and her visitors could be seated and which served at night as her bed; and a chest to keep her clothes. She hung a Crucifix on the wall and set a small lamp to burn beneath it.[94]

In all things material Catherine chose simplicity and poverty that her entire energy and passion could be devoted to the service of her beloved Spouse and Lord.

Catherine of Siena's family, church, political milieu and early spirituality prepared the saint to ultimately embrace a sacred covenant of caring for the sick. As noted at the outset of this chapter it is one's philosophy of life and worldview which both stimulate and support the undertaking of any committed lifestyle. For Catherine, ministry to the sick, although not immediately perceived to be a focus of her vocation, emerged as flowing directly from her love of Christ, her love of family and neighbor and her love of the Church. The painful challenges to her envisioned calling predisposed Catherine to accept the sufferings she would later encounter in her ministry to the ill and the infirm. The young Catherine initially believed that her love of God and neighbor would be fulfilled through a life of intense and solitary prayer and penance. As she grew in maturity and in her commitment to Christ, Catherine learned to accept the truth that, as biographer Augusta Theodosia Drane so aptly observed: "He is pleased to abide in other sanctuaries than the solitary cell"; Catherine came to the knowledge that she could indeed seek and find her Beloved Savior in the person of the poor and the sick. The saint's response to that knowledge was formalized in her decision to enter the

"Sisters of Penance of St. Dominic," the Dominican Mantellate, as revealed in the following chapter.

Chapter 2. "On Two Wings You Must Fly"
The Call to Active Ministry

"On two feet you must walk and on two wings you must fly to heaven."

God's Message to Catherine

Solitude

A daughter of Saint Dominic,
she sought to contemplate
God's love.

A daughter of Saint Dominic,
she learned to proclaim
God's love.

A soul enflamed in solitude; a
heart transformed in
service.

Catherine of Siena
contemplative and caregiver,
mystic and minister,
lover and beloved.

Blessed Raymond of Capua declared that while Catherine was "wonderfully compassionate towards the poor... for those who were ill, her pity was unbounded."[95] Raymond added that, as a result of that compassion, Catherine "performed unprecedented labours" in ministering to the ailing which many may find incredible.[96] Nevertheless, Raymond assured the reader of his *Legenda* that reports of the saint's selfless care of the sick were documented by those who knew her well; some of these informants included Catherine's first confessor, Fra Tommaso Della Fonte, her friend and confidante Fra Bartolommeo di Domenico, her sister-in-law Lisa and her mother Mona Lapa.

In fact, in an attempt to be as transparent as possible, after describing Catherine's call to active ministry, Blessed Raymond added the following disclaimer: "I have said... that I would write nothing down that was untrue, imaginary or exaggerated, but would restrict myself to what I had actually heard from the virgin herself or from others."[97]

Raymond admitted that he might have forgotten some things about the virgin's life because of responsibilities he was obliged to assume since last meeting with her, as well as from the personal incursion of the aging process, however, he explained:

> When memories come back into my mind, I use the words which seem to me most likely to have been said by her; but to the honour of Almighty God and his bride Catherine, I am bound to confess that, thanks to her, many things come back before my eyes which I had previously never even thought about. In fact she seems at times to be with me, telling me what to write.[98]

Catherine's active ministry of caring for the sick poor was initiated when she began the public dimension of her life as a Dominican Sister of Penance. Prior to her nursing role within the community of Sisters, Catherine was prepared spiritually during many months of solitude and prayer as the following pages reveal. For it was in prayerful interaction with her Beloved Spouse that Catherine heard the call to serve Him through serving her neighbors; to do for the sick poor what she could not now do for Christ.

Catherine's Vocation
The "Sisters of Penance of St. Dominic"

From the time of her childhood Mass attendance at the Church of San Domenico, Saint Catherine had daily witnessed the prayerful presence of the lay community of the "Sisters of Penance of St. Dominic," commonly called the "Mantellate," and desired to join them. Biographer Don Brophy conceded that "there is some question as to when Catherine first became interested in the Mantellate."[99] Brophy cites the opinion of Raymond of Capua that Catherine was already thinking of the Order before telling her family of her lifetime vow of virginity. Raymond recounted one of Catherine's dreams "in which St. Dominic appeared to her, holding in His hands the habit worn by the Sisters of Penance and saying: 'Dearest daughter, be of good courage; do not lose heart no matter what the odds against you. Be assured that you will one day wear this habit which you long for.'"[100]

The "Order of Penance of St. Dominic" was over 100 years old and associated with the first Dominican communities founded in the 13th Century. In the late 13th Century, the Master of the Order wrote a rule for the lay community giving them recognition as permanent members of the Third Order of St. Dominic.[101] The lay Brothers and Sisters of Penance are described as having sprung:

> From the Dominican Order as a branch from a trunk filled with life. Wherever a convent of Friars was established, friends of the order, both men and women, inspired by their spirit, nourished by their teaching, and edified by their example, endeavored to live according to the Dominican spirit and to promote the Dominican apostolate. The name of Third Order was given to societies of men and women who, under the spiritual direction of the Fathers, wished in their own way and in the degree possible to them to share the religious and apostolic life of the Dominican Order.[102]

It was also reported that "the Dominicans were the first actually to set up an Order of Penance that would formally be part of the larger Order, under the jurisdiction of the Master of the Order; this was done in 1285."[103]

In the early part of the 14th Century, communities of Dominican Sisters of Penance were found in Italian cities such as Florence, Pisa and Siena; the women were devoted to prayer and works of mercy, especially visiting and caring for the ill and the infirm.[104] The Sisters worked together with the Friars; their primary ministries involved "serving in the hospitals, visiting and caring for the sick in their homes, ministering to prisoners and comforting those in spiritual distress."[105] Members of the Dominican Third Order remained in their residences, among their families, adopting a lifestyle of simplicity and poverty appropriate to the identified ministries. Although lay, the female Third Order members wore a Dominican habit and lived very much like nuns. They did not have community chapels or oratories but met once a month in churches belonging to the Dominican Friars.[106]

The "Sisters of Penance" were commonly referred to by the local community as the "Dominican Mantellate." This name was derived from the fact that their habits consisted of a white tunic over which they wore a black mantle. Although Catherine had long admired the Sisters from afar, a problem for her was that the majority of Mantellate were older widows who, after their husband's deaths, had committed the remainder of their lives to Christ and to the service of their neighbors. It was not usual for the community to accept a young, single woman. Because a significant dimension of the Mantellata's role was to visit the ill in their homes and in the hospitals, it was considered unseemly, in that era, for a young, unmarried woman to travel the streets of Siena engaged in such ministries.

Catherine would not be dissuaded from her desire, regardless, and she pleaded with her parents, now well aware of their daughter's vow of virginity, to intercede for her; she begged the Mantellate community to accept her and grant her the longed-for Dominican habit. Mona Lapa Benincasa still believed that her daughter might be swayed from such an austere lifestyle; to further that end she initiated several strategies with the potential to change Catherine's mind. One of those interventions was to insist that Catherine accompany her to the local "sulphur baths" in the hope that the saint would become attracted to more worldly comforts. Although Mona Lapa's goal was to introduce her daughter to the pleasure of the soothing waters, Catherine, seeking a penance, secretly immersed herself in an area of the baths containing boiling sulphurus waters, which burned her skin. The young woman's self-chosen suffering finally convinced Mona Lapa to accept her daughter's commitment to a life of prayer and penance. Thus she reluctantly agreed to visit the Mantellate community and attempt to advocate on her daughter's behalf.

The Sisters' first response to the entreaty was negative. They replied that it was simply not their custom to accept unmarried girls, rather that they primarily admitted only older widows who had already devoted their lives to the Lord's service. The community felt this was necessary as the Mantellate had no formal enclosure as cloistered nuns.[107] It was understood that those accepted to the Sisters of Penance must be mature and responsible; the Sisters feared that a young attractive woman in their ranks might become involved in some scandal in the city.[108]

Catherine, nevertheless, continued to trust in the Lord, praying "day and night" that she might be accepted as a Mantellata; she begged her mother to meet again with the Sisters to plead her case.[109] Within the preceding weeks, Catherine had experienced a serious illness brought on by the scalding with boiling water experienced during her trip to the sulphur baths; her skin became disfigured by blisters and swelling. During this time Mona Lapa, concerned for her daughter's very life, remained daily at the bedside showering her with loving care.[110] Finally, in fear of losing Catherine, Mona Lapa told the Mantellate Sisters of her daughter's illness and pleaded that they visit Catherine to evaluate her fitness for the community. This time the Sisters replied that if Catherine was not too attractive and was judged to be of good character they would consider accepting her. And, after a face-to-face meeting with the saint, the Mantellate community acquiesced to her desire. Raymond acknowledged that Catherine was indeed not beautiful because of her skin lesions and explained that when the Sisters "heard the way she expressed herself and explained the seriousness of her intention they welcomed her sound sense and wisdom, first with amazement and then with increasing delight, realizing that though young in years she had an old head on her shoulders and excelled many older women in the sight of God."[111]

Following their visit, the Sisters of Penance recommended Catherine to the Friars and received consent for her admission to the Dominican Third Order. They sent word to Mona Lapa that, when her daughter had recovered from the illness, she should bring her to the Community.[112] Within a few weeks, Catherine's health was restored and she was formally accepted into the Sisters of Penance of St. Dominic, receiving the black and white habit of a Mantellata in the presence of her Sisters and the local Dominican Friars. Blessed Raymond commented that the habit was most appropriate for the young initiate because of its religious symbolism: a black mantle for humility and white tunic signifying innocence.[113]

Catherine was clothed in the Mantellata habit in the Capella delle Volte, in the Church of San Domenico, where the Sisters of Penance held their meetings; the clothing was presided over by Dominican Fra Bartolommeo Montucci, a Friar of the parish.[114] It was reported that, when Catherine returned home from the ceremony, she mused to herself:

> Look, now you have entered into religion and it is not fitting that you should go on living as you have done hitherto. Your life in the world is over, a new life is beginning. The white robe you are wearing signifies that you must be girded with sheerest purity. The black cloak means that you must be wholly dead to the world. And henceforth you must walk in the narrow path, trodden only by very few.[115]

While biographers differ to some extent on Catherine's exact age at the time of her reception of the habit, it is generally believed that she was around 16 or 17 years old.

After officially becoming a member of the Sisters of Penance of St. Dominic, or a Mantellata, Catherine returned to her small room in the Benincasa home. Augusta Drane described the space as "a little cell under her father's house, no more than five metres long and three in width. It was lighted by one small window to which a few brick steps led up... on which it is said the saint often rested her head when sleeping."[116] "Here," Drane added, "she retired as into the solitude of a desert, giving herself up to rigorous penance and uninterrupted prayer."[117] At this time Catherine continued her practice of fasting from meat, most breads and sweets to the point that swallowing more than a few bites of herbs or salad would make her ill. Desiring to imitate her holy Father, Saint Dominic, Catherine scourged her body several times a day in atonement for her sins and those of others.

Initially, Catherine left the solitude of her cell only for Morning Mass at the Church of San Domenico. She treasured donning the habit of a Mantellata and loved to say that she would never cease wearing it. A moving anecdote is told, however, that one day while walking to church Catherine met a poor man begging for alms. The saint apologized for having no money, so the beggar asked for her mantle, which she immediately gave him. When her Mantellate Sisters learned of the gift they retrieved the mantle substituting alms in exchange. The Sisters asked Catherine how she could possibly have given away the mantle, the symbol of her commitment to Christ; she replied: "I would rather be without my mantle than without charity."[118]

As noted earlier, a primary ministry of the "Sisters of Penance of St. Dominic," the only religious community to which Catherine aspired, was that of visiting and caring for the sick in their homes and in the hospitals. Yet, we do not know if Catherine ever felt called, as a young person, to care for the ill and the infirm. Often those who choose nursing, medicine or a related healthcare ministry, describe having been attracted to the work during their early years. For some, the interest comes about through reading stories of compassionate caring by those who minister to the sick. Other healthcare professionals report their vocational choice as motivated by having cared for an ill family member or having provided support to an elderly relative in his or her final years. And, for a few, it is a personal bout with illness that becomes the impetus for the chosen vocation; the experience of having been lovingly cared for by a dedicated physician, nurse or chaplain moves these individuals to consider a healthcare vocation for themselves. Such youthful forays into the world of illness or disability can frequently become the catalyst for a career in caring for the sick.

Although Catherine was not literate in childhood, we are told that she attended daily Mass and listened each morning to the reading of the Gospel, as well as to the homilies given by the Dominican Friars. Thus, even though she could not read the words of scripture, one must assume that the saint had heard repeatedly the Lord's mandate to care for the least of His brethren as documented in Matthew 25: 35; 40: "I was hungry and you gave me food, I was thirsty and you gave me something to drink, I was a stranger and you welcomed me, I was naked and you gave me clothing, I was sick and you took care of me, I was in prison and you visited me... Truly, I tell you, just as you did it to one of the least of these who are members of my family, you did it to me." Surely, this message of Catherine's Beloved Savior, the assurance that the carrying out of these caring activities for those in need was the same as ministering to Him, must have moved her heart to admire such a calling.

In terms of family caregiving, Catherine, as the second youngest child in the Benincasa family, probably did not have much opportunity to care for siblings during illness, nor do we know of visits to elders within her extended family. Catherine was only an infant when the first outbreak of the plague decimated Siena; blessedly, her own family was spared significant loss at that time. What we do know of Catherine's young life experience, which might be related to her choice of vocation, were several personal experiences of bodily illness and suffering. As a very young child, with the nickname of "Euphrosyne" for her joyful nature, Catherine seemed a healthy, happy youngster, described by biographers as a delight to her family and neighbors. As Catherine matured in her childhood spirituality, however, she became aware that even small acts of penance such as fasting and sleeping on boards could be painful; she understood, early on, the meaning of physical suffering.

Catherine's first recorded personal bout with illness was that which followed her visit to the sulfur baths with Mona Lapa. While Blessed Raymond described Catherine's sickness as "a complaint that often attacks young adolescents," he admitted that "it may have been a result of the excessive heat that she had to endure from the boiling waters."[119] It was during this time that Catherine experienced the devoted nursing care and compassion bestowed on her by her mother who sought desperately to restore her beloved daughter to health. Mona Lapa stayed at Catherine's bedside "and nursed her faithfully and tirelessly. She attempted to console her sick child with caresses and loving words, and did everything she could to make her well again."[120] Surely Catherine must have been touched by her mother's tender ministrations and may, during that time, have begun to consider a day when she herself could provide such compassionate care to others who were ill and suffering.

Solitude as a Preparation for Active Ministry

Despite Catherine's entrance into a community whose primary apostolic work was ministering to the sick poor of the city in their homes and in the hospitals, the new Mantellata initially retreated to a private cell in her family residence for a period of three years. Her seeking to be immersed in a contemplative spiritual life may have been related to Catherine's youth and inexperience with the world; the adolescent saint was at a very different developmental stage than that of her widowed Sisters in the Mantellate community. Just as young medical or nursing students of today need to be educated and mentored prior to their initiation into a clinical environment, perhaps the Lord in his tender love, sought to prepare Catherine spiritually for the caregiving ministry to which He would ultimately call her.

Dominican Friar Martin Gillet wrote of Catherine that, as a "true daughter of St. Dominic, she labored, in her solitude, through prayer and penance for the salvation of souls."[121] While, being illiterate, Catherine could not become formally educated in courses of philosophy and theology, she nevertheless "imbibed all her sacred doctrine at its very source, in contemplation and under the direct dictation of God."[122] During her period of seclusion the young saint experienced many mystical interactions with the Lord as the previous statement indicates. Blessed Raymond testified that he had found "four full written records left by the saint's first confessor, Fra Tommaso della Fonte, packed with information about the marvelous visions and unheard of revelations she had."[123]

Catherine's solitary commitment to her Blessed Spouse was guided not only by her earlier pronounced vow of virginity but also now by additional vows of obedience and poverty. Although religious vows were not required of the Mantellate, Catherine chose to observe them privately. She resolved to be obedient to the Director of her community as well as to her confessor and she chose to keep very few personal possessions for her own use. Even though not formally bound by the letter of religious vows, Catherine fully embraced the spirit of the evangelical counsels as she understood it.[124] The saint was able to do this because during the years of prayer and contemplation Christ instilled in his daughter the inner meaning of the vows she had pronounced.[125]

Of the three vows, poverty posed the most difficult because of Catherine's commitment to living in the world rather than within a cloistered convent. But the Lord taught her that:

> Those who wish to attain great perfection despise the world's goods literally and spiritually... If you possess the world's goods you should do so with humility, not with pride, holding them as a thing lent, not a thing which is your own... You have them only when I bestow them; you keep them only when I leave them in your possession, and I leave them and give them only when I judge it well for your salvation.[126]

Catherine took to heart the Lord's words, seeking to possess only the basic necessities for her daily life and distributing to the poor, as alms, even some of her treasured possessions. Throughout these three secluded years Saint Catherine continued to leave her cell only for morning Mass and often stayed awake much of the night in prayer; she did not even join her family for meals.[127] It was during this period of austerity in her small cell that the young Catherine was also blessed with the grace of a spiritual union with Christ.

The Mystical Marriage

According to Blessed Raymond's *Legenda* Catherine's mystical marriage to the Lord occurred near the end of her experience of solitude.[128] In that time Catherine had been well schooled in the love of God and filled with grace. She prayed that her devotion to Christ would be continually increased and the Lord replied, "I will espouse you to me in faith."[129] Raymond explained, it was near Lent:

> And "the virgin was to be found alone in her little room seeking through prayer and fasting the face of her eternal Bridegroom, praying endlessly for the same thing. Then the Lord said to her, "Since for love

of me you have forsaken vanities and despised the pleasure of the flesh and fastened all delights of your heart on me, now, when the rest of the household are feasting, and enjoying themselves, I have determined to celebrate the wedding feast of your soul and to espouse you to me in faith as I promised."[130]

In her vision, Catherine saw the Son of God holding a beautiful golden ring, which he placed on her finger, saying, "There, I marry you to me in faith, to me, your Creator and Saviour. Keep this faith unspotted until you come to me in heaven and celebrate the marriage that has no end."[131]

Catherinian biographer Igino Giordani has created an idealized description of the mystical marriage, which bears repeating:

> Catherine's espousal occurred when she was twenty years old, in the flower of her youth, on Shrove Tuesday 1367, when Siena was wildest in its carousals and the populace poured through the streets dancing, singing, ogling, abandoning itself to collective madness... Manners had become increasingly frivolous, and the populace, floundering in economic instability and political ineptitude, sought to drown its bitterness in orgies.
>
> Catherine, perhaps the only citizen of the town completely detached from the carnival madness, kept to that little room, high ceilinged, heavy with silence, into which penetrated only an occasional echo of distant voices, more a lament than merrymaking, only to die there. And she was firmly convinced that hers was the true joy, there in that silence, and that against the noisy background of unthinking youth the only true reality was the Crucified Christ: Truth and Love.
>
> 'Lord, strengthen my faith', she prayed again and again in the midst of that insanity of pleasure. 'Lord, grant me the fullness of faith'. Again, and again she repeated the invocation, until at last Our Lord appeared to her and called to her in the tender terms He had used before: 'Since you alone have rejected all these vanities and for love of Me have fled them, and in Me alone have placed all the devotion of your heart, I have determined to celebrate with you the feast of your espousal to me.'[132]

The "heavenly nuptuals" were portrayed as:

> More joyful and more impressive than any that Siena had ever devised... Jesus Christ... placed a ring on Catherine's finger (and) then

as the angelic choirs paused in silence He pronounced the ritual formula: 'I, your creator and your Savior, wed you in this vow which, until you celebrate with Me in heaven our eternal nuptuals, will preserve you spotless... armed with the power of this faith you will successfully overcome all your adversaries.'[133]

Giordani's narrative concluded with the assertion that, from that moment on, Catherine "never took from her finger that ring, which only her own eyes could see and which even she could not see if for a moment her thoughts strayed from her bridegroom."[134]

It was also during these years of prayerful seclusion that Catherine reportedly achieved a degree of literacy. The saint had long desired to be able to read the Holy Scriptures and the Psalms of the Divine Office prayed by the Dominican Friars. She sought help from her Sisters, one of whom gave Catherine a copy of the alphabet which she studied diligently; her efforts, nevertheless, proved fruitless. Finally, as Catherinian biographer Augusta Drane recounted, Catherine "prostrated upon the ground in prayer and thus made her petition: 'Lord, if it be agreeable to Thee that I may know how to read, in order that I may recite the Divine Office and sing Thy praises, vouchsafe to teach me what I cannot learn of myself.'"[135] Catherine assured the Lord, however, that she was also "content to remain in ignorance" and spend her time in "simple meditation" if that be His will.[136] God heard his daughter's prayer and endowed her with such a facility for reading that she "at once procured the necessary books and began to say her Office daily with great devotion."[137]

From Catherine's solitary spiritual experiences was derived the primary content of her *Dialogue*. This process was described by biographer Claire Mary Antony: "Here in a quiet cell, away from the noise of the house and of the streets, Catherine absorbed full draughts of that Divine wisdom which shortly before her death, her secretaries wrote down from her lips in the form of the celebrated *Dialogue*.[138]

Catherine was able to be present to listen to the instruction of the Lord because, during this time, she spoke very little except with her confessor, Fra Tommaso della Fonte.[139] She tried as much as possible to maintain the "'great silence' of the Cistercians, that silence which, together with solitude, has always been a favorable climate to spiritual development."[140] Catherine's spiritual growth was reflected in the fact that she was possessed of only one fear, one anxiety, "the anxiety to please God."[141] This concern for pleasing God, combined with a lack of fear of anything else that might happen to her, served the saint well in her later apostolic ministries, especially in her care of those with infectious diseases such as leprosy and the plague.

Although Catherine lived initially in a solitary cell she did not choose the path selfishly with no concern for others. Catherine viewed herself as "a daughter of the Church, overflowing with love… and (filled) with intense sadness (when) she thought of the majority of mankind without love, without Christ."[142] Catherine believed that it was her responsibility to pray and do penance for the salvation of others; for her family, for her neighbors, for her religious Sisters and for her Brothers, the Dominican Friars.

The saint presented an external image of a hermitess at the time, living alone within a small room, but as will be seen in her service to the sick, Catherine of Siena was a community-oriented Mantellata; she was deeply solicitous of the spiritual, psychological and physical well-being of her brothers and sisters in the human family. It was, in fact, that concern for others that kept Catherine awake and at prayer during many long nights. As a means of sharing in the common life of the Dominican Friars, Catherine frequently prayed the Divine Office during the darkest hours, while the Brothers slept, offering her prayers in their stead.[143]

The Mantellate rule required its members to pray the Divine Office, attend daily Mass and generally remain close to their own homes, except when visiting the sick and the poor, usually going about the city in groups of Sisters. One biographer pointed out that Catherine had modified her own pastoral activity in that when she did ultimately quit her reclusive lifestyle, "she often went about town by herself" to accomplish her ministry to the ill and the infirm.[144] As the following pages will reveal, Catherine chose this path in keeping with her understanding of the Lord's mandate to leave her solitude and embrace the service of her neighbors.

Call to the Service of the Sick and the Poor
"On Two Feet You Must Walk"

Dominican Suzanne Noffke observed that following a "youthful plunge into an all-but-absolute solitude… Catherine was brought to the graced insight that changed her life: in the Incarnation, God so identified the divine with humankind that God and neighbor are henceforth inseparable."[145] Catherine came to the realization that if she was to love God completely, "she must serve others and so she began to wait on the material and physical needs of those around her."[146] Noffke concludes that the experience of this "simple material service," combined with "the gradual recognition of her gifts," led Catherine to "a more and more explicitly pastoral service."[147] As well as providing nursing care for the sick in their homes, in the hospitals and in the streets of Siena, Catherine was also blessed with the gift of healing and was credited with performing many "miraculous cures."[148]

As Suzanne Noffke indicated, Catherine's early plan for solitude was the result of her "youthful" desire for intimacy with God. The adolescent Catherine may indeed have needed those years of contemplative meditation and intimate interactions with the Lord to prepare her for the apostolic work to come. For, it was, in fact, during one of her prayerful conversations with God that Catherine heard the call to active ministry; to the service of the sick and the poor. The Lord's call was not, at first, happily embraced by the saint.

Blessed Raymond explained that when Catherine received the message "from the lips of her Shepherd and Heavenly Bridegroom that she was to be called from rest to labour, from silence to noise, from the seclusion of her cell to public life" her heart was torn.[149] She was distraught at the thought of leaving the prayerful solitude she had treasured for three years and wondered: "How was she to pray if she had to be with people all day long?"[150] The saint conceded that when she initially heard the Lord's command that she leave her cell, "she felt such a sharp pain in her heart that it seemed as though it was about to break, and that no one except the Lord would have been able to make her do it."[151] Catherine begged God not to ask her to abandon her seclusion with the words: "Why, sweetest Bridegroom, are you sending me away? Woe is me! If I have offended your Majesty, here in this little body of mine, let it be punished at your feet before you; I myself will be perfectly happy to do this. But do not let me be obliged to endure the harsh punishment of being separated from you."[152]

In His loving response the Lord continued to teach Catherine with the words:

> Be quiet, sweetest daughter; it is necessary for you to fulfill your every duty, so that with my grace you may assist others as well as yourself. I have no intention of cutting you off from me; on the contrary, I wish to

31

bind you more closely to myself, by means of love of the neighbor. You know that the precepts of love are two: love of me, and love of the neighbor; in these, as I have testified, consist the Law and the Prophets. I want you to fulfill these two commandments. On two feet you must walk... and with two wings you must fly to heaven.[153]

Catherine admitted to Blessed Raymond that the Lord then reminded her of her early desire to join the Order of Preachers and participate in their ministry for the salvation of souls; God reiterated Catherine's great admiration for Saint Dominic who founded the Order out of love for others and suggested that He was only now leading her to what, as a child, she had wished to do.[154] The Saint responded: "Let Your will be done, in all things"; she did, nevertheless, express concern about how she might minister to her neighbor as she viewed herself as a "frail" woman, "not highly considered by men."[155] The Lord reassured Catherine with the words: "Nothing is impossible to God... am I not He who created the human race, and divided it into male and female?... In my eyes there is neither male nor female, rich nor poor, but all are equal, for I can do all things with equal ease... It is written of me that I made whatever I willed to make, for nothing is impossible to me (Psalm 113)."[156]

Having heard this promise of support for her apostolic ministry, Catherine went immediately to join the family in response to the Lord's wishes; she responded "with the true Dominican spirit, beginning to give forth to the world, at first at home, but soon throughout her native city, the fruits of her contemplation."[157]

Blessed Raymond penned a defense of Catherine's initial hesitancy to accede to the Lord's call to leave her solitude for the service of neighbors; he asserted:

> A soul that has tasted how sweet the Lord is finds it very difficult to detach itself from this perfect sweetness. If this has to happen, the soul cannot help grumbling a little, resenting the fact that it has been called by God to produce sons and supply them with all they need... her own "door" is already open" to God; now she is being called to open not only her own "door" but the "door" of other souls.[158]

Igino Giordani also offered an interpretation of Catherine's hesitation to leave her seclusion in noting that the Lord's asking His daughter "to serve her fellow men, to love Him in them, to achieve the full measure of

His love… meant that just when she had achieved supreme renunciation of the world, she must return to the world to participate in all the drama of its tragic incidents in order to love God in men."[159] And, Friar Martin Gillet shared a similar understanding of Saint Catherine's reluctance to quit her solitary life in admitting: "How well we understand the objection of Catherine. She does not actually refuse to collaborate with Jesus in the salvation of souls, but she fears that a renewed contact with the world she had left long ago in order to find God may make her lose Him again."[160]

Saint Catherine's example of what she originally perceived as a drastic change in her spiritual calling, the move from contemplative to active ministry, and her ultimate response provides a powerful example for all of us. There may indeed arise occasions, for those who minister to the sick, when the direction of planned caregiving activities is forced to change, sometimes not according to our preference or even to our liking. Such redirection might be related to leadership turnover or structural reorganization within a healthcare setting. Catherine teaches us that although such transitions may be painful at first, acceptance with trust in the Lord and His Divine plan will ultimately bring peace and fruitful outcomes in the ministry of caring for our neighbors in need.

Joseph Marie Perrin OP observed, "It is impossible to love God without also being led to love the neighbor truly; and it was Catherine's mission to reiterate this truth. This is the heart of Christianity because the union between God and man is one of the consequences of the Incarnation. That is why whatever we do for the least of Christ's brethren we do for Him."[161] Perrin added: "Of all the mystics, Saint Catherine in particular seems to have had the special mission of proclaiming the essential connection between love of God and love of neighbor."[162] This is reflected in paragraph 7 of Catherine's *Dialogue*, as follows:

> Since the soul truly loves Me, it also truly serves its neighbor. It cannot be otherwise because love for Me and love for the neighbor are one and the same thing; the more the soul loves Me, the more it loves its neighbor because love of him proceeds from love of Me. This is the means that I have offered you so that you may practice virtue and may experience it in yourself because, since you cannot profit Me in any way, you should be helpful to your neighbor. This will be the sign that you possess Me by grace in your soul.

The soul enamored of My truth never ceases to make itself useful, in general and in particular, to a greater or a lesser degree, according to the dispositions of him who is to benefit by it and according to the fervor of him who offers it.

When this love of union with Me has disposed the soul to love its neighbor and to extend its desire to include the salvation of the world in general, then the soul, having been rendered useful to itself by conceiving virtue which gives it the life of grace, exercises its ingenuity to see to the needs of each of its neighbors in particular. It then gives aid to those near it according to the different graces that I have granted it so that it may dispense them. It will teach some by word, will give advice to others, and by example will be a model for living. Each one is bound to edify his neighbor by a good, holy and upright life.

These are the virtues that are born of love of neighbor, and there are so many others that you could not name them all... Love of neighbor is perfected in love for Me. When love of neighbor is attained, the law is observed. He who is bound by love does everything it is possible to do.[163]

One of Catherine's earliest biographers, lay Dominican Claire Mary Antony, pointed out that the saint's time of solitude and interaction with God alone, learning to love and serve her neighbor, was time constrained: "To many of the saints it has been granted to spend, not three years, but the whole of a long life, in such heavenly intercourse, in the silence of the hermitage or the peace of the cloister. Catherine was not one of these. Her lot was cast in the world; her life is inextricably woven into the history of her times."[164] "But," Antony added:

In those three years she learned the lessons of a lifetime. No hermit of the desert, no Carmelite or Carthusian mystic has surpassed in his supernatural knowledge of the hidden mysteries of Christ, Catherine Benincasa, the dyer's daughter of Siena, who was so soon to become one of the most important political figures of her day; and who was to die at thirty-three, worn out and broken by her labors. For she had learned, not only to think on God, but to forget herself.[165]

In this ministry of serving the neighbor, God was gentle with Catherine allowing her to begin her active apostolate with baby steps,

34

first joining her parents and siblings for meals and helping with domestic duties. Catherine undertook a variety of household tasks in humble service to her immediate family. Johannes Jorgensen cites the words of Catherine's disciple and friend Fra Tommaso Caffarini: "Now when that gentle maiden" says Caffarini, "saw that it was the will of her Bridegroom that she should live among her fellows, she resolved to live in such a manner that she might serve them as an example. Above all she began to serve the others, not as before, under compulsion, but of her own free will."[166]

Even in her own home, the Lord seemed to have been readying his daughter for her future nursing ministry. One of the Benincasa family servants fell ill, at the time of Catherine's move back into the bosom of the household, and Saint Catherine undertook the task of caring for her; she not only attended to the servant's physical needs but also assumed responsibility for her household duties.[167] It is reported that ultimately, Catherine "nursed the poor woman back to complete health."[168] From ministering within the Benincasa household, Catherine soon began to go forth to care for the sick poor in the homes and hospitals of the city of Siena.

Sister Mary Ann Fatula OP declared: "the same undivided energy that she had given to solitude, Catherine now devoted to caring for the Lord she found in the poor and the sick"[169]:

> Siena knew the largesse of lay people dedicated to the poor by giving their wealth and lives to maintain hospitals, hospices and foundling homes. As one of the Mantellate, Catherine now entered wholeheartedly into the movement so obviously prompted by the Holy Spirit. She served those whom no one else would touch; the leprous and reviling… the abusive… the dying…

"Wherever she turned," Fatula added, "she saw Christ's face in the poor and the suffering."[170] Because Catherine saw the poor and the sick as her brothers and sisters in the human family, and thus also saw Jesus Christ in them, she treated them as if each one was the Son of God Himself."[171]

Igino Giordani described the beginnings of Catherine's apostolic ministry:

35

Each morning, setting out on her first works of charity, bearing a cargo of bread, wine, oil and other supplies, Catherine climbed the stairs of the poor, opened their rickety doors, left her gifts and, being careful not to make her presence known, moved on to other hovels. She was able to do this because as a tertiary, she was not obliged to conventual residence. Here was a new possibility in monasticism, we may call it public monasticism, religious life, not distinct, but fused and infused in the life of the world.[172]

As Dominican Thomas Schwertner reflected, because Catherine "loved God, she loved God's handiwork. Because God is beauty, she would see His beauty reflected as fully and unbrokenly as possible in the mirror of every human soul"; he added that, "through her prayers, her sympathy, her helpfulness, her personal devotion to the sinner, the criminal and the infirm, she tried to free the window of the soul from the dust and grime which sin had spread over it, thereby shutting out the light of God's grace and goodness."[173] Schwertner believed that Saint Catherine had no plan or social program other than to return each individual to God's love.

Catherine was deeply devoted to caring for the ill and infirm in whatever milieu they were to be found. The saint "who endured suffering so courageously, could not bear to see others suffer, especially when their suffering separated them from God instead of drawing them nearer to Him. Catherine, today the patroness of nurses, hovered lovingly around the beds of the sick and in certain instances carried her devotion to the point of heroism."[174] Friar Martin Gillet commented that Catherine's apostolate among the sick and the poor reflected the fact that, "for her, love of one's neighbor was no idle word. As soon as anyone came to seek her aid, even materially, she was ready to do anything even at the risk of her life. As a true daughter of St. Dominic, who sold his books to get money for the poor, Catherine was ingenious in finding ways to assist them."[175]

The accounts of Catherine's tender and compassionate ministry to the ill and the suffering have been documented in the writings of myriad biographers, as well as by the historians of professional nursing. In order to better understand Saint Catherine's "lived experience" of a spiritually oriented ministry to the sick, an exploration of her caregiving activities was undertaken employing the method of hermeneutic phenomenology; this research, together with its conceptual orientation, is explained in Chapter Four; also included in the chapter are numerous excerpts from

Catherine's own writings, supportive of her care of the sick, as contained in the *Dialogue*, the *Letters* and the *Prayers*. The findings of the study, and their importance for contemporary caregivers, are also presented in Chapters Five, Six and Seven. In the immediately following pages, Chapter Three, the personal spirituality which guided Catherine's ministry to the ill and the infirm is described.

Chapter 3. "Lose Yourself on the Cross"
The Spirituality of Serving

"Lose yourself on the Cross (for) the more you lose yourself, the more you will find yourself."
Catherine of Siena: Letter T 316

The Cross
Lose yourself on the Cross,
Catherine taught,
for
It is the Cross that gives
Light,
It is the Cross that gives
Peace,
It is the Cross that gives
Joy,
and,
in the loving wisdom
of our gentle God,
It is on the Cross that the
Word made flesh gives
Life unto eternity.

In discussing the spirituality of the "Christ-Bridge" allegory, described later in this chapter, Catherinian scholar Thomas McDermott OP noted that Saint Catherine does not speak of "'the bridge of Christ' but most often of 'the bridge of Christ crucified.'"[176] McDermott explains that this is "to underscore that it is by the passion, death and resurrection of Christ that God makes possible the gift of communion with himself."[177] For many of us, the cross, while a deeply beloved icon, can at times be a fearful image. We long to follow Christ, to participate in the "gift of communion" with Him, yet when we approach the exigencies of the cross our faith begins to waiver. We are like Peter walking trustingly on the water until, encountering strong winds, we also become afraid that we might drown (Matthew 14: 22-29). Catherine teaches us, by her words and by her example, that the Cross of Christ is a blessed gift, not to be feared but to be treasured and embraced; it is the heart of the spirituality of service.

Catherine's love of the Cross, as well as the joy she experienced in becoming a servant of her Crucified Savior, is revealed in the following pages. The Saint also found light, peace and life in the spirituality of serving her neighbor in need, most especially in the person of the poor and the sick.

In his inspiring narrative poem, written in 1911, Algernon Charles Swinburne offered a poignant meditation on the city of Siena and, pointedly, on its most distinguished citizen Caterina Benincasa, known today simply as Saint Catherine of Siena.[178] The work describes the saint's spirituality of serving those in need and reads in part:

> Then in her sacred saving hands
> She took the sorrows of the lands,
> With maiden palms she lifted up
> The sick time's blood-embittered cup,
> And in her virgin garment furled
> The faint limbs of a wounded world.
> Clothed with calm love and clear desire
> She went forth in her soul's attire,
>   A missive fire.
>   Siena,
>   Algernon Charles Swinburne[179]

Swinburne begins his narrative by introducing the reader to the idyllic beauty of the small Tuscan city of Catherine's birth. He then guides one on a virtual pilgrimage from Siena's great fountain, the Fontebranda, up a hill to Catherine's home, within which Swinburne mused, the saint's "beautiful" face burned with the "light of fiery love."[180] The poet goes on to explain that this "sweetest of saints" lived her life in unceasing "quiet," until the "cries" of those in need called her forth to an active ministry.

In stanza 7 of the ode cited above, Swinburne proposed a poetic description of the saint's spirituality of serving those in need. Catherine's hands, described as "sacred and saving," the poet declared, took within them all of the "sorrows of the lands." For those living in Siena and the neighboring countryside, in the later 14th Century, the "sorrows of the lands" were monumental. The populace of the cities and smaller villages had borne the brunt of two horrendous outbreaks of the bubonic plague, resulting, for many families in poverty, famine and death. The political scene, both national and local, was in a constant state of flux and the Church was, in certain quarters, beset by disorganization and disarray. The result of the latter was the sad fact that many churches were faced with empty pews during worship services; the sick and dying were left with limited access to the comfort and support of the sacraments.

As a consequence of the poverty and famine, as well as the struggles for power among ruling families, cities such as Siena experienced the onset of a multiplicity of diseases and other health related problems. Inadequate hygiene and sanitation, combined with substandard nutrition, resulted in infections, gastrointestinal problems and a variety of illnesses associated with deficient growth and development among the poor. Diseases such as leprosy and bubonic plague were passed from one person to another because of unfamiliarity with the vectors of contagion. And traumatic injuries, at times causing the serious maiming of a victim's body, were the product of the physical conflicts which occurred between feuding families.

All of these "sorrows," as Algernon Swinburne so accurately acknowledged, Catherine took within her "sacred, saving hands" in the carrying out of her Mantellata vocation of caring for the sick and the poor. Catherine's spirituality of serving embodied Swinburne's observation that the saint "lifted up" to the Lord, and enfolded within her treasured Dominican mantle, "the faint limbs" of the "wounded world" in which she found herself. As taught by her Divine Spouse, Catherine poured herself out in the service of the sick and the poor; she fed the hungry, gave drink to the thirsty, clothed the naked, visited those in prison, welcomed strangers and cared for the sick (Matt. 25: 35-36). The saint trusted that in caring for these least of His brothers and sisters, she was in truth caring for Christ.

As recounted in the preceding chapter, Saint Catherine did not, at first, choose to follow a path of active ministry. Yet, as the poet Swinburne affirmed, when called upon by God to serve Him by serving her neighbor, Catherine responded with a soul attired in zeal to follow a vocation of apostolic ministry. The saint, with her heart enflamed by the suffering she encountered, did indeed go forth as "a missive fire," her caregiving bolstered by a spirit of loving service and infinite compassion.

"The Service You Cannot Render Me"

Catherine: Dialogue 7

Blessed Raymond of Capua tells us that, after several prayerful interchanges with God, Saint Catherine finally accepted the fact that He was calling her not to remain in contemplative solitude but to enter actively into caring for the needy.[181] The saint thus began immediately to move into the arena of service to the sick poor through visiting the ailing in their homes, in the hospitals, in the prisons and even in ministering to the injured fallen in the streets of the city. Catherine later described the mandate to serve her neighbors in her letters as well as in a compendium of writings describing her mystical interactions with the Lord known only as the *Dialogue*.

In paragraph seven of her *Dialogue*, Catherine reveals the Lord's teaching that "selfish love deprives (our) neighbors of... charity and affection."[182] The message continues to explain that "all virtues are built on charity for (our) neighbors."[183] The unselfish and loving care of one's neighbors, God told Saint Catherine, "is the means that I have given you to practice and prove your virtue. The service that you cannot render me, you must do for your neighbors."[184] The Lord's teaching on service to the neighbor becomes more precise with the message that his servant must "go beyond a general love for all people" and "set her eye on the specific needs of her neighbors and come to the aid of those nearest to her according to the graces (He) has given her for ministry."[185]

The Lord admitted to Catherine that He had bestowed dissimilar gifts on individuals and made them "ministers" in "different positions and different ranks" for there are many rooms in His house.[186] God concluded with the message that, in loving Him, Catherine would realize love for her neighbors and advised: "If you are bound by this love, you will do everything you can to be of service wherever you are."[187] These words constituted both the catalyst and the heart of the saint's selfless commitment to care for the sick and the poor.

In paragraph 8 of her *Dialogue* Catherine conceded that she heard the Lord's mandate that one must go even "further" in love of Him and of neighbor.[188] Christ's teaching was that His followers must learn to be humble in the service of their neighbors, accepting even responses that may sometimes be "unjust," "cruel," or even "wrathful."[189] It is when this occurs that true virtue will be tested, most especially the virtue of "steadfast courage."[190] Those ministering within the present day healthcare system are acutely aware of the many instances when their vocation demands unselfish and loving care for their patients. Today's caregivers are also cognizant of the fact that they might at times experience unjust treatment related to system dysfunction or simply lack of communication. In such instances humility can be sorely tested.

The spirituality of service is also explored later in the *Dialogue*, in paragraph 64, where Catherine again relates hearing the Lord's instruction that we have been put among our neighbors "so that we can do for them what we cannot do for" Him.[191] The fullness of this service to neighbors, God added, is to "love them without any concern for thanks and without looking for any profit for yourself."[192]

The Lord's ordinance of selfless service to neighbors, of not seeking gratitude or profit, is one of significant relevance to those engaged in contemporary care of the sick, including nurses, physicians, chaplains, pastoral care staff, and a variety of others who minister to the ill and disabled. While admittedly most 21st-century healthcare professionals receive financial compensation for their work, the majority of those who consider caring for the sick a spiritual ministry deny the prominence of monetary reward. A cadre of present day nursing leaders, interviewed to explore the meaning of nursing as a calling of service, spoke passionately about the spiritual meaning of their vocation to care for the sick. The comments of these practicing nurses are reflections of the spirituality of serving the sick as taught by Saint Catherine:

> There is a sacredness in the work we do as nurses, as servants, in our ministry of caring. There is a sacred trust that we hold in the relationship between the nurse and the patients... It makes me think of the Florence Nightingale quote that the nurse often holds in her hands "God's precious gift of life." What a truly sacred trust has been given to us in our ministry of nursing; what a sacred heritage has been left to us in serving for the sick.[193]

Additionally, other nurses reported that, "Nursing is the opportunity to be God's hands and His feet and His voice in serving the people that He has entrusted to me"[194]; "I believe every nurse has a call to service... I am a servant to my patients, to my team to the physician and to the entire nursing staff. Each day we deal with patients who need our service. Each day we deal with staff who need our service... (it) takes compassion, takes caring"[195]; "You don't do nursing for a paycheck. You really need that spiritual force inside you that moves you beyond ordinary patient care; otherwise, you can't do nursing. I know that if I didn't have that spiritual calling; this idea of a calling to serve, I wouldn't have been (working) in the hospital for 29 years"[196]; and "Nursing is something that is a part of you. It is ingrained in the spirit and everything that is you. It is wanting to serve the needy, wanting to serve humanity, and wanting to extend yourself in a service-oriented profession."[197]

In his *Legenda*, Blessed Raymond of Capua described the spirituality of Catherine's ministry of serving as explained by Catherine herself, as well as by direct witnesses to her kindness and compassion. Raymond reported that once Catherine realized that the more loving she was toward her neighbors, the more she would please the Lord, "she prepared and equipped herself as thoroughly as she could to succor the needy."[198] Aside from prayer, we do not know precisely how Catherine "prepared and equipped" herself to care for the sick. Raymond and other biographers do, however, tell us that Catherine in her youth began to reach out to the poor of Siena, seeking her father's permission to distribute alms from the Benincasa household. The saint delivered food and clothing with her own hands to needy families of the neighborhood; she sometimes carried heavy loads of goods at great cost to her own fragile body.

Blessed Raymond described five specific occasions reflecting Saint Catherine's service to the poor in Siena. As those to whom she ministered were in dire need of either housing, food or clothing, and sometimes all three, they were at risk for a variety of potential health threats. Thus, Catherine's early ministry to poverty stricken neighbors might well be considered the beginning of her commitment to community and public healthcare as described later in Chapter Six.

In the first incident, Raymond reported that when Catherine heard of a needy family whose members were suffering from hunger but were ashamed to beg for alms, she immediately gathered grain, wine and oil and delivered the provisions to their home, leaving quickly that her personal charity would remain hidden.[199]

A second anecdote describing Catherine's largesse for the poor reflected not only her spiritual response to Jesus' message – "I was hungry and you gave me food" – but also her concern for the health of those living in poverty. Upon learning of the grave physical distress of a poor widow and her children, all of whom were said to be dying of starvation, Catherine carried a large parcel of food and container of wine to the family. The saint was, herself, unwell at the time with an illness that caused her body to swell; nevertheless, she begged the Lord for strength to be able to carry out the ministry of charity and return home without others being aware of her sacrifice.[200] Saint Catherine had been feeling so ill she spent the entire previous night "praying to our Lord that he would give her strength enough to go and help the poor woman."[201]

In a third interaction, a beggar, who described himself as desperate, asked Catherine for any help she might be able to give him. The saint had no food or alms to give at the time, but she remembered a small silver cross, which was attached to the prayer beads she always carried. Generously, she removed the cross and gave it to the suppliant. It was reported that when the poor man "had received this alms at Catherine's hand, he went his way, and was seen no more to beg that day, as though his coming had been for the cross only."[202]

The fourth narrative described a young man, who was homeless and poverty stricken, begging for some clothing to cover his almost naked body. Saint Catherine gave the man her own woolen tunic which she had worn as protection against the cold.[203] And, in a final scenario, Catherine reportedly gathered a large bag of eggs to feed a frail pauper who was ill and dying of hunger.[204]

Catherine's outreach to the sick poor, as portrayed in these anecdotes, provides a powerful model for contemporary caregivers not only in terms of the assistance we might give but also in being willing to sacrifice our own comfort, if need be, to practice such a ministry of service.

"Lose Yourself on the Cross"
Catherine of Siena: Letter T 316

Many years ago, as a young Sister, I kept a small wooden Cross on my bed; this was a tradition in the community. The devotional item was not a Crucifix, containing the image of our Blessed Lord, but a simple Cross; the symbolism served as a reminder that this was not Jesus' Cross but one's own. On the Cross were inscribed the words of Saint Andrew's beautiful prayer: "O good Cross, long desired and now made ready for my longing soul. With great confidence and joy I come unto thee; do thou then with gladness receive me, the disciple of Him who hung on thee."

I love this prayer, which is so reminiscent of Saint Catherine's teaching that we must "lose" ourselves "on the Cross." It is, admittedly, a challenge to consider losing oneself on a Cross and especially to look forward to the losing with "confidence and joy." But the heart of Saint Andrew's prayer, and the precious treasure given to all who embrace it, is the gift of being able to say of the Cross, that we are "disciples of Him who hung on thee." The blessing and the honor we celebrate, and in which we rejoice, is that of being *His* disciples!

In a letter written to her dear friend Daniella, Saint Catherine spoke of the importance of having the light of truth in order that we may walk "along the way of Christ Crucified, a well-lighted way that gives us life."[205] Catherine added, "Without this light we would be walking in darkness" and may end up in chaos and bitterness.[206] Ultimately, Catherine wrote, each individual must "lose yourself... on the Cross."[207] She explained that, "the more you lose yourself, the more you will find yourself."[208]

In order to fully comprehend Catherine's unwavering advice to "lose oneself on the Cross," it is helpful to remember the illness and healthcare era in which the saint had been called by God to care for the sick and to consider the kinds of diseases and illnesses which she and her companions faced: leprosy, plague and serious traumatic injuries, as well as all manner of untreated conditions such as advanced cancer. These are discussed in later chapters but suffice it to say that the young "nurse" Catherine and her Sisters in the Mantellate Community were most probably ill prepared for the kinds of suffering they would be called upon to encounter when visiting the sick in their homes or in the local hospitals.

At one point we are told, Catherine's mother, Mona Lapa, became very angry with her daughter for her embrace of a ministry of caring for those suffering from leprosy. Mona Lapa not only feared for Catherine's life, but also accused her of potentially carrying the infection home to other members of the Benincasa household. Catherine had, however, as she advised others, lost herself in the Cross of the Crucified Christ. And it was thus that she was able to "turn away from her mother's wrath with soft answers convincing her that she had no reason to fear for her daughter's health and insisting that it was impossible for her to give up a job that had been laid upon her by the Lord."[209] It was this powerful spirit of obedience and trust in God's care that allowed Catherine to peacefully continue her service to the sick, even to those with the life threatening communicable diseases.

This sense of spiritual security was especially important for Catherine during her ministry to those suffering from the "Black Death," the Western European bubonic plague epidemic of the later 14th Century. Pondering Catherine's ministry to plague victims brings to mind the anecdotes told of the courageous firefighters and police officers during our own country's "9/11" tragedy, when thousands perished in the burning towers of New York City's "World Trade Center."[210] Observers of the disaster reported that, while others rushed away from the burning buildings, the firefighters and police officers rushed toward them.[211] These brave caregivers may truly be considered to have "lost themselves in the Cross of Christ," risking their lives for brothers and sisters in need, just as Catherine did when she traversed the streets of Siena seeking those who had fallen ill with the plague. While many rushed away from plague victims, Catherine, as the firefighters and police officers of "9/11," rushed toward those suffering from the deadly disease.

The Joy of Serving the Sick

In reviewing the contemporary healthcare literature, one does not find a great number of writings focused specifically on the "joy" of serving the sick. Yet, in talking with today's practicing caregivers to the ill and infirm, frequently the experiences and anecdotes they share reflect the joy and satisfaction found in their ministry to the ailing. As one individual, educated as both nurse and chaplain, put it:

> I thought that in my interactions with patients, I would be giving to them; I would be bringing my caring and support to ease their suffering a little. Well, I hope I do some of that but really I'm the one on the receiving end in this ministry of caring for those who are sick. It's such a blessing to be allowed to serve the Lord in this way. And it's such a joy! It's the joy of serving Christ in His most fragile brothers and sisters.

Three recent nursing journal articles explored the concept of finding joy in caring for the ill. In discussing the issues of nursing shortage, as well as other problems in the present day healthcare arena, clinical nurse specialist Jeffrey Albaugh concluded: "It may seem difficult to find passion and joy in nursing during these tumultuous times, but it is essential. Now more than ever, nurses need to feel a strong passion for work that brings about joy... Passion will continue to propel the nurse forward toward the joy he or she discovers in nursing."[212] Beverly

47

Malone also describes the "joy of nursing" in such a way that "the passion creates a fire and an ability to touch and reach my patients in a healing way."[213] Additionally, Associate Dean of Nursing, Donna Middaugh, associated joy in caring for the sick with "thriving," which, she asserted, fuels the caregiver with "energy."[214]

In his book dedicated to the need for compassion in our wounded world, Precious Blood Missionary Joseph Nassall C.PP.S. relates the ability to be joyful to the virtue of compassion; he notes: "Ironically, when we increase our capacity for compassion, we make room for joy."[215] In her ministry to the sick and poor, Saint Catherine of Siena is described by those who knew her as being unfailingly and unequivocally compassionate, as well as being unfailingly and unequivocally joyful. The source of Catherine's joy in serving the ill was the fact that she had truly lost herself, her own concerns, her needs and her desires, in the Cross of her Beloved Spouse. Loving Him, in loving service to her neighbor, constituted the heart of the saint's joy.

As mentioned in Chapter One, from early childhood Catherine was observed to be joyful thus meriting the title "Euphrosyne"; this label was associated with that of the Greek goddess of joy whose own name was derived from the word "euphrosynos," meaning "good cheer" or "merriment." The young saint was perceived as "so sweet that she was constantly being lent to friends and neighbors who wanted her to spend a day with them."[216] Clearly this joyful temperament continued into her young adult years also as early biographer Theodosia Drane wrote of Catherine, citing the testimony of her companions: "She is ever joyful and smiling and counts her own sufferings as nothing; thought she has always the sharp knife in her side, yet she makes light of it with her spouse, and recreates herself cheerfully, praying the while for those who have need of pardon... From the crown of her head to the soul of her feet, she is full of Christ, and sings His glory day and night."[217] Drane added:

> In fact there was an ever springing fountain of joy in Catherine's heart which habitually found expression in her words and countenance At times this joy could take the form of playfulness, and in the frank and happy intercourse which existed between her and her spiritual children there was nothing of restraint. They gathered about her and gave her the tenderest and most familiar titles; 'Nostra dolcissima mamma' was the ordinary name by which they addressed her.[218]

Saint Catherine's joy in her Mantellata role of serving the sick was a true reflection of her Dominican vocation. Our holy Father Dominic was described as ever joyful, and the second Master of the Order, Blessed Jordan of Saxony, embraced the gospel message of Saint Matthew: "Enter into the joy of the Lord" (25: 21) "as an invitation to become a Dominican."[219] As Paul Murray OP pointed out in *The New Wine of Dominican Spirituality*: "There were many different kinds of men and women who followed faithfully the path of Dominic in the early centuries of the Order. But they did have one thing in common. All of them, after the example of Dominic, had learned to drink deep from the wine of God's word. And they became, we can say, not only witnesses of certain great moral and doctrinal truths, but witnesses also of an unimaginable joy."[220] Catherine of Siena had indeed drunk deeply from the "wine of God's word" and demonstrated in all of her ministries this "unimaginable joy"; she was not a woman who loved God, but a woman "in love" with God.

Myriad anecdotes describing Catherine's ministry to the ill and the infirm, as well as general reports of her healthcare activities exemplifying the saint's joyfulness in the service of the sick, are reflected in the following pages. Descriptions of Catherine's joy in caring for the ailing are included in comments by both early and later biographers. Fra Tommaso Caffarini, the saint's Dominican disciple and comrade, wrote in the 14th Century of her care for the plague victims: "Never did she appear more admirable than at this time. She was always with the plague stricken; she prepared them for death, she buried them with her own hands. I myself witnessed the joy with which she tended them."[221] And, writing some six centuries later, Richard Cardinal Cushing, observed that as Catherine moved about Siena, caring for the sick and the poor, the citizens "felt the joy of her presence" and "caught the gladness of her countenance that ever wore a smile."[222]

The secret to Saint Catherine's ever present joy in serving her sick brothers and sisters was the fact that she had indeed chosen to lose herself by embracing the Cross of her Beloved Spouse. Those whom Christ loved, Catherine loved, and in caring for them she trusted that she was caring for Him as well. What greater joy could she possibly know than to be blessed with the gift of serving those whom Jesus loved?

The "Christ-Bridge" Allegory
"I am the Way, the Truth and the Life"
John 14: 6

Perhaps the best known spiritual teaching advanced by Saint Catherine of Siena was that contained within her "Christ-Bridge" allegory, or, as Catherine preferred to put it, the "Bridge of Christ Crucified." In the allegory, Catherine identified Christ's body as metaphor for a bridge upon which pilgrims must travel in order to achieve salvation. Thomas McDermott OP suggests that the saint's "Christ-Bridge" allegory is the central "image on which she hangs many of her most important teachings"; it is a bridge which reaches from earth to heaven.[223] Because the original road to heaven was destroyed by Adam's sin, "out of love the Eternal Father made of his Son a bridge so that we could approach him and become like him by sharing his life, joy and beauty."[224] Saint Catherine, relating to Christ's words recorded in the Gospel of John: "I am the way, the truth and the life," envisioned the Christ-Bridge as the only way for a person to reach his or her eternal goal. She taught that all of us are "obliged to pass along this bridge" on our spiritual journey.[225]

Catherine's early biographer, Edmund Gardner, interpreted the image of the "Christ-Bridge" as the "figure of the Word... Catherine laying stress upon the doctrine that the eternal truth has created us without ourselves, but will not save us without ourselves."[226] In a similar vein, the bridge was described by Joseph Marie Perrin OP as related to the primary mission of Christ "who became man... to permit us to reach Him who loves us so greatly that He seems unable to do without us"; he added that, "under the bridge thunders the river that sweeps to perdition those who will go there by refusing to cross over by the bridge of salvation... Only through love can we set foot on and cross over the bridge."[227] Dominican Giacinto D'Urso observed that there are two facts which "presuppose the bridge: original sin and the incarnation... (God) sent His Son to earth to be our mediator and to re-open the gates of heaven with the Cross and with his blood."[228]

The "Christ-Bridge" concept first appears in paragraph 26 of the *Dialogue.* Catherine teaches that the bridge of Christ connects our earthly home with that of heaven by reason of God having "joined" Himself with our humanity.[229] In Letter T354, written to one of her disciples, the saint asserted: "Christ crucified is our road, and he is truth itself, and he is life. He said so himself: 'I am the way, the truth and the life.'"[230] Also, in *Dialogue #26*, Catherine described the three *scaloni*, or stairs, of the "Christ-Bridge," which correlate to three stages of the spiritual life. These stairs are associated with the Lord's feet nailed to the Cross; His wounded side, "that was pierced to reveal the ineffable love of the heart; and Christ's mouth, where the bitterness of gall and vinegar is turned to peace... These three steps represent the three powers of the soul: will, memory and understanding; as likewise the three states of the soul in God's service, by which she passes from servile fear and mercenary obedience to true fidelity and friendship and, lastly, to perfect filial love."[231] Catherine also wrote of the steps in a letter to a community of Augustinian nuns explaining that in approaching Christ's feet nailed to the Cross, we try to humbly rid ourselves of selfish self-will.[232]

At the first stair, one attempts to discard disordered affections and to separate his or her feet from being anchored in the material world and place them on the nail pierced feet of Jesus.[233] This symbolism was popular in the Middle Ages, when the image of Christ's feet was viewed as a reflection of the soul's journey, while Christ's hands "represented the good works that each Christian did."[234] Arrival at Christ's feet, at this first scalene, or stair, on the Christ-Bridge, represents the beginning of an individual's spiritual journey. The first stair initiates "the ascent on the Christ-Bridge in which the Divine likeness increases" in the pilgrim traveler.[235]

At the second stair, we experience Christ's deep love in the pouring out of blood from his wounded side; at that stage, one seeks a love of friendship with Christ, which involves serving the Lord not for any personal gain or comfort, but rather "in the simple hope of pleasing him."[236] The "characteristic feature" of this stair is described as "the discovery of God's love in Christ, an immense love which embraces the whole of humanity and calls it to him but which is more personal for each soul the more docilely each one surrenders himself to it."[237] As an individual traversing the Christ-Bridge grows in love, "more joy and consolation are experienced."[238]

Finally, coming near to the Lord's mouth, we find the peace experienced in perfect obedience to His will and to the gospel message which He taught; when we arrive at the mouth of Christ, we receive "his kiss of peace."[239] At this third stage on the Christ-Bridge the "last vestiges" of one's selfish will are obliterated: "The 'war' between one's higher and lower self has been won by the former and peace ensues."[240] The third stage on the Bridge reveals an inner unity because all the powers of one's soul "now cling to God for His sake alone."[241] Thomas McDermott explains that the three *scaloni* on the Christ-Bridge, representing the stages of an individual's spiritual development, also reflect "different degrees of love of God and neighbor."[242]

Although only three stairs were initially identified in the allegory, Catherine later introduced a fourth "stage" as being that time after death when a pilgrim traveler arrives at the gate of heaven; it is a time of perfect union with God and envisioned as the "fruit" of the third stage.[243] The fourth and final stage symbolizes the pilgrim's anticipation of heaven, the "quiet of the soul now at peace with God."[244] This stage indicates arrival at the place where one can "glimpse the other side."[245] McDermott reflects that here "the soul experiences a pledge or a foretaste of the final end of the Christ-Bridge."[246] This is the time when death separates the soul from the body, and the individual is united with God in love.[247]

In her book *A Retreat with Catherine of Siena*, Elizabeth Dryer commented that, in Catherine's spirituality, "the most visible and compelling truth about God is Jesus, the Christ."[248] Thus it was that in the *Dialogue*, Dryer pointed out, Catherine "developed at great length the image of Christ as the bridge."[249] In Dryer's perception, at the first stair we obey Christ "out of fear rather than love"; at the second stair we do obey out of love but that love remains "tinged with selfishness." At the third stair, however, our obedience is derived from a deep loving response to Christ's truth.[250] Dryer added: "The way of truth is the way of Christ, and Catherine warns her readers to take heed that they not take the path beneath the bridge... for it is not the way of truth."[251]

Saint Catherine's Christocentric spirituality, as reflected in the allegory of the "Christ-Bridge," was the driving force of her contemplative life as well as her apostolic ministry. As Dominican Thomas Schwertner remarked:

> Catherine sought nothing more earnestly than to put on Christ, and Him crucified. She would be the spouse of the King of the Five Wounds. Therefore she realized early in life the need of putting off herself completely and entirely. Strong woman that she was, it called for no mean nor unheroic battling to drive away the faults-impatience, censoriousness, a spirit of criticism-which are the inevitable

accompaniments of a nervous, vivacious temperament like hers. Outward persecution, indeed, helped to bring under control the hastiness and impetuosity of her nature; but it was within that all the finer battles were fought out. By drawing the sword of penance daily against herself... she succeeded in crucifying the carnal spirit with its sensitive appetites, in constraining her will to accept the 'hard sayings' of Christian reason, and in submitting her mind to the guidance of truth.[252]

Schwertner concluded that, "The sum total of (Catherine's) spiritual teaching, as also the mainspring of all her striving was charity... She lived to love. She loved to love. She made all things oil and fuel to feed the living flame of her love."[253]

The allegory of the "Christ-Bridge" resonates with today's caregivers to the ill and the infirm as it must have for Catherine in her care for the sick poor. The pain and suffering experienced by those who are ill may challenge beliefs about the meaning and purpose of life for contemporary healthcare ministers. It is only in marveling at the immense love of a Crucified Savior that both caregivers and those they serve can find peace; it is by casting away earthly cares and choosing to trust in the One sent by his Father to be "The Way, the Truth and the Life," that acceptance is possible. Catherine, who herself lost beloved friends and family members to the horrors of the "Black Death," taught this in many letters reflecting her desire to offer compassion and comfort to others.

Saint Catherine recognized the pouring out of Jesus' blood from His wounded side as a model for the kind of love that was needed to minister to those beset by devastating diseases such as leprosy and plague. In her spirituality of serving the sick, Catherine's caring was unequivocally self-giving, a ministry of love of God and of neighbor with no thought for her own safety and security. Such selfless love is also demanded of 21st-century caregivers who daily negotiate medical minefields, encountering unfamiliar diseases and untested therapeutic protocols, which may or may not result in the cure or alleviation of symptoms.

For those ill with life-threatening, degenerative conditions, such as Alzheimer's disease or ALS (amyotrophic lateral sclerosis), and for their caregivers, the allegory of the "Christ Bridge" holds the hope which can be supported only by faith in God's love and mercy. Catherine was never without hope for those she served, despite their physical or spiritual challenges. She begged the Lord a thousand times over, to accept her embrace of suffering, as a stipend for His comfort and compassion for those to whom she ministered.

Whoever Wishes to be My Servant

"Whoever wishes to become great among you must be your servant...
for the Son of Man came not to be served but to serve."
Mark 10:43, 45

The spirituality of serving is both very old, as taught by Jesus Himself, and very new, in light of a contemporary interpretation described as the theory and practice of servant leadership.[254] Servant leadership is considered a necessary attribute of those who care for the sick.[255] Nurse historian Josephine Dolan explained that early Christian ministers to the ill modeled Jesus' example of serving: "Instead of saying the word and healing the sick, Christ gave individual attention to the needs of all by touching, anointing and taking the hand."[256] Jesus has been labeled as the "enduring model of servanthood... The form of Christ's servanthood included self-emptying, identification with the needy and self-giving."[257] This image is supported by authors of the book *Lead Like Jesus*, Ken Blanchard and Phil Hodges, who assert that Christ was the pre-eminent figure of a servant; they add: "The call by Jesus to servant leadership is clear and unequivocal... Servant leadership is to be a living statement of who we are in Christ, how we treat one another and how we demonstrate the love of Christ for the whole world."[258]

In the current understanding of service in healthcare settings, such as the hospital or clinic, servant ministers place others' needs before their own; the servant leader wishes first to serve. Saint Catherine is described as a role model for 21st-century servant leaders who care for the sick, especially for those ministering to the ill and infirm in the community; this label is derived from her service to sick poor in Siena, particularly to persons stricken with the plague.[259]

From data elicited in a study of 75 contemporary nursing leaders, all of whom considered their vocation to be guided by a spirituality of service, a model of servant leadership for those who minister to the ill was developed. The key elements of the model include five attributes describing one's attitude toward serving the sick and eight themes identifying behavioral characteristics of the servant in healthcare. The attitudinal attributes included viewing the vocation to care for the sick as "A Blessed Calling," including within it an attitude of "Passionate Caring"; the vocation being "Ingrained in one's Spirit"; caregivers being willing to go "The Extra Mile" and considering their service "A Privilege."[260] The behavioral themes reflecting actions of servant leader caregivers are: "Listening with the Heart," "Giving of Yourself," "Doing Ministry," "Assessing Needs," "Becoming an Advocate," "Discerning Decisions," "Making a Difference," and "Being There to Serve."[261]

In analyzing Catherine of Siena's ministry to the sick poor, in context of this model, we may describe the saint as providing a true example of servanthood for current caregivers to the ill and the infirm. In terms of attitude, Catherine decidedly considered her ministry to the sick as "a blessed calling"; in fact she did not want to leave her contemplative solitude until she was convinced that it was within this apostolic vocation that the Lord was calling her to serve. Catherine had a "passionate caring" for those to whom she ministered as reflected in the instances of ministry when she was treated unkindly by her patients yet continued the loving service which had become, it seemed, very quickly "ingrained" in her "spirit." To say that Catherine would go "the extra mile" is an understatement considering the sometimes stressful nursing conditions she embraced, and her tender, compassionate, and continuous care demonstrated the "privilege" with which she viewed her vocation to minister to the sick.

As to Catherine's servant behaviors, we know that she "listened with her heart" to the sufferings of others; this is reflected in the many letters in which she responded to the spiritual, emotional and/or physical pain of the recipient. In the "case examples," described in the following chapters, Catherine's ministry of service is shown to represent a "giving of self," the "assessing" and "discerning" of needs for the sick she encountered, the practice of "becoming an advocate," especially for Sienese citizens involved in domestic disputes, the gift of "making a difference" in the lives of those who were ill, and, finally, always "being there" to serve the sick whenever called upon.

Catherine of Siena's spiritual approach to caring not only supports the contemporary model of servanthood in healthcare but is an exemplar par excellence of both the concept's theory and practice. Catherine's servant oriented attitudes and behaviors are clearly demonstrated in the many caregiving anecdotes contained in Chapters 5 and 6, as well as in those described in the analysis of her "sacred covenant of caring" presented in Chapter Seven.

Catherine as Mystic and Minister
"The Cell Within Your Soul"
Catherine: Letter T 41

Saint Catherine of Siena was a multidimensional woman. She was a scholar, teaching others to live the gospel message of Jesus, a nurse and a minister who cared for the physical and spiritual needs of the ill and infirm and a mystic who experienced multiple Divine visitations sometimes culminating in miraculous occurrences. In his *Legenda*, Blessed Raymond of Capua related many mystical encounters, including ecstatic interactions with the Lord, which occurred during the saint's life.

Author Laurie Feldman suggests that a "fascinating aspect of Saint Catherine's mysticism was the frequency and familiarity of her conversations with God."[262] Feldman asserted that "To Catherine, God was an intimate acquaintance."[263] Such mystical occurrences were not uncommon in the medieval era: "Advocates of mysticism in the middle-ages believed that the soul could have direct contact with God and that it was thus possible for believers to have a conscious relationship with Him. They encouraged others with the possibility of union with God in this life, that is, a direct and intimate consciousness of the divine presence."[264]

A difference noted in Catherine's mysticism, however, was the fact that "the Dominican tertiary witnessed to the movement out in the world with a universal message... the saint's mystical gifts... were given to her not only in private but also in the public forum."[265] That is, the saint "combined contemplative union with Christ and a divinely given apostolate of preaching and peacemaking."[266] Although a contemplative and mystic, Catherine was also a practical caregiver to the sick, ministering to the needs of the ill in the hospital, in the home and in the community. The mystical Catherine who spent hours in contemplative prayer, interacting only with her Divine Spouse, was also the nurse and minister Catherine who walked the streets of Siena at night, armed only with her small lantern and scent bottle, seeking to bring comfort to those fallen ill with the plague.

A further dimension of Catherine's mystical spirituality, combined with her apostolic ministry to the sick, is reflected in the healing miracles attributed, to her intervention, which occurred after the Virgin's death.[267] Blessed Raymond asserted: "When Catherine's earthly pilgrimage had ended and she had received her reward, the Divine power that had always accompanied her did not cease revealing the merits of her sanctity to the faithful."[268] For some, the healings involved the ill or injured person touching a piece of cloth which had, in turn, been touched to the saint's remains; in other cases, healings were the result of a sick person touching Catherine's body as it lay in the coffin in St. Dominic's chapel.

The healing miracles described by Raymond included: the restoration of use of a Franciscan Sister's wasted arm, the healing of a young boy with a badly contracted neck, return of the ability to walk for a man with a paralyzed leg, the erasure of a leprous mass from the face of a young girl, the cure of consumption which no treatment had been able to effect, the healing of gout, cures of several serious eye problems, and healing of a variety of other diseases and illness conditions.[269] Blessed Raymond ended his narration of Catherine's healings with the comment: "I can recollect hearing tales of many more miracles but even my memory is growing old and I cannot remember them all clearly."[270]

The important point about Saint Catherine's miracles, in context of this chapter, is that even in death, the saint continued to shower her mercy and tender care on those who were ill, disabled or injured. Those who had known Catherine and had confidence in her service to the sick in life, trusted her service to the sick in death as well; their faith in the saint's compassion did not go unrewarded.

When attempting to comprehend Saint Catherine's mysticism it is important to remember that accounts of mystical actions and interactions, such as those related to ecstasies, Divine visitations and even miracles, were in the 14th Century often the norm in descriptions of the lives of holy people. Thomas McDermott noted that "every legenda… had the purpose of edifying the Christian faithful so as to build up spirituality."[271] "Miracles," he added, "were a standard part."[272] As a student of the medieval period put it, in "broaching the issue of saints, miracles and relics… we have to recognize that, in the Middle-Ages, believing in these phenomena was absolutely normal and a part of everyday life."[273] Miracles were central to the texture of Christian experience.[274] Miraculous occurrences and mystical union with God were viewed as a part of a saint's experience, not simply a matter of "theory" or "belief."[275]

In the introduction to Blessed Raymond's *Legenda Major*, or major account of the life of Catherine, Thomas Gilby OP admitted that the "signs and wonders (Catherine's) companions thought so admirable" may be difficult for the contemporary reader to accept, but he advises that we "have to remind ourselves that she is our model for the general design of her desire, not all the details."[276] Father Gilby's advice might well pertain to Catherine's practice of fasting from a variety of foods and liquids, a mortification which began when the saint was still a young child. Raymond reported of Catherine that "When she was fifteen she gave up wine and drank nothing but water"; this was a significant mortification in an Italian household.[277] He added that Catherine "gradually learned to do without any kind of cooked food except bread, and soon reached the point of living entirely on bread and raw herbs."[278]

Later students of Saint Catherine have described her practice of fasting as "anorexia mirabilis" or holy anorexia. Physician Fernando Forcen points out that this was not anorexia as we understand it today for "self-starvation was a common behavior among religious women in the middle-ages... suffering was considered a way to imitate Jesus in remembrance of Christ's torments during the passion."[279] Forcen's observation is supported by scholars Maria Reda and Giuseppe Sacco who explain that, "in the medieval period, the control, renunciation and torture of the body were understood not so much as a rejection of the physical but as a way of achieving the Divine."[280]

"The Cell within Your Soul"

Saint Catherine's concept of establishing a cell within one's soul is found in Blessed Raymond's *Legenda*.[281] The spiritual concept is also found in a letter which Catherine wrote to her first confessor, Fra Tommaso della Fonte.[282] Catherine was particularly close to Fra Tommaso as he had been raised in the Benincasa household from the age of ten after being orphaned by the plague.[283] In the letter Catherine tells her confessor and adopted brother, now a Dominican priest, that she longs to see him "united with and transformed in God."[284] The saint offered the thought that if we were to ask God how to discover His holy will his response would be as follows: "Dearest Children, if you wish to discover and experience the effects of my will, dwell within the cell of your soul."[285] Catherine explained that within the heart's interior cell: "We see that our being is from God... we get to the living water, the very core of the knowledge of God's true and gentle will which desires nothing else but that we be made holy... if we dwell there, we will necessarily come to know both ourselves and God's goodness."[286]

It was because of the presence of this interior cell that Catherine could incorporate both the "mystical" and "ministerial" in the spirituality of her service to the sick and the poor. The "mystic" Catherine desired only to live and love in intimate union with her beloved Spouse to whom she had dedicated her virginity at the age of seven. Yet, the "minister" Catherine, in her Mantellata role of caring for the ill and infirm, could not but respond to her Blessed Lord's call to "render to her neighbor" the caring which she could not now physically provide to Him. Quite simply, the saint who had created a "cell" within her heart was able to proceed with her apostolic ministry while never abandoning her contemplative vocation. Suzanne Noffke observed that "Catherine's life of prayer joined with action is in itself the pinnacle of her teaching."[287] Catherine ultimately learned and affirmed, by her example and her writing, that embracing the service of one's neighbor was the truest way to demonstrate love and filial obedience to God.[288]

Chapter 4. "Ablaze with Loving Fire"
Care for the Sick Neighbor

"I long to see you so totally ablaze with loving fire that you become
one with the gentle first Truth"
Catherine of Siena: Letter T 137

Loving Fire
Ablaze with loving fire
she embraced the beloved
neighbor,

In the desolate homes of the
sick and the poor,

In the bleak wards of the hospitals
and the leper house,

In the abandoned streets of the
anguished city,

In the barren cells of the
cheerless prisons.

Catherine of Siena
Hope of the hopeless,
Consoler of the inconsolable,
Lover of the unloved.

Although as observed in the opening pages of this book, Saint
Catherine of Siena has long been identified as the Patroness of those who
care for the sick, a number of her biographers have paid scant attention
to her activities of ministering to the ill and the infirm. An exception is
Blessed Raymond of Capua whose well-known 14th-century *Legenda*
includes a chapter entitled "Charity Toward the Infirm." In this
discussion, Raymond presents the details of three "case-studies"
describing individual patients whom Catherine cared for, one in the

hospital, and two in their homes. Blessed Raymond also identified a number of Catherine's other services to the sick; they are, however, scattered throughout the *Legenda*'s following chapters and sometimes buried amidst theological or spiritual discussions.

Powerful examples of Catherine's caregiving are also found in the *Supplemento Alla Vita di Santa Caterina da Siena* by Fra Tommaso d'Antonio Caffarini; this work was written in the 14th Century, as well, shortly after Catherine's death. One of the goals of Fra Tommaso Caffarini's research was to support the process of canonization for Catherine of Siena "whose way of life had given the Dominican Penitents a new inspiration and sense of focus."[289]

Other biographers, both early and later, such as Augusta Theodosia Drane, Edmund Gardner, Johannes Jorgensen, Alice Curtayne, Catherine Meade, and Thomas McDermott to name only a few, have included information on Catherine's healthcare ministries in various detail. Material suggestive of Catherine's concern for the sick neighbor is also found in the saint's own works: the *Dialogue*, the *Letters*, and the *Prayers*.

The goal of the this book is to identify, describe and analyze information describing Catherine's ministry to the sick, as documented by her biographers, in the accounts of nurse historians, in the reflections of authors of scholarly articles and in selected passages from Saint Catherine's personal writings.

Documentation of Catherine's Care for the Sick

In order to collect and interpret data reflecting Catherine's lived experience of caring for the sick in the later middle-ages, the research method of hermeneutic phenomenology, as articulated by Max van Manen, was employed.[290] For van Manen, phenomenology "aims at getting a deeper understanding of the nature or meaning of the everyday experience."[291] Hermeneutic phenomenology, which is both descriptive and interpretive, posits an approach which consists of a retrospective reflection on a "lived experience"; it is "reflection on experience that has already passed or been lived through."[292] Thus it is an appropriate method to attempt to understand the lived experience of Catherine's ministry of caring for the sick in the 14th Century.

According to van Manen, hermeneutic phenomenology must be "presuppositionless," that is without predetermined ideas or concepts which could bias the research.[293] While I have, in the past, written briefly about the nursing ministry of Catherine of Siena, the work was abbreviated and descriptive. For the present research more complete data reflecting Catherine's thoughts and experiences were collected through extensive review of the autobiographical, biographical/hagiographical, theological, spiritual and historical literature. Pre-conceived notions were "bracketed" or set aside during the conduct of the study.[294]

A "Literature Review Guide" was created to focus the data collection on the following topics: Catherine's world (the Church, politics and family life in 14th-century Siena); Catherine's early spirituality; the saint's experience of contemplative solitude; the Mantellata vocation and call to active ministry; health and illness issues in the Italian later Middle Ages, especially hospital care in such facilities as *Santa Maria della Scala*, *Casa della Miseracordia* and *San Lazzaro*; and Catherine's apostolic activities of caring for the sick in the community, in the home, in the hospital and in the prisons. Selected concepts identified in Sister Suzanne Noffke's conceptual schema for "Exploring Catherine's Theology and Spirituality" were also employed to focus the research.[295]

Conceptual Orientation

Suzanne Noffke introduces her conceptual schema by suggesting that, in order to "learn from the spirituality of a saint such as Catherine of Siena," three interrelated levels of concern may offer guidance. These levels include: (1) Catherine's "personal spirituality"; (2) "her thought concerning spirituality (as this had expression in writing, preaching)"; and (3) "the application of her example and teaching to one's own spirituality or that of others."[296] While Noffke's entire comprehensive schema is more complex than appropriate for the present exploration of Catherine's spirituality of caring for the sick, a number of key concepts are ideally suited to providing a conceptual orientation for the study.

Conceptual Level 1

In examining Catherine's personal spirituality selected concepts included: understanding "how Catherine actually perceived and lived out her relationship with the mystery of God," "what convictions most strongly motivated her response in faith"[297] and, importantly, the influences of history, tradition and culture on Catherine's attitudes and behavior.[298] Data sources identified for this study were Catherine's autobiographical and heuristic writings, as well as biographical/ hagiographical and historical materials descriptive of her spirituality and ministry. Also of interest were contemporary reflections on Catherine's personal spirituality and theology.[299]

Literature reviewed for the research on Catherine's spirituality of caring for the sick included both primary and secondary sources.

Primary Sources

The primary data sources included: *Catherine of Siena: The Dialogue* (translation and introduction by Suzanne Noffke OP); *The Letters of Catherine of Siena*, Volumes 1-4 (translated with introduction and notes, by Suzanne Noffke OP); *The Prayers of Catherine of Siena* (translated and edited by Suzanne Noffke OP); the *Legenda Majore* or "The Life of St. Catherine of Siena" by Blessed Raymond of Capua; the *Leggenda Minore di Santa Caterina da Siena e Lettere dei Suoi Discipoli*, and the *Supplemento Alla Vita di Santa Caterina da Siena* by Fra. Tommaso D' Antonio Caffarini; and "The Miracoli of Catherine of Siena" written by an anonymous author.

As well as Catherine's own writings, the classic *Legenda* by Blessed Raymond was considered a primary source of information in describing Catherine's ministry to the sick. While Raymond's account of Catherine's life does appear to belong in the literary genre of hagiography, her confessor is to be commended for his meticulous documentation of sources for the work. For example, at the end of each chapter describing some aspect of Catherine's spirituality and/or ministry, Raymond concludes with comments such as: "All that is contained in the present chapter I heard from the Virgin herself and from Lapa her mother"[300]; "I must insist that all that I write was either confessed to me by Catherine herself or I found it amongst the writings of Fra Tommaso, her first confessor"[301]; and "the bulk of its (i.e., the chapter's) contents are guaranteed by the Virgin herself, and by her words and open acts, and by my predecessor as her confessor."[302]

Examined as primary sources, as well, were selected passages from Fra Tommaso Caffarini's *Supplemento Alla Vita di Santa Caterina da Siena*, which was composed as a supplement to the original *Legenda* of Blessed Raymond of Capua and *Caffarini's Leggenda Minore Di Santa Caterina Da Siena E Lettere Dei Suoi Discepoli*. In the *Supplemento Alla Vita*, Fra Caffarini described a number of instances of Catherine's ministry to the sick not included in Raymond's *Legenda*. In a 2010 Italian language edition of the *Supplemento Alla Vita di Santa Caterina da Siena*, the publisher noted that the book was "born from the wish of disciples of Caterina who pointed out to Fra Tommaso... that in the main biography of the saint, *La Leggenda Majore*, compiled by Blessed Raymond, important facts of her life were missing."[303] It was suggested that the *Supplemento* is a primary source "for those who wish to gain a thorough understanding of the figure of Saint Catherine."[304]

In Fra Caffarini's *Leggenda Minore*, also, certain reports of Catherine's ministry to the sick, not found in the *Leggenda Majore*, are included; an example is the anecdote describing the saint's care of a young prisoner condemned to death for minor political indiscretions.

"The Miracoli of Catherine of Siena," believed to have been written around 1374, presents a brief picture of Saint Catherine "as a young woman who was already known locally for her visions, asceticism and patient service to the poor and the sick."[305] This abbreviated biography is believed to have been composed by someone who knew Catherine personally and wanted to share a condensed account of her life with the common people.

Secondary Sources

Twenty-eight additional works, reviewed for data on Saint Catherine's care of the sick, included the writings of such authors as: Augusta Theodosia Drane, Edmund Gardner, Johannes Jorgensen, Claire Mary Antony, Martin Gillet, Igino Giordani, Joseph Marie Perrin, Thomas Luongo, Giuliana Cavallini, Suzanne Noffke, Mary Ann Fatula, Arrigo Levasti, Alice Curtayne, Mary O'Driscoll, Sigred Undset, Catherine Meade, Thomas McDermott and Giacinto D'Urso. Three early publications were considered particularly important as the authors reported their examination of a number of Catherinian materials in their original Italian or Latin formats; these were the works of Augusta Theodosia Drane, Edmund Gardner and Johannes Jorgensen.

A comprehensive biography entitled *The History of St.Catherine of Siena and Her Companions* was first published in 1880 by Augusta Drane. In the preface, Drane noted that the objective of the work was to place facts of Catherine's life, identified by others, in correct chronological order and to address previously neglected supplemental material.[306] As well as drawing upon the famous *Legenda* of Raymond of Capua, Drane cited passages from 35 other biographical/hagiographical writings such as the *La Leggenda Minore* and the *Supplemento Alla Leggenda di Santa Caterina* by Fra. Tommaso D'Antonio Caffarini, the *Processus Contestationem* edited by Tommaso Caffarini, and the *Lettere di Santa Caterina*, as well as numerous other works. Augusta Drane concluded her preface with the comment that, in describing the life and ministry of Saint Catherine of Siena, a "rule has been strictly adhered to of excluding all imaginary details and introducing nothing for which there does not exist unimpeachable authorities."[307]

In *Saint Catherine of Siena: A Study in the Religion, Literature and History of the Fourteenth Century in Italy*, published in 1907, Edmund Gardner, like Augusta Drane, was conscientious in describing the sources used in his research on Catherine's life. Five key resources identified were: the "Vita" or "*Legenda*" (*Legenda Prolix* or *Leggenda Maggiore*) by Blessed Raymond of Capua; the "*Leggenda Abbreviata*" (*Leggenda Minore*), the *Supplementum* and the *Processus* by Fra Tommaso d'Antonio Caffarini; and Catherine's *Letters*.[308]

Johannes Jorgensen's biography *Saint Catherine of Siena*, published in 1939, also included identification of original sources: the "*Singularia et Mira Sanctae Caterinae Senesis*" (Jorgensen considered this document, containing the notes of Saint Catherine's first confessor Fra Tommaso della Fonte, as her original biography); *La Legenda Majore* of Blessed Raymond of Capua; *La Laggenda Minore* and the *Supplementum* authored by Fra Tommaso Caffarini; and the "Process of Venice" containing accounts of the witnesses to Catherine's life and miracles which Fra Caffarini compiled in support of the process of canonization.[309]

Also reviewed as secondary sources for the present study were 31 journal articles which contained discussion of Catherine's ministry to the sick and/or illness and healthcare issues relevant in the later Middle Ages; particular attention was focused on diseases, such as leprosy and the "Black Death," as well as the environment of Siena's largest hospital where Catherine served *Santa Maria della Scala*.

Information about Saint Catherine's healthcare activities was obtained, as well, from 15 classic nursing history texts, including the works of: James Walsh, Sr. Charles Marie Frank, Adelaide Nutting and Lavinia Dock, Josephine Dolan, Isabel Stewart and Anne Austin, Victor Robinson, Agnes Pavey, Minnie Goodnow, Lena Dietz and Aurelia Lehozky, Anne Austin, M. Patricia Donahue, Josephine Dolan, H. Louise

Fitzpatrick and Eleanor K. Herrman, Gladys Sellew and C. Joseph Nuesse, Lucy R. Seymer and Deborah Jensen, John Spaulding and Elwyn Cady. Comments supportive of Catherine's influence on contemporary care of the sick were also found in two current nursing texts, in which the saint is described as a role model for all those who minister to the sick.[310]

A source of criticism of early Catherinian scholarship which should be mentioned is the work of French scholar Robert Fawtier. Fawtier authored two books on Catherine of Siena, and co-authored a third (1921-1930). His writings caused great angst among students of the saint as Fawtier questioned the historical value of many biographical and autobiographical works about and by Catherine.[311] Robert Fawtier claimed that Saint Catherine's early biographers "fabricated their accounts in order to promote Catherine's canonization and the glorification of the Dominican Order."[312] Fawtier's criticism, nevertheless, proved to be the catalyst for a renewed interest in Catherinian study, reflected in Siena University establishing a chair in "Studi Cateriniani."[313] Contemporary Catherinian scholar Thomas McDermott OP observed that today "few scholars would completely dismiss the historical value of the biographical sources" of Saint Catherine's life.[314] McDermott also cited the opinion of an eminent Dominican, Pierre Mandonnet, who asserted of Catherine: "I do not believe that there exists in the XIV century, in all of hagiography, a personality whose life presents itself in its whole and its detail, with similar guarantees of historicity."[315]

Conceptual Level 2

Catherine's "theory about the spiritual life" is also found both in her own writings and those of her biographers.[316] Suzanne Noffke notes that it is important to understand how Catherine's behaviors and teachings may have changed or been modified as the saint matured.[317] Noffke also suggests that one must consider Catherine's words and actions in terms of "the common sense of another place, time, culture and cast of mind."[318]

Level 2 data describing Catherine's theory relating to her spiritual life, for this study, that which includes changes in philosophy and spirituality over time and the influence of 14th-century healthcare concepts, was also found in the saint's autobiographical writings, biographical/hagiographical works on Catherine's life, scholarly journal articles and historical accounts as identified for level 1 sources. As to changes over time, it is telling to note the finding that, while the young Catherine was herself austere in terms of fasting from food and drink, even during periods of physical illness, an older and wiser Mantellata Sister counseled sick followers not to abstain from health giving food and drink when suffering from illness or disability.

Conceptual Level 3

Finally, Suzanne Noffke's level 3 "Practical Application of Catherine's Example and Teaching" suggests that one "cull from Catherine's example and thought the greatest benefit" for the individuals concerned.[319] In this level there is a presumption that, were it possible, Catherine would be "willing to enter into a conversation" about her experiences and teaching as relevant to issues of this age.[320] Noffke issues a caveat, however, that one "must respect, as a sincere listener, the reality of what Catherine has to say to the present, and not merely pick over the data as if it were a box of ingredients out of which to make a dish of our liking."[321]

Through the method of hermeneutic phenomenology, the present study explored and analyzed the lived experience of Catherine's philosophy, spirituality and practice of caring for the sick in the 14th Century as applicable to 21st-century ministry to those who are ill. Catherine's beliefs and behaviors identified in the saint's writings and in those of her biographers, were ultimately interpreted in light of a contemporary theory of caregiving: the "Sacred Covenant Model of Caring for the Sick."[322] This model, explained as a guiding framework for interpreting Catherine's teaching, is described in Chapter Seven.

The Challenge of Hagiography

The issue of hagiography has been addressed briefly in the preface and will be discussed here only in relation to the sources used for the study of Saint Catherine's ministry to the sick. Inspirational lives of the saints, especially those written in the Middle Ages, are often considered to fall within the genre of hagiography, rather than biography. That is, while the authors focus on the uplifting virtues of the saint, they are sometimes remiss in admitting to any faults or failings which might be attributed to the individual. For this reason, the label "hagiography" is viewed by some critics as a pejorative term. In order to avoid such negative stereotyping, Thomas Heffernan, an analyst of the biographies of medieval saints, has described such works as "sacred biographies" rather than hagiographies.[323]

Several of the primary sources employed for the present study of Catherine's care for the sick might certainly be considered to fall within the category of hagiography; these include the *Legenda Majore* of Blessed Raymond of Capua, the *Legenda Minore* and *the Supplemento Alla Vita di Santa Caterina da Siena* authored by Fra Tommaso Caffarini and "The Miracoli of Catherine of Siena." As noted earlier, however, Blessed Raymond took great care in documenting the sources for his accounts of Catherine's life and ministries, as did Fra Tommaso to a lesser degree. To provide information for their works both Friars reviewed original notebooks describing Catherine's spirituality compiled by her first confessor, Fra Tommaso della Fonte; they solicited observations from Saint Catherine's family members and friends as well.

We are cautioned by Suzanne Noffke not to "romanticize" Saint Catherine for fear of tarnishing her image.[324] What Noffke suggests, and what has been the goal of this present work, is to "study Catherine's life and writings to discover the principles that formed her thought, the principles out of which she responded to her own questions and out of which she can in a very genuine way respond to today's questions."[325] The hope is that Catherine's 14th-century understanding of her vocation to minister to the ill and infirm, lived out as a sacred covenant of caring for the sick, can serve as a guide for 21st-century caregivers seeking to embrace a similar calling.

Catherine's Writings

While Catherine's writings did not specifically address her personal care for the sick, the saint's early Mantellata activities graphically expressed this dimension of her vocation. And, in carefully exploring the *Dialogue*, the *Letters* and the *Prayers*, one encounters the powerful and compassionate understanding and faith, which both directed and supported Catherine's healthcare ministry. It was in communion with the Lord, as recounted in the *Dialogue*, that Catherine first heard the call to apostolic ministry, a ministry of serving the neighbor in need. During this meditative interaction with God, Catherine received the message that solitary prayer was not enough; Catherine must fly to heaven on "two wings," one demonstrating her love of the Lord, and the other, her love of neighbor.

Nothing documented of Saint Catherine's early background would lead one to expect that she would choose a life of serving the sick in their homes or in the hospitals. These duties were an important aspect of the Mantellata role to which Catherine aspired; however, while she wished to follow the Dominican charism of laboring for the salvation of souls, she did not, initially, seem drawn toward caring for those who were ailing. Nevertheless, as her biographers attest, Catherine undertook, especially in her first five years of service as a Mantellata, a tender and compassionate commitment to care for the sick, particularly the sick poor; she carried out this ministry in multiple venues and with persons suffering from a variety of diseases and illnesses. It is this important dimension of Saint Catherine's vocation that leads us, to this day, to consider her the patron of nurses and of all those who minister to the ill and the infirm.

The *Dialogue*

Biographer Edmund Gardner described the *Dialogue* as a "book concerned with the whole spiritual life of a person in the form of a prolonged dialogue, or series of dialogues, between the eternal Father and the impassioned human soul, represented as Catherine herself."[326] Suzanne Noffke, in the Foreword to her translation of the *Dialogue*, notes that while the work reflects "some of Catherine's earlier letters and recorded mystical experiences… here all is drawn together and expanded into a more cohesive whole, in the form of an exchange between God and herself."[327] The Dialogue's aim, Noffke points out, is "the instruction and encouragement of all those whose spiritual welfare was her concern."[328] She observed that, "while Catherine's letters are the better window to her personality, growth and relationships with others, the Dialogue is her crowning work, her bequest of all her teaching to her followers."[329]

Catherinian scholar Guiliana Cavalleni asserted that the *Dialogue* represents a "singular conversation between Catherine and a mysterious voice responding to her desires in the depths of her soul (which) is at the same time the story of mankind in its fall and redemption, and that of every single soul striving for perfection."[330] In the *Dialogue*, Sister of St. Joseph Catherine Meade commented: "Catherine connected to her own inner power and authority and took control of her own experience; she clarified for herself, as well as for others, God's action in her life."[331]

Probably written between 1377 and 1378, the *Dialogue* is described by Dominican Sister Mary O'Driscoll as a "compendium" of Catherine's "theological teaching."[332] It reflects a spirit of familiarity between Catherine and God, by whom the saint tells us, she trusts that she is "being listened to with immense love and mercy."[333] O'Driscoll admits that the *Dialogue*, "being wordy and repetitious," can be difficult to read and suggests that it "it is a book to be dipped into and prayed with" rather than "read from cover to cover."[334]

For contemporary men and women engaged in caregiving ministries to the ill, Catherine Meade's point that Catherine "clarified for herself as well as for others, God's action in her life" is important. There are times when those of us caring for the sick need to stop and take stock of our lives, to reflect on God's role in the ministry. We do this in order to understand His will as it relates to our service to others. While engaging in such reflection, Sister Mary O'Driscoll's advice that the *Dialogue* be "dipped into and prayed with" is both a wise and comforting suggestion.

While, as noted, Catherine's *Dialogue* does not deal directly with the saint's own ministry to the ill and infirm, there are many passages which focus on love of and service to one's neighbors. One passage which is especially relevant for those involved in 21st-century healthcare is paragraph 144, which reads, in part: "Your hands... were made to serve your neighbors when you see them sick and to help them with alms in their need... your feet were given you to serve by carrying your body to places that are holy and useful to you and your neighbors for the glory and praise of my name."[335]

For today's ministers to the ailing, the concept of hands being "made to serve" and feet to "carry" us to those who need our caring is both a humbling and a blessed message. Many healthcare facilities and universities educating those who minister to the sick hold annual ceremonies of "blessing and anointing of hands" for their staff or students. The spiritual concept underlying such rituals is related to the well-known teaching of Saint Teresa of Avila, who reminded us that Christ has no body now on earth but ours, no hands or feet but ours; we must, as Catherine taught, use our hands to serve as His hands, our feet as His feet. This is reflected in the following "Nurse's Prayer" entitled "The Sacred Covenant":

Gentle God,
        You alone are the source of my strength and the

Center of my life;
Bless my nursing that it may always
Be guided by the sacred covenant
Of your loving care.
Use me as Your instrument in serving the sick:
Use my eyes to look with Your compassion on those
Who are broken in body or in spirit;
Use my hands to touch with Your tenderness those
Who suffer illness or injury;
Use my lips to speak Your words of comfort to those
Who are anxious or afraid.
Dear Lord,
Let me recognize every sickroom as a tabernacle where
You dwell;
And
Let me never forget, as I care for the ill, that
The ground on which I am standing is holy,
The vocation to which I am called
Is holy.
Help me to be worthy.[336]

Twenty-two paragraphs in the *Dialogue* were identified as containing data relevant to the research on Catherine's healthcare ministry; 14 of the most significant passages are examined here in terms of their importance for care of the sick. These messages address the service one's neighbor in attending to both spiritual and material concerns.

Paragraph 6 of the *Dialogue* contains the mandate: "It is your duty to love your neighbors as your own self. In love you ought to help them spiritually with prayer and counsel, and assist them spiritually and materially in their need... Every help you give them ought to come from the affection you bear for love of me."[337]

It may be assumed that the requirements of those who are ill, both for counseling and physical care, would be included in the spiritual and material needs of our neighbor.

Another important point in interpreting this teaching of Saint Catherine is presented in the words "every help... ought to come from the affection you bear for love of me." It is not enough that we who care for the ailing treat them well as fellow members of the human community. Catherine's expectation is that we see, as she did, Our

Blessed Lord in the person of the sick and the poor and that we care for them as we would care for Him. This thought brings to mind a moving "Night Nurse's Prayer," written some years ago, which contained the lines: "I looked at my patient there in his bed, but I felt I was seeing the Thorn-Crowned Head."[338] This, I believe, is how Catherine would ask us to approach our care of the sick.

In Paragraph 7 of the *Dialogue*, we find the teaching: "Love of me and love of neighbor are one and the same thing: since love of neighbor has its source in me, the more the soul loves me, the more she loves her neighbor. Such is the means I have given you to practice and prove your virtue. The service you cannot render me, you must do for your neighbors."[339]

This passage from Catherine's *Dialogue* provides a clear and blessed teaching for those who care for the sick. Our Lord Jesus is no longer present in human form that we might comfort Him or wipe his bleeding countenance as the holy woman Veronica did on the journey to Calvary. We can, however, wipe away the pain and the tears from the face of a suffering patient. This is reflected in a meditation on modeling the caregiving of Saint Veronica.

Veronica: A Nurse's Meditation
Standing at the fringes of the crowd,
   She feels the restlessness.
She shades her eyes from the hot Jerusalem sun
   And peers down the road;
It's so dry and dusty, she can't see anything
   But she senses His coming.
Her heart begins to beat fast and her
   Temples pound.
How could they do this to her dear and
   Gentle rabbi; the One who taught
    Her to love in His Father's
     Name?

Then, over the rise of a hill, she catches
   The first painful glimpse.
The soldiers surround Him; as if He had
   The desire, or even the strength

To run.
The Cross is fearful; its wood so heavy,
   Its beams so rough.
He can barely drag it down the path; only
   The young, strong arms of Simon make
   The humiliating procession possible.

As He draws near she sees the beautiful face;
   Now caked with the dirt of the streets and
   Blood from the cruel beating.
Crimson droplets trickle into His loving
   Eyes; Her King is crowned with brambles
   And thorns, not with gold and jewels.
Her heart breaks and her soul weeps bitter
   Tears; she feels so helpless.

She has no towel or cloth to wipe the precious
   Wounded face; only a poor woman's veil,
   Simple muslin, but soft and clean; put
   On that very afternoon to preserve
   Humility before the eyes of her Lord.
Modesty is no longer relevant; now she must
   Bare her head to blot the blood and tears
   From those same beloved eyes.
She is rewarded with the blessed image of
   The Divine Son of God.

I see him stumble into the E.R., leaning
   Heavily on his comrade's arm.
"He's homeless," his friend from the
   Family of the streets reports:
"They beat him up, those young punks,
   Just because he's old."

His body is caked with the dirt of the
   Streets, and blood from the cruel
   Beating.
His eyes are moist with unshed tears; alive
   With the pain of loneliness and fear.

I wash the gentle, weathered face with
  a clean soft towel, and I think of
    Veronica.
I am rewarded with the Blessed image of
  The human Son of God.[340]

Continuing her *Dialogue* with God, as recorded in paragraph 7, Catherine was taught and teaches us that numerous virtues are "brought to birth in love of neighbor."[341] God explained to Catherine that virtues are given "in different ways so that one virtue might be, as it were, the source of all the others:

> To one person I give charity as the primary virtue, to another justice, to another humility, to another a lively faith or prudence or temperance or patience, and to still another, courage. These and many other virtues I give differently to different souls and the soul is most at ease with that virtue which has been made primary for her. But through her love of that virtue, she attracts all the other virtues to herself.[342]

This passage speaks especially to those who minister within the vast diversity of specialty areas in the contemporary healthcare system. For all who serve the sick, each of the virtues is important but one can also identify individual moral traits which would seem to be primary for those ministering in certain venues and with defined populations. For example, charity is critical for those caring for the poor and the underserved; justice, for ministers in correctional facilities; hope and faith, when supporting the terminally ill at the end of life; patience in tending to persons with cognitive disabilities and courage when ministering in settings such as infectious disease units or military combat zones.

Saint Catherine goes on to remind us, in paragraph 8, through recounting her conversation with the Lord, that the virtues with which each person is gifted will be tested:

> You test the virtue of patience in yourself when your neighbors insult you. Your humility is tested by the proud, your faith by the unfaithful, your hope by the person who has no hope. Your justice is tried by the unjust, your compassion by the cruel, and your gentleness and kindness by the wrathful. Your neighbors are the channel through which all your virtues are tested and come to birth.[343]

How often are virtues of those who care for the ill not tested to the max in the practice of our professions? For the sick and suffering, those who are in pain, those who are without hope, those who are angry over their illness, even the greatest gentleness on the part of a caregiver can rankle a frustrated temperament. An angry patient response may represent reaction to overwhelming fear; fear of loss of friends, fear of loss of income or even fear of loss of life related to one's illness. As a result a healthcare minister might be told "leave me alone," when the underlying message is "please don't leave me," or "you don't understand," with the real meaning being "you are not going through this suffering. I am." The humility and compassion of a caregiver may be sorely tried in such situations, but it is, in these very trials, that Catherine would have us learn that our virtues are not only tested but are strengthened in the testing.

A *Dialogue* passage contained in paragraph 64 expands the Lord's message to Catherine, cited earlier in paragraph 7, which teaches that we must do for others what we cannot now do for God. In this passage the Lord underscored the importance of gratuitous love in the service of others:

> Whatever love you have for me you owe me, so you love me not gratuitously but out of duty, while I love you not out of duty but gratuitously. So you cannot give me the kind of love I ask of you. This is why I have put you among your neighbors: so that you can do for them what you cannot do for me – that is, love them without any concern for thanks and without looking for any profit for yourself. And whatever you do for them I will consider done for me.[344]

This is not an easy message for those of us living in contemporary society, especially for those whose calling is to minister to the sick. Most care providers for the ill and the infirm, serving in such arenas as nursing, medicine, or chaplaincy, understand that they may never receive words of appreciation for their care; this might be due not to a lack of gratitude on the part of a sick person, but rather expressions of thanks may simply be hindered by the patient's physical or cognitive impairment. The majority of caregivers might, however, hope for some small personal "profit" from their ministry, such as that provided by a superior's acknowledgement of positive services rendered.

Nevertheless, many caring tasks in ministering to the sick are hidden, known only to the patient and to God and thus one must be prepared to love, as Catherine teaches, without looking for profit or reward.

In a later section of Paragraph 64, a significant dimension of the lesson is recorded in God's question to Catherine: "Do you know when you can tell how your spiritual love is not perfect?" The Lord's response was: "If you are distressed when it seems that those you love are not returning your love or not loving you as much as you think you love them."[345] This comment is pertinent especially for those who care for the sick in the home or in a long term care facility. Family members, friends or professional caregivers often spend long hours selflessly tending to a physically or cognitively challenged individual, sometimes with little response or recognition. Yet, it is this continued faithful service, without expecting return, which the Lord desires of his followers and which Catherine wishes us to embrace.

In paragraph 69 of the *Dialogue* Saint Catherine recounts the Lord's instruction regarding those who seek their own comfort, even if spiritually, at the expense of their neighbor's need:

> These people find all their pleasure in seeking their own spiritual consolation, so much so that often they see their neighbors in spiritual or temporal need and refuse to help them. Under pretense of virtue they say, 'It would make me lose my spiritual peace and quiet... but they are deceived by their own spiritual pleasure, and they offend me more by not coming to the help of their neighbors need than if they had abandoned all their consolations... they offend me more by abandoning charity for their neighbor for a particular exercise or for spiritual quiet, than if they had abandoned the exercise for their neighbor. For, in charity for their neighbors they find me.[346]

The Lord added: "In other words, those who are willing to lose their own consolation for their neighbors' welfare receive and gain me and their neighbors, if they help and serve them lovingly."[347]

The first thought which comes to mind, in reading the above teaching from Catherine's *Dialogue*, is the situation of the nurse, physician, chaplain or other healthcare team member who is called upon to leave home, family, perhaps even a worship service to respond to a medical emergency. Any healthcare professional or pastoral care provider who has been in the situation of being "on call" understands the meaning of being forced to put aside personal activities, be it sleeping, eating or even praying, if a neighbor requires immediate care. When the young community of Daughters of Charity was beginning their ministry of visiting and caring for the sick poor in their homes, their founder Saint Vincent de Paul advised the Sisters that there would be instances when they must quit their chapels to meet the needs of the ailing. Saint Vincent is reported to have said of such occasions: 'There will be times when you will need to leave God to go to God." This is surely a case of ministers to the sick being "willing to lose their own consolation for their neighbors' welfare."

Catherine is taught by the Lord, in paragraph 74, that He gives the soul a share in His love, "which is the Holy Spirit, within her will, by making her will strong enough to endure suffering and to leave her house in my name to give birth to the virtues in her neighbors. Not that she abandons the house of self-knowledge, but the virtues conceived by the impulse of love come forth from that house. She gives birth to them as her neighbors need them, in many different ways."[348]

This teaching may seem, at first blush, not to have relevance for those who minister to the sick in terms of a caregiver "giving birth to virtues in her neighbors." On reflection, however, it is really most appropriate. An example might be the nurse or chaplain attending a hopeless or depressed patient. In such a situation, it sometimes happens that the ill person will not listen to the consoling words of the minister. Some patients lash out in anger, especially if topics involving religion or spirituality are raised. It is at that point that caregivers must set aside personal feelings of frustration at being blocked in their attempted ministry and respond with infinite patience and kindness, listening with love and absorbing the ill person's pain. Such caring behavior, reflecting the healthcare minister's understanding and compassion, may ultimately generate a virtuous response of trust and acceptance on the part of a patient.

In paragraph 77 Saint Catherine reveals to us the instruction she received on the virtue of being humble in service to others. Some souls, the Lord taught Catherine, "hide their virtue only through humility, never through fear":

> If their neighbors have need of their service, they do not hide their virtue for fear of suffering or for fear of losing their own selfish comfort. No, they serve them courageously, with no concern for themselves. In

whatever way they use their lifetime for my honor, they are happy to find spiritual peace and comfort. Faithfully they serve their neighbors, paying no attention to their lack of recognition or gratitude or to the fact that sometimes vicious people insult and reprove them for their good works.[349]

The combined concepts of serving one's neighbor courageously with no concern for oneself, the lack of recognition or gratitude and the fact of possibly being reproved for good works cannot help but remind one of military medical personnel who have served and continue to serve in combat operations caring for wounded troops. As a faculty member who has mentored many military students, both those about to enter the service and those who have spent many years in their respective nursing corps, I have learned that members of military healthcare teams do, at times, experience a lack of public recognition and gratitude other than that provided by the wounded being immediately cared for. It takes great personal courage to risk one's life serving in the midst of combat; this bravery is even more impressive when witnessed among military healthcare providers serving injured combatants in an "unpopular" war, for which the caregiver may, in fact, be "insulted and reproved." These courageous men and women do indeed hide their virtue but they do it, as Catherine taught, through humility, never through fear.

In paragraph 86 of the *Dialogue*, Saint Catherine relates a conversation with God in which He teaches her the importance of both self-knowledge and knowledge of His will; the Lord admonishes Catherine that one must see with the "mind's eye" and hear with a "feeling ear":

> If you would serve yourself and your neighbors in the teaching and knowledge of my truth. For, I told you in the beginning that one comes to knowledge of the truth through self-knowledge. But self-knowledge alone is not enough; it must be seasoned and joined with knowledge of me within you. This is how you found humility… along with the fire of my charity, and so came to love and affection for your neighbors and gave them the service of your teaching and your holy and honorable living.[350]

It is important for those who minister to the sick or who teach those who care for the ill and infirm to have self-knowledge and knowledge of God in order to communicate the concept of service to others. A dimension of this dual knowledge is the Lord's directive that one see with the "mind's eye" and hear with a "feeling ear." These mandates are germane to both a teacher's interaction with students in the healthcare professions and also in the care of patients and their families. Sometimes the symptoms presented by a patient may seem, on the surface, to indicate a particular diagnosis, but if one looks deeper with the "mind's eye" or listens with a "feeling ear" a very different scenario can be at work within an individual. Saint Benedict advised that one should "listen with the ear of the heart" in order to discern the true intent behind a speaker's words; this is the meaning of the Lord's teaching to Catherine, and, to us, that we observe and listen with a caring heart.

Later, in paragraph 86, the theme of serving one's neighbor by teaching and by example is continued:

> I have set you as workers in your own and your neighbor's souls...in yourselves you must work at virtue; in your neighbors...you must work by example and teaching. For I have already told you that every virtue...is realized and intensified through your neighbors. Therefore, I want you to serve your neighbors and in this way share the fruits of your own vineyard.[351]

Here again, the Lord and Catherine are educating us in the importance of being holy ourselves, so that we can serve "by example" as well as by teaching. For members of the healthcare professions, who advise not only students, but also patients and families, the example of the teacher can be a critical element in enhancing communication between the educator and the learner. It is very difficult to accept information from a person a learner does not respect; a mentor's inspiring witness may be the key to important information being communicated, accepted and received by a student, a patient or a family member.

In paragraph 100 of the *Dialogue*, several messages about the behavior of a virtuous person are presented. First, the Lord describes a holy individual as finding the positive "in everything": "This is true not only of good things; even when they see something that is clearly sinful they do not pass judgment, but rather feel a holy and genuine compassion, praying for the sinner and saying with perfect humility, 'Today it is your turn; tomorrow it will be mine unless divine grace holds me up.'"[352]

The moral person is further described as not wasting time "passing false judgment" either against the Lord's servants "or the world's servants. They are not scandalized by any grumbling on anyone's part; if it is against themselves they are happy to suffer in my name and when it is against someone else they bear with it in compassion for their neighbor, grumbling neither against the grumbler nor the victim, because their love for me and for their neighbor is well ordered."[353]

There are two powerful messages in this passage of the *Dialogue* for those of us who care for the sick. First, the Lord presented an ideal image, as it were, of holiness to Saint Catherine in stating that those who are holy do not pass "false judgment" against others or "grumble" against their neighbors. How easy it can be, in a healthcare setting, to judge that one ailing person is a "good patient," docile and perfectly compliant with a therapeutic regimen? We can, just as quickly, however, label an ill person a "difficult patient," non-compliant, ever questioning a treatment protocol. Yet, the latter behavior may represent the sequellae of anxiety and stress rather than the symptoms of a disagreeable temperament. As discussed in a later chapter, during her hospital ministry at *Santa Maria della Scala* , Saint Catherine was always willing, and, in fact, chose to serve the most unruly and noncompliant patients. She saw in their personalities not simply unsavory characteristics but instead the pain and distress of a suffering child of God. And it was that child, deeply loved by God, whom Catherine also loved. And it is that wounded, yet beloved, child of God whom the Lord asks us to love as well.

In another teaching, in paragraph 100, God presents the holy individual as one who not only does not judge others but who accepts with humility the fact that, without God's grace, it could be his or her "turn" next. The teaching is reminiscent of the comments of a head nurse in a large shock-trauma unit who admitted that she sometimes had to interact with patients who had engaged in serious criminal behavior. "But," she asserted, "I can't judge them as criminals, just as persons. They are here to be cared for; that's my job as a nurse and I try to treat those patients as I would any other admission to the unit. And, I have to remember that, there but for the grace of God, go I."

It would seem that both the Lord and Catherine sought to forcefully affirm the importance of not sitting in judgment of one's neighbors for the theme continues in paragraph 105 of the *Dialogue*. God's message was:

I also told you, and I will tell you again, that nothing in the world can make it right for you to sit in judgment on the intentions of my servants, either generally or in particular, whether you find them well or ill disposed… their reasons you cannot judge, and that if you do you will be deluded in your judgment. But compassion is what you must have, you and the others, and leave the judging to me.[354]

For those of us who minister to the sick, in whatever venue, the gift of compassion for an ill person's suffering is, perhaps, the greatest blessing we can bring to an interaction. As well as pharmacological intervention, often what an ill person needs is a healthcare provider, whether medical, nursing or religious, who is compassionate toward his or her suffering. A caregiver's act of compassionate listening to a patient's pain can be one of the most healing therapies available. To know that a professional person within the healthcare community is truly sympathetic to one's experience of illness can greatly alleviate the felt loneliness of living with suffering. From the descriptions of her ministry in the hospitals, in the home, in the community and in the prisons, we know that one of Catherine's greatest gifts to those for whom she cared was her compassion. This compassion is also reflected in her myriad letters to those experiencing a variety of painful life challenges.

Paragraph 148 of St. Catherine's *Dialogue* reflects, perhaps, the most important description of God's will for the human family as a group of people who would truly be "community" in service to each other. As the Lord taught Catherine:

In this mortal life, so long as you are pilgrims, I have bound you with a chain of charity. Whether you want it or not, you are so bound. If you should break loose by not wanting to live in charity for your neighbors, you will still be bound by it by force. Thus, that you may practice charity in action and in will, I, in my providence, did not give to any one person or to each individually the knowledge for doing everything necessary for human life. No, I gave something to one, something else to another, so that each one's need would be a reason to have recourse to the other. So, though you may lose your will for charity… you will at least be forced by your own need to practice it in action… Each has the need of the other because neither knows how to do what the other does. So, also the cleric and religious have need of the layperson, and

82

layperson of the religious; neither can get along without the other. And, so with everything else.

God concluded: "Could I not have given everyone everything? Of course. But in my providence I wanted to make each of you dependent on the others, so that you would be forced to exercise charity in action and will at once."[355]

In our contemporary healthcare field, with its diversity of specialty areas within research, education and practice, it would be impossible for any one researcher, educator or practitioner to possess the knowledge and the skill to understand, to teach or to practice comprehensive care for those experiencing illness or disease. The beauty of our ministries resides in each individual caregiver's unique and different gifts and talents which may be shared with others. It is in the coming together of a community of persons, such as those who populate the healthcare professions, that a complete tapestry of care may be created for the sick and the disabled.

The *Letters*

Saint Catherine is described by Edmund Gardner as "one of the greatest letter writers of her century."[356] "Some of her letters," he noted, "are purely mystical, ecstatic outpourings of Catherine's heart... others are nearer to familiar domestic correspondence, in which daily needs of life become ennobled."[357] In describing the *Letters*, Father Martin Gillet OP wrote: "Catherine would not have been a true daughter of Saint Dominic if she had not been concerned about preaching to souls the marvelous doctrine of love that God Himself had revealed to her."[358] Gillet added: Saint Catherine's letters are, however, not just a "doctrinal exposition," but rather "they are the accents of a fiery soul who addresses herself personally to her correspondents and teaches them doctrine... but only after it has passed through the fire of her contemplation."[359]

Currently we have 381 of Catherine's *Letters*, "the earliest written perhaps around 1370" and others spread out "until her death in 1380."[360] The *Letters* were written to a diverse group of recipients, some of whom the saint knew, others she had never met.[361] The purpose of the *Letters* was "always deeper than the mere social or informational";

Catherine "was interested primarily in the eternal dimension of personal lives and social affairs."[362]

Saint Catherine's desire to strengthen the spiritual lives of the persons to whom she wrote was always the focus of the letter. She wished her recipients "to be constant in faith, warm in charity; to practice humility or temper justice with mercy; to be courageous in fighting abuse or patient in bearing offense."[363] "It is evident," wrote Mary O'Driscoll OP, "that Catherine delights in the uniqueness of each person. She displays delicate sensitivity and good common sense as she deals with different temperaments, needs and situations of one correspondent after another."[364] The "secret" of Catherine's ability to touch varied individuals with her letters, O'Driscoll asserts, lay in her "exceedingly deep, compassionate love for each person with whom she corresponds."[365] "Through her letter writing, Catherine of Siena found a way to bring together her love of God and her love of neighbor."[366]

The *Letters*, which were dictated to disciples who served as secretaries, often consisted of responses to questions or requests Catherine had received; at times, however, "she assumes the initiative" in giving spiritual advice.[367] In the *Letters*, "Catherine shows us how to use our particular gifts to spread the good news of the truth to others and to the suffering world."[368]

Twenty-first-century ministers to the sick can be both inspired and supported by the broad range of individuals who Saint Catherine counseled. Today's caregivers also serve a variety of ill and the infirm persons: those of different ages, different races, different ethnic and religious traditions and individuals from myriad socio-economic backgrounds. We, as Catherine, are called upon to treat each person individually, with concern not only for his or her physical needs but for the "eternal dimension" as well. One of the comments by Dominican Sister O'Driscoll could easily be read as a guide for present day ministers to the sick: that we, as Catherine, should "delight in the uniqueness" of each person, and display "delicate sensitivity and good common sense" as we deal "with different temperaments, needs and situations" in our caregiving."

From a review of the Letters, 29 documents were perceived as providing data relevant to the saint's healthcare activity in the 14th-century, as well as containing important lessons for contemporary ministers to the ill and infirm. The identified communications fell into such categories as: letters of comfort and consolation for those suffering from physical illness or psychological challenges; letters of encouragement to members of the Sisters of Penance of St. Dominic (the Mantellate) in their ministry to the sick poor; letters of support to a "Rector" (administrator) and lay members of religious confraternities serving in Siena hospitals such as *Santa Maria della Scala* and *Casa della Miseracordia*; letters to Knights Hospitallers of St. John of Jerusalem who provided nursing care for the Crusaders; a letter to prisoners, whom Catherine often visited, expressing her concern for their eternal salvation; and a letter to Blessed Raymond of Capua describing Catherine's accompaniment of a prisoner to his beheading. While in the latter communique, the prisoner's name is not included, the execution was generally believed to be that of the young Perugian nobleman Niccolo di Toldo; this is considered to be Catherine's most famous letter.

Excerpts from 19 of the 29 letters considered were analyzed for their value in helping to explicate Catherine's healthcare ministry in Siena and the neighboring cities. The content reflects Catherine's support and encouragement for: five members of the Sisters of Penance of St. Dominic (the Mantellate); four lay members of religious confraternities of Brothers serving in Siena hospitals; a "Rector" and head of a confraternity of Brothers serving at the *Casa della Miseracordia* hospital (two letters); the Prior of the Knights Hospitallers of St. John of Jerusalem; two bereaved widows and five individuals suffering from illness (three suffering from a physical illness; two experiencing mental anxieties). The letter describing Saint Catherine's support of Niccolo di Toldo at the time of his execution is discussed in Chapter Seven.

As well as writing to those who were ill, it's important to acknowledge that Saint Catherine also ministered to "ministers," those who provided comfort and care for the sick. She exhorted her own Mantellate Sisters to continuously grow deeper in their love of God and thus to provide loving and tender service to the sick poor for whom they cared. Catherine encouraged lay members of the religious confraternities of Brothers who served in hospitals to live lives of holiness, totally dedicated to meeting the physical and spiritual needs of those in their charge. And it was in this vein that the saint also wrote to leaders of healthcare facilities and communities such as the "Rector" of a Siena hospital, and the Prior of the Knights Hospitallers of St. John of Jerusalem.

Letters to Sisters of Penance of St. Dominic (Mantellate)

Of Saint Catherine's written communications, the 5 letters to the Sisters of Penance of St. Dominic provide examples of the saint's concern for the physical and spiritual welfare of her Mantellate Sisters; the documents are identified as Letters: T40, T50, T53, T132 and T213.[369]

In Letter T40, identified simply as having been written to "certain of her daughters in Siena," Catherine first begs her Sisters to become "faithful servants of our Creator" in visiting the sick; that this will become their "holy desire." The saint advises that the Sisters must, in prayer, continually acknowledge "God's unspeakable love for you." To achieve this, Catherine explained:

> There is no service you can do for God, and so you will extend your love to your neighbors, doing for them the service you cannot do for God. You will visit the sick, help the poor, and console those who are troubled. You will weep with those who weep and rejoice with those who rejoice. I mean you will weep with those who are grieving in deadly sin by being compassionate and by offering continual prayers for them in God's presence. And you will rejoice with those who are glad because they are true servants of Jesus Christ crucified, always happy to be in their company.[370]

Letter T50 is written to a Mantellata of Siena, Caterina di Ghetto, who is described as "one of Catherine's earliest disciples."[371] In writing to this Mantellata Sister, Saint Catherine reiterates some of her teaching in the *Dialogue*, in pointing out that virtues conceived in God are brought to birth in service to our neighbors, and that this love and service to our neighbors must be gratuitous, as we are loved by God.[372] Catherine concludes the letter with the counsel:

> You have been made a servant to your neighbors, to serve them in everything to the extent that you can. Just as you are a spouse to Christ, so you must become a servant to your neighbors if you would be a faithful spouse. Because we cannot be of any profit or service to God in our love for him, we must, as I've said, serve our neighbors with a genuinely heartfelt love. There is no other way, nor any other vehicle through which we can serve God.[373]

Letter T53 is one of several letters which Catherine wrote to Agnesa Malavolti, a widow and also a member of the Siena Mantellate. In the letter, Saint Catherine admits to her Sister that she longs to see her "bound in the bond of divine Charity." She asserts that this charity will be found in self-knowledge through which the Sister will learn God's deep love for her. Catherine explains:

> Once you have discovered love and come to know it within yourself, you will not be able to keep from loving. And the sign that you have discovered and conceived love will be that you bind yourself in charity to your neighbors by loving them and by serving them lovingly. For the good and the service that we cannot do for God we must do for our neighbors, enduring with true patience whatever burden they may be to us.[374]

In a letter intended for a group of Mantellate in Siena, Letter T132, Saint Catherine exhorts the Sisters to be humble, not seeking their own will but simply being "clothed in God's will."[375] Catherine wrote: "This my dearest daughters in Christ," Catherine writes, "is the sort of meekness our gentle Savior wants to find in us: that with a completely peaceful and tranquil heart we be content with everything, as he disposes and arranges it for us, that we not want times and places to be according to your liking but only to God's."[376]

And, in a letter to the Mantellata Daniella, Letter T213, Catherine discussed the "need for discernment" in serving one's neighbor.[377] She pointed out that: "The principal thing discernment does is this: once we have seen by discerning light what we owe and to whom, perfect discernment makes us give it right away. So, we give glory to God, and praise to God's name... By the same light (we) give (our) neighbors their due."[378]

In the five letters to members of her Mantellate community in Siena, Saint Catherine reminds the Sisters that since they cannot now serve God, they must respond to his love by serving him in their neighbors, especially in the sick, the poor and those who are grieving and that their service must be done with love and with enduring patience. Twenty-first-century ministers to the sick can identify with Catherine's advice to her 14th-century nursing sisters. Many of today's caregivers to the sick and the poor also live out a calling to serve God in serving their neighbor, and seek to serve with love and with enduring patience.

Letters to Lay Members of Religious Confraternities Serving in Hospitals

Of the four letters chosen to describe Saint Catherine's commitment to lay Brothers of the religious confraternities serving in hospitals, three were written to Brothers serving at *Santa Maria della Scala* in Siena and one letter was written to a Brother ministering in a hospital near Florence. These letters are identified as: T184, T69, T122 and T72.

In Letter T184, Catherine addresses the Prior and all the members of the lay confraternity, the "Company of the Virgin Mary" serving at *La Scala* Hospital. In the introduction to Letter T184, Sister Suzanne Noffke provides information about the confraternity's origins in the 4th Century: "The Confraternity's church and quarters were located beneath the hospital. Its coat of arms bore an image of the virgin, a cross and a discipline, symbol of the brothers' life of asceticism. Their ministry was to shelter the poor; to serve the hospitals, both within and outside the city; to aid needy girls, pregnant women, pilgrims and prisoners; and to educate young men."[379] Clearly the confraternity was still active in the 14th Century as Noffke supports the notion of Catherine having been given a small room where she could rest when working beyond curfew and "in which she could join the brothers for prayer without being seen."[380]

Saint Catherine seems to support the asceticism of the confraternity life of hospital service, in Letter T 184, by reminding the brothers that "God wants nothing else but that we be made holy, and that whatever he gives or permits us-trials or consolations or persecution or distress or derision or abuse-everything is given so that we may be made holy in him."[381] Catherine also addresses the humility and poverty which the brothers practice by advising that we:

> Keep ourselves in check and not pursue honor or prestige or greatness; nor will we be avaricious in our possession of wealth. In fact, if we do not have wealth we will become Christ's stewards of it for the poor. Living virtuously always brings us joy, and peace with God and with our neighbors. Once we have risen above rancor we feel a familial charity, and so we love our neighbors as we love ourselves... We should try as hard as we can to be tolerant and put up with (our neighbors') shortcomings, hating the vice that may be there, but not hating the person.[382]

In a letter, T69, written specifically to a wool-worker, Sano di Maco di Mazzacorno, also a member of the confraternity of the Company of the Virgin Mary at *La Scala*, Saint Catherine admitted that she was writing to encourage him; she wrote:

> I long to see in you in the same power of holy faith and perseverance as the Canaanite woman had... Realize that in this life we, like the Canaanite woman, can have only the crumbs that fall from the table; I mean the graces we receive that fall from the Lord's table. But when we reach everlasting life, where we will see God face to face and will taste him, the food on the table will be ours. So never evade hard work. I will send you crumbs, and food as well, as to a son. As for you, fight and preach, like a man.[383]

Letter T122 was written to a third lay Brother of the Company of the Virgin Mary at *Santa Maria della Scala*, Salvi di Messer Pietro. In this letter Saint Catherine reminds the Brother of the fact that virtues are given birth in our neighbors, especially in the achieving of the virtue of patience: "We do this through the mediation of our neighbors, when we mutually put up with and share the burden of each other's shortcomings."[384] Catherine added:

> It is through our neighbors that our love of God is proved. Why? Because we can be of no service to God, but God wants us to do him service through the intermediary he has given us, our neighbors, by bearing with their shortcomings, by carrying them before God with compassion, by enduring with patience the wrongs they do us and by treating God's servants with due reverence.[385]

Catherine wrote, finally, to Brother Romano (Letter T7), a flax dresser of the Company of Bigallo in Florence, "a confraternity founded in the 13th Century by the Dominican Peter of Verona" which had in Catherine's day directed its efforts "toward care of the sick, and had been entrusted particularly with a ministry to the Hospital of Santa Maria del Bigallo" south of Florence.[386] In the letter Catherine appears to be encouraging perseverance in Romano's vocation to serve the sick as a lay Brother:

> I long to see that you are persevering in virtue and not turning back to look at what you have already plowed. For you know that only

perseverance is crowned… I beg you, for the love of Christ Crucified, respond courageously and don't be remiss. Remember that simply beginning, putting one's hand to the plow, is nothing… Holy thoughts begin the plowing, and perseverance in virtue finishes it.[387]

In the four letters to lay members of religious confraternities, Saint Catherine advised the Brothers to live holy lives, not seeking honor, prestige or greatness; this was to be accomplished by the power of their faith, by enduring with patience wrongs done to them, and by continued perseverance. While the laymen and laywomen serving in today's hospitals in roles such as: nurses, physicians, or technicians are generally not members of religious confraternities, they also are called to carry out their tasks with no thought of honor or greatness and with patience and perseverance. The desire to serve was initially and remains the catalyst for their embrace of a ministry in healthcare.

Letters to a Hospital Rector: Matteo di Fazio dei Cenni

Within a fairly short period of time Saint Catherine wrote two letters to her friend and disciple Matteo di Cenni who was "Rector," the title for the administrator and superior of the confraternity of Brothers serving at *Casa della Miseracordia* Hospital. As Suzanne Noffke explains in the introduction to the first letter, T137, the Brothers "vowed obedience to the rector… and lived in common. They wore a long tan tunic with a leather belt and black mantle with a cross on the left side."[388] In Catherine's era, in Italy, serving the sick poor in a hospital was considered a serious religious commitment; the hospital Brothers gave away their wealth and possessions and dedicated their lives to ministry to the ailing.

In this first letter to Matteo, Catherine, mindful of the *Casa della Miseracordia* Hospital Rector's responsibility to the sick under his care as well as to the Confraternity of Brothers, counseled him to be "ablaze with fire": "I long to see you so totally ablaze with loving fire that you become one with the gentle First Truth."[389] She added: "I beg you, I command you: always be conscientious about consuming all the dampness of selfish love, of indifference, of foolishness. Let the fire of boundless holy desire grow (til you are) drunk with the blood of God's Son," and if we "throw ourselves with blazing desire into God's measureless goodness," we discover His goodness in ourselves and in our neighbors, and this is the "tender fruit which He wants us to share with our neighbors."[390]

Once Saint Catherine recognized her own call from the Lord to abandon the solitude of her cell, she herself became "ablaze with loving fire" in the service of the sick and the poor. She longed to communicate that fire to all of her disciples, most especially those caring for the ill and the infirm. Contemporary hospital administrators can welcome Catherine's mandate. For there are many occasions in this sometimes blessed, sometimes confusing, sometimes frustrating culture of hi tech healthcare, when only a heart "ablaze with loving fire" may help an administrator survive the day. Many 21st-century healthcare executives, while accepting their roles as leaders in attending to the sick, are also deeply aware that they are "servant leaders," sorely in need of spiritual support for their chosen ministry.

In a second letter to Matteo, T210, Catherine follows the theme of her desire for the rector to be "immersed" in "the precious blood of God's Son" because she asserted "It frees from cruelty and gives compassion."[391] The saint provides the rationale for her solicitude:

> I long, then, to see you immersed in this river so that you may absorb from it the kind of tender compassion and mercy you must constantly exercise in your way of life. I do want to see you exercise this virtue for Christ's poor with your material possessions. But I am not satisfied with that. No, I am inviting you, as God invites my soul, to extend your fervent loving desires, with compassionately tearful eyes in the presence of divine compassion, to the whole world.[392]

In a footnote to Catherine's comment about Matteo possessing compassion and mercy in his way of life, Suzanne Noffke observed that "As rector of a hospital, Matteo would especially need these qualities."[393]

In the two letters to Rector Matteo di Cenni, Saint Catherine urged conscientiousness and compassion, characteristics vitally important to his role as both administrator of the hospital and superior of the confraternity of Brothers of the Company of the Virgin Mary. Today's hospital directors are also called upon to display such qualities in the exercise of their duties and in their attitudes toward patients and staff. And it is, in fact, in the practice of these virtues that healthcare executives find the fulfillment of their vocations.

Letter to a Prior of the Pisan Knights Hospitallers of St. John

In Letter T256, written to Niccolo dei Strozzi, Prior of the Knights Hospitallers of St. John of Jerusalem, Catherine reveals her awareness that the Hospitallers would soon be engaged in a Crusade and wishes to encourage them:

> I long to see you a courageous knight, stripped of selfish self-centeredness and clothed in divine love. For a knight who is put on the battlefield to fight should be armed with the weapon of love, the strongest weapon there is... this is the glorious armor that rescues us from eternal death and gives us light and delivers us from darkness... To this battle you have to go armed not only with material weapons but with spiritual ones. For if you didn't have the weapons of love for God's honor... you would win little success... I want you, dearest father and son, you and your whole company, to take Christ crucified as your focus... I hope that by God's infinite goodness you will fulfill his will (for that is what he is requiring of you) as well as my desire.[394]

Catherine's message in this letter, that the Knights Hospitallers go to battle "armed with the weapon of love," is a beautiful and consoling thought for contemporary military medics who serve the wounded in theaters of combat. Our physicians, nurses, corpsmen and chaplains in the armed forces, deployed during wartime, risk their lives daily and must indeed be armed with the love which Saint Catherine described as "the strongest weapon there is."

Letters of Consolation to Bereaved Widows

As well as the ill themselves and those who minister to the sick, Catherine was not insensitive to the suffering of individuals who were grieving over the suffering and death of a loved one. Two letters written to bereaved widows were those addressed to Madonna Bandecca, Letter T68, and Madonna Jacoma, Letter T264. In both instances the deaths of the women's spouses were violent, one executed during "a popular uprising," the other "assassinated by political enemies."[395]

In her letter to Madonna Bandecca, Catherine invites the widow to "true patience" and advises:

> when for God's sake we bear with any trial, whether God sends it through death or through life or in any other way, every bitterness becomes sweet and every heavy burden light under this sweet yoke, taken upon our shoulders with God's gracious and agreeable will...

whatever God gives or permits us he gives for our good, so that we may be made holy in Him. So, don't take it ill, dearest mother and sister in Christ Jesus, because the doctor of everlasting life came into the world to heal our illness.[396]

In the letter to Madonna Jacoma, St. Catherine repeats her request for patience and reminds the widow: "Worldly enjoyments or consolations are so unenduring that they are inevitably either taken from us or we from them. Thus, God sometimes permits them to be taken from us, as when we lose earthly goods or even the physical life of those we love. Or, it happens that we leave them, as when God calls us from this life through physical death."

Catherine continues her counsel by acknowledging that Madonna Jacoma has had a traumatic experience and admits how painful it is when the world "fails" one; thus she advises the widow to draw near to the Crucified Christ. Catherine declared that God loved her husband with a special love because he "died in the service of the holy church," and added: "If you say to me 'This burden is too great for me to bear,' I answer you, dearest sister, that... our burden is only as great as time is long... once we have left this life our burdens are gone."[397]

With the exception of chaplains, consoling bereaved family members is not generally the responsibility of those who care for the sick; nevertheless, it sometimes becomes an important informal dimension of the caregiver's role. Family members, who have lost loved ones to illness, may seek comfort from those who provided physical care to the deceased during the final days. Some families develop close bonds with these healthcare providers during an illness experience and wish to remain connected during a time of bereavement. The support of such caregivers can be a source of significant consolation during the grieving period.

Letters to Persons Suffering from Physical Illness or Mental Distress

In three letters to those who are ill, Saint Catherine comforts persons coping with physical illness; in two communications she give solace to individuals suffering from psychological challenges.

The introduction to another letter to Rector Matteo di Cenni, reveals that Catherine was aware that her friend was physically ailing. The letter, T63, is brief, perhaps in sensitivity to his illness. As, previously,

Saint Catherine begins by advising Matteo of his responsibilities as rector:

> I long to see you carrying other people's burdens with love and with desire for God's honor and their salvation. I long to see you a true shepherd conscientiously taking care of the little sheep that are or have been entrusted to you… take care of them with courage… See that you don't try to escape hard tasks, but accept them gladly. Go to meet them with holy desire, saying: 'You are very welcome.' And, 'What a favor my creator does me by letting me endure suffering for the glory and praise of his name!'[398]

An interesting and compassionate conclusion to Matteo's letter comes in Catherine's nursing advice regarding his illness: "I've heard you have been and are still suffering a great deal… I am with you in continual prayer. In no way in the world do I want you to have any more suffering, so that you will be better able to bear what you do have. See that you don't do any sort of penance right now, but take as much comfort as you can get. This is my order!"[399]

The saint's advice might seem surprising given the fact that she so often advised her letter recipients to embrace pain and infirmity as a gift from God, a mentality that she herself had adopted. We trust that she knew Matteo well enough to understand that he would accept whatever suffering he was experiencing but needed, nevertheless, to recover his strength in order to resume his ministry to the sick as rector of *Santa Maria della Scala*.

In Letter T 335, written to a Carthusian monk, Don Christofano, it is clear that Catherine was aware of his ongoing physical and spiritual suffering. She writes:

> I long to see you in the light and fire of the Holy Spirit, the light that dispels all darkness… according to what you wrote me, you are suffering from trials and sufferings both physical and spiritual and for these you need this light… We see that whatever physical illness or spiritual temptations God permits us in this life are for our good, and we judge it all by God's standards… We realize that not a leaf falls from a tree without God's providence. God allows us to be tempted in order to test our virtue and make us grow in grace, not that we may be conquered but that we may conquer by trusting in divine help rather than our own strength.[400]

Catherine concludes with the mandate: "Clothe yourself in God's gentle, eternal will, which has permitted you every one of these physical and spiritual sufferings. God has done and continues to do this for your sanctification. He has given you this out of special love, not out of hatred."[401]

A third letter dealing with physical illness, Letter T 81, was written to one of Catherine's Mantellate Sisters, Francesca di Francesco di Tato Tolomei, whom the saint had been told was very sick. In this letter Catherine tells her Sister that she longs to see her "with a true and holy patience, so that you may courageously bear with illness and anything else God may permit you... Be happy, my daughter, be happy, that God in his mercy makes you worthy to suffer for him...in this way God's will is fulfilled in you, as well as my soul's desire for to see you with a true and holy patience."[402]

Two additional letters selected as examples of Catherine's ministry of correspondence, were addressed to a priest and nun, respectively, both of whom were experiencing mental challenges manifested in anxiety and depression. In her letter to a Pisan priest, Nino da Spazzavento, Letter T158, who was depressed about aging, Catherine suggests that he be "immersed in the blood of Christ Crucified" and explained:

> Those who clothe themselves in it never grow old but are constantly rejuvenated. It makes them fresh with virtue; it strengthens and enlightens them and unites them with their creator. For in Christ Crucified they find the Father and share in his power. And they find the wisdom of God's only begotten son, who enlightens their understanding. They see and experience the mercy of the Holy Spirit. Even if all our other works and all our physical activity should fail, our love must never fail.[403]

And, Saint Catherine's letter to cloistered nun, Suor Bartolomea della Seta, Letter T221, reminds the Sister that her anxiety and depression may be caused by the devil who God allows to test her virtue. The Saint advises Suor Bartolomea: "Be careful not to become depressed or unduly dismayed. And don't give up on the exercise of prayer... (but respond to temptation firmly). I would rather do my duty in pain, darkness and struggle for Christ Crucified than not do it at be at rest."[404] Catherine continued:

But you will say to me: "When I am experiencing so much pain and darkness and struggle I can see nothing but desperation, and I have no apparent grounds for hope at all, so miserable do I seem." I answer you, my daughter, that if you search you will find God in your good will. (And if you say to the Lord) "Oh, good gentle Jesus! And where were you when my soul was in such distress?" The gentle Jesus, spotless lamb, answers: "I was with you. For I am unchanging. I never leave anyone who does not leave me first through deadly sin"(p. 182).

Catherine concluded: "Keep living in God's holy and tender love, finding your rest always on the wood of the Cross."[405]

Catherine's five letters to individuals experiencing physical illness or psychological challenges, contain words of faith and encouragement; she asks that the suffering be endured in the praise of God. The saint issues a reminder that nothing happens without God's knowledge and begs for holy patience. Those in pain, whether physical or emotional, are asked to cling to the Crucified Christ for comfort. Catherine's messages of hope, consolation and spiritual support are as appropriate for the 21st-century person experiencing illness or infirmity as they were in the saint's era of medieval healthcare.

The *Prayers*

In the "Introduction" to her volume of *Saint Catherine's Prayers*, translator Suzanne Noffke notes that the 26 prayers we currently have "are all from the last four years of Catherine's life."[406] Thus, they "along with her *Letters* of that same period, express Catherine's spiritualty at its most mature."[407] Noffke explains that "the principle Catherine emphasized in her teaching found constant expression in her own prayer: knowledge of God as loving Redeemer and of herself as loved sinner, the centrality of truth and love, the primacy of desire, the call to enter fully into the redemptive mission of Christ by laying one's own life on the line for others."[408]

Catherine's *Prayers*, which "afford a precious opening into her intimacy with the Godhead," were not dictated but rather recorded by her disciples when she prayed aloud."[409] When Catherine's followers recognized the importance of her prayers "they wrote down her words."[410] The *Prayers* "impress us by their simplicity, their intense concentration on God who is repeatedly praised and thanked, and their constant desire for the salvation of others."[411]

Dominican Mary O'Driscoll points out that while Saint Catherine was "a great intercessor," her prayers reveal that she does not "regard intercession as merely a passing prayer to God on behalf of one or other person in time of crisis, but rather as an expression of her deep loving permanent commitment both to God and to her neighbor."[412] Because Catherine wrote the *Prayers* near the end of her life, Sister Catherine Meade believes that the saint "conscious of her impending death" chose to "restate ideas and beliefs, symbols and images, concerns and directives" by encapsulating "the more lengthy instructions in the *Letters* and the *Dialogue*."[413]

For present day Christian ministers to the sick, Catherine's *Prayers* provide powerful spiritual grounding and guidance for their healthcare service; especially important is the teaching of perceiving God as "loving Redeemer" and the call to follow Christ by placing one's life on the line for others if need be.

While currently it may not seem, for many of us, that we are risking our lives for those we serve, there are, in fact, instances of contemporary hospital and clinic nursing which demonstrate such a response. For a more dramatic example of service to the sick, one might remember the early days of the HIV/AIDS pandemic when physicians, nurses and chaplains caring for human immunodeficiency virus infected patients had little knowledge of how the devastating disease was actually transmitted; fears of the infection abounded. These front line ministers to HIV/AIDS patients, as Catherine during the era of the "Black Death," risked their own lives to care for those infected with the virus. As well as caring for victims of contemporary infectious diseases, a number of today's medical professionals risk their lives in volunteering for healthcare missions to developing countries, some of which are fraught with conflict and violence.

Prayer 9

> You want us to serve you in your way, Eternal Father, and you guide your servants in different ways along different paths. And so today you show us that we neither may nor can in any way, on the basis of the action we see, judge what is within a person. Rather we should judge all things according to your will... This is why the soul is happy when in your light, she sees the light of the endlessly different ways and paths she sees in these servants of yours. For though they travel by different ways, they are all running along the fiery road of your charity... some of

them in a living faith, others in mercy; and others in letting go of themselves totally opened out in charity for their neighbors. By acting in such ways the soul grows fat... In everything they see your will, and so in everything your creatures do, they look for your will, never passing judgment on the intentions of others... Grant that I may follow your truth with a simple heart; give me the deep well and fire of charity... give my eyes a fountain of tears with which to draw your mercy down over all the world.[414]

In Prayer 9, Saint Catherine teaches us that we must not judge others except in the light of God's will for we do not truly know what is within another person's heart; we should "never pass judgment on the intentions of others." This is a very important message for those of us who minister to the sick. Professional caregiving always involves some dimension of judgment, as contained within the concept of assessment. We, as caregivers, are taught to assess an ill persons' physical, psychological and spiritual challenges and needs; such assessment can be critical in guiding the individual's therapeutic regimen. How, then, can we as healthcare providers, not judge others? It would seem, from the message contained in Catherine's prayer, that the guidance for our judgment must lie in the fact that it be carried out prayerfully, seeking the light of God's will. If our assessments are conducted in such a way, and always tempered with mercy, they will reflect the loving care for our neighbors so often stressed in the mandates of Saint Catherine.

Prayer 12

Oh Fire ever blazing! The soul who comes to know herself in you finds your greatness wherever she turns, even in the tiniest t things, in people and in all created things, for in all of them she sees your power and wisdom and mercy (p. 112)... Eternal goodness, you want me to gaze into you and see that you love me, to see that you love me gratuitously, so that I may love everyone with that very same love. You want me, then, to love and serve my neighbors gratuitously, by helping them spiritually and materially as much as I can, without any expectation of selfish profit or pleasure. Nor do you want me to hold back because of their ingratitude or persecution, or for any abuse I may suffer from them.... You, high eternal Wisdom, did not leave the soul alone but gave her the company of her three powers, memory, understanding and will. These are so united among themselves that whatever the one wants, the others follow. Thus, if memory sets itself to consider your blessings and your boundless goodness, the mind at once want to understand them and the will wants to love and follow your will. And because you did not leave the soul alone, you do not want her to be alone, without love for you and affection for her neighbors.[415]

In Prayer 12, Saint Catherine again meditatively pursues the concept of gratuitously loving and serving others, a theme which emerges repeatedly in both her *Dialogue* and her *Letters*. Catherine is very specific about the meaning of gratuitous service; that is, to assist our neighbors both spiritually and materially without any expectation of personal profit or pleasure. Additionally, we are asked not to hold back on our love and service to others because of ingratitude, persecution or even abuse.

While this is indeed a challenging message, it contains within the blessing of selfless service to those who are sick. There are, of course, occasions in healthcare ministry when we receive satisfaction and even pleasure in the response of grateful patients or family members thankful for our service. At other times our heartfelt care and commitment may seem to go unnoticed and unappreciated even by those to whom we minister. It is precisely in those situations that we are blessed with the opportunity for the gratuitous service which the Lord asks of us.

Prayer 15

Oh God eternal! Have compassion on us! You, high eternal Trinity, say that compassion blossoming in mercy is your hallmark (for mercy is proper to you and mercy never lacks compassion, so it is through compassion that you have mercy on us)… through compassion alone you gave up the Word, your Son to death for our redemption. And that compassion sprang as from a fountain, from the love with which you had created your creature… God eternal…you show us that your compassion will avail us not at all unless we ourselves are compassionate… You want us, merciful and compassionate Father, to look at your boundless compassion for us, so that we may learn to be compassionate, first of all to ourselves and then to our neighbors… You, Light, make the heart simple… so big that it has room in its loving charity for everyone… for a neighbor's physical good, such a heart will give up its material possessions. Such a heart is so open that it is false to no one; everyone can understand it.[416]

Prayer 15 teaches that we must have compassion both for ourselves and for others. Compassion is surely one of the most important virtues for those of us engaged in caring for the sick. In the following meditation, a nurse's prayer for the gift of compassion is described:

Clothed with Compassion
"Dear Lord Jesus,
    You who had compassion
      For all humanity.
Teach your nurses
    The spirituality of
Compassionate caring.

Teach us compassion for the frightened child,
    tearfully begging to return to home
    and family.

Teach us compassion for the stressed preop
    patient, anxiously anticipating the
    outcome of surgery.

Teach us compassion for the frail elder,
    fearfully pondering an uncertain
    future.

Teach us compassion for the terminally ill
    person, solemnly awaiting the
    final exit.

Teach us compassion for the worried family
    member, desperately hoping for
    a word of reassurance.

Teach us, O Lord, to be nurses
    clothed in compassion for
    our fragile brothers and
    sisters for whom we
    care."[417]

The purpose of this chapter, as well as briefly describing the methodology guiding the study of Saint Catherine of Siena's ministry to the sick, has been to identify and analyze selected passages of the saint's own writings which have relevance for contemporary caregivers. While Catherine did not write specifically about her personal activities of caring for the sick, she taught extensively her divinely inspired spirituality of serving one's neighbor. These directives for selfless caring, included in Saint Catherine's *Dialogue*, in her *Letters*, and in her *Prayers*, provide the direction, and guidance for contemporary healthcare ministry to the ill and infirm in the home, in the hospital and in the community. Through describing and analyzing relevant excerpts from Catherine's writings, the spirituality of the saint's 14th-century ministry to the sick poor comes alive for the 21st-century caregiver.

Chapter 5. "Make Yourself a Channel"
The Spiritual Ministry of Healthcare

"Make yourself a channel for giving each person what he or she needs, according to their disposition and what I, your Creator, give to you."
Catherine of Siena: Dialogue 109

A Channel
She walked the streets of Siena
to become a channel
of caring.

She traversed the halls of the hospitals
to become a channel
of solace.

She graced the cells of the prisons
to become a channel
of hope.

A channel for the sick and
the suffering,
A channel for the poor and
the destitute,
A channel for the fearful and
the abandoned.

A channel for all in need of
her loving care
was the young
Dominican Sister
of Penance.

In order to fully comprehend the challenges faced by Saint Catherine of Siena in her ministry as a channel for the needy, especially in her care for the sick poor, we must first explore the association between religion and healthcare in the later Middle Ages, including such topics as diagnosis and treatment of illness and disease, medical education and the medieval hospital. Also of interest is the prevalence of certain diseases and injuries of the era; foremost among these were the bubonic plague, often referred to as the "Black Death," leprosy, and traumatic bodily insults incurred as a consequence of the numerous and sometimes deadly feuds of the period. Regardless of a sick person's illness condition, religious and spiritual support were considered central to any plan of therapeutic intervention.

Religion and Medicine in the Middle Ages

In exploring the relationship between religion and medicine in the Middle Ages, there are three primary areas of concern: the limited understanding of diagnosis and treatment of illness and disease, the circumscribed medical education of the physician, and the multidimensional caring environment of the medieval hospital. Religious and spiritual beliefs were of influence in all three arenas. For example, if the etiology of an illness condition was thought to possess a spiritual or religious component, the treatment might have been difficult, if not impossible, to ascertain. Most physicians were trained in theology as well as the basics of medical practice, and the religious ministries of the medieval hospital were often considered as important as the physical care of the sick. Many medieval hospitals had been established out of Christian piety; they were "all-purpose institutions for social stress of every sort" including the "care of invalids and beggars."[418] *Santa Maria della Scala*, the primary hospital where Saint Catherine served, "received and educated foundlings, lodged pilgrims, and distributed alms to the needy outside its walls" as well as providing care for the sick.[419]

Diagnosis and Treatment

The state of medical and nursing knowledge and practice was decidedly primitive during the Middle Ages. Signs and symptoms associated with many of today's disease conditions were virtually unknown in that era. This was related to the state of medieval medical education as well as to the severe limitations on diagnostic techniques available to practicing physicians.

One author observed that "the truth about the much slandered medical science of the middle ages is that it had probably advanced as far as was possible in an age when no one had yet dreamed of the microscope, and sciences such as chemistry and biology were in their infancy."[420] As to the medications that the medieval physicians did use, the practitioners had no way of analyzing their effectiveness: "any understanding of their effects could only be based on mere theorizing and speculation and were often quite fantastic."[421]

In terms of objective diagnosis, medieval physicians relied primarily on visual inspection of a patient's urine, blood and skin color for signs of illness or some deviation from healthy bodily functioning. Treatments generally consisted of such interventions as "Dietary guidance, bleeding and cautery... corrective measures designed to maintain or restore a patient's health by adjusting his or her humerol balances."[422] Herbal remedies were also employed to alleviate certain symptoms. While these early physicians had only minimal understanding of germ theory, which was not fully explored until several centuries later, they did recognize the seriousness of infections. They realized that an injury could be "fatal if it were infected, but they had no other method of cleansing a wound than the red-hot iron of the surgeon or the method used in the Bible, bathing it in wine and covering it with oil."[423]

What must be kept in mind is the centrality of both the medieval patient's and the medieval physician's spiritual and religious beliefs related to health and illness. The Middle Ages was sometimes described as "the age of faith" which was "certainly borne out by the numerous instances in which people relied on prayer and divine intervention to heal illnesses, either mental or physical."[424]

Medical Education

Some early medieval physicians and surgeons, the latter frequently described as "Barber Surgeons," had received no formal medical school education; these men were often the practitioners of last resort for the poor and underserved of the cities and countrysides. Other physicians and surgeons, especially in the later Middle Ages, had matriculated at one of the great universities such as those of Salerno and Bologna. However, much medical education of the time relied on ideas inherited from the past such as "Hippocrates' Aphorisms, the assumption of a basic knowledge of the humors and complexions, the reference to diagnosis by urine and pulse."[425] Such rudimentary medical knowledge taught throughout the Middle Ages was limited in terms of etiology and treatment of most diseases. There was, in fact, "an enormous amount of faulty knowledge and superstition, the greater part of it passed down from the ancient world as well as from the tribal ancestors of medieval Europeans."[426]

Medieval healthcare practitioners were both physician and theologian. Medical students of the time "turned toward theology and philosophy" to understand why certain things worked to cure sickness.[427] The "learned men of the middle ages reasoned that as it is good for the soul to raise itself above such feelings as fear and disgust, the same must apply to the body; and as they thought in analogies they sometimes prescribed cures which were quite worthless, simply because they were bound to cause aversion among normal people."[428] On a positive note, the physicians of the period did "know enough about infection to institute quarantine for travelers who came from places where epidemics were raging"; unfortunately, "they were far from sure which illnesses were infectious."[429]

The European university medical education embraced the importance of both science and religion in caring for the sick. All "throughout the middle ages physicians possessed one fundamental source upon which they could draw when asserting the legitimacy of their profession, the Bible."[430] The Book of Sirach, Ecclesiasticus, 38 was used "to supply scriptural authority to a general argument in favor of the medical profession in Christian society"[431]:

> Honor physicians for their services, for the Lord created them; for their gift of healing comes from the most High and they are rewarded by the King. The skill of physicians makes them distinguished, and in the presence of the great they are admired. The Lord created medicines out of the earth, and the sensible will not despise them... And He gave skill to human beings, that he might be glorified in his marvelous works. By them the physician heals and takes away pain... God's work will never be finished; and from Him health spreads over all the earth (Ecclesiaticus (Sirach) 38: 1-8).

The text in Ecclesiasticus goes on to support the importance of an ill person's faith, freedom from sin and prayer rather than relying on medicine or medical treatment for healing: "My child when you are ill, do not delay, but pray to the Lord, and he will heal you. Give up your faults and direct your hands rightly, and cleanse your heart from all sin"

(Ecclesiasticus 38: 9-10). Nevertheless, the message ultimately returns to recommending the value of the physician: "Then give the physician his place, for the Lord created him; do not let him leave you, for you need him. There may come a time when recovery lies in the hands of the physicians, for they too pray to the Lord that he grant them success in diagnosis and in healing for the sake of preserving life" (Eccles. 38: 12-14).

For some medieval Christian patients and their physicians the "concept of illness was almost one of an experience to be cherished, since they believed that the more one suffered on earth, the better one's chances of getting into heaven."[432] Even in the later Middle Ages spiritual and religious beliefs "still remained an essential part of the practice of medicine. Prayer and spiritual care had precedence over drugs and physical care."[433] An example is given of the medieval physician's awareness of the positive influence of spiritual support in the course of treating illness and disease: "he recommends that the patient should be asked to confess and receive the Sacraments of the Church before the doctor sees him, for if mention is afterwards made of this, the patient may believe that it is only because the doctor thinks there is no hope for him."[434]

Medieval Hospitals

A number of institutions that were identified as "hospitals" during the earlier Middle Ages were not hospitals as currently understood. Many were "actually almshouses... residences for people who were poor but not sick."[435] The facilities labeled "hospices," in distinction, were way stations for traveling pilgrims. "Hospitals" built by the very early Christian communities were labeled *Xenodochia* (inns or hostels) and housed a variety of travelers and pilgrims as well as the ill.

By the later medieval period, hospitals, although still offering a variety of other charitable services, were generally acknowledged to primarily be facilities for care of the sick: "Along with wards for housing the patients, these hospitals typically had chapels, kitchens, laundry facilities and domestic accommodations for the staff. The patients' wards were generally depicted as long, open halls with rows of beds along the walls."[436] Most institutions had long curtains attached to the ceiling which could be draped around a bed for patient privacy.

The Spiritual History of Christian Healthcare: Catherine's Heritage

Saint Catherine, in her 14th-century ministry to the sick, had inherited a rich legacy of Christian caregiving. For the early Christian healthcare provider the healing activity of Jesus was seen as the model for attending to the sick. In ministry to those who were ill or injured, Jesus "touched the sick, visited their homes, allowed them to touch him and showed compassion whenever asked for mercy by one who was in need of his caring support."[437]

Following the death of Jesus, care of the sick was considered a blessed and treasured ministry of the young Christian church. A primary role of the deacon was visiting the sick in patients' homes and providing care as needed; some church deacons even took the ill into their own homes housing them in *Diaconia* (from the Greek verb *diakonen* meaning to serve) or "Christrooms," where the ailing were clothed, fed and cared for.[438] Deacons were "obliged, by their positions, to visit and nurse the sick."[439] The *Diaconia* might be considered the earliest precursor of the Christian hospital suggesting an association with Jesus' teaching: "I was a stranger and you took me in."[440]

Another group of individuals who ministered to the sick in the early Church were the Roman Matrons who had converted to Christianity in the era of the third and fourth centuries. The Matrons, many of whom were widows, "were able to use their power and wealth to support the charitable work of nursing the sick; they founded hospitals and convents, living ascetic lives dedicated to the care of the ill and the infirm. Three of the most famous Roman matrons, involved in healthcare, were Saints Helena, Paula and Marcella."[441] Saint Helena, the mother of Constantine, founded the first nursing home for the aged infirm called a *gerokomion*.[442] Saint Paula established the earliest pilgrim hospice.[443] And Saint Marcella organized a community of women religious whose primary ministry was care of the sick poor.[444]

The Church's "religious ethos of charity continued with the rapid growth of monastic orders in the fifth and sixth centuries and extended into the middle ages. Monasteries added hospital wards, where to 'care' meant to give comfort and spiritual sustenance."[445] Although early monasteries, such as those of Saint Benedict of Nursia, were centers of prayer and study, ultimately "nursing of the sick became a chief function and duty of community life."[446] Initially, the monks cared only for their

108

own monastics who were ill; eventually they began to welcome the sick poor from the surrounding villages. Monastic women also founded communities whose work included nursing of the sick; three of the most well-known Abbesses engaged in ministry to the ill and infirm were Saint Radegunde of Poitiers, Saint Hilda of Whitby and Saint Brigid of Ireland.[447]

The monastic concern for those who were ill was the catalyst for other religious communities of men and women to undertake a variety of forms of care and devotion to the sick. This "duty to treat" ethically "stemmed from the powerful Christian virtues of charity and service" to the poor and needy rather than any sense of professional obligation.[448] Biblically the Christian commitment to care for the ailing or injured was derived from "Christ's parable of 'The Good Samaritan'; mercy and compassion for anyone in need."[449]

It was during the Christian era that hospitals began to be identified as places where the sick could be housed for extended periods of time to receive treatment and care. The Christian populace "supplied significant impetus to hospital development by their establishment of caring facilities for the sick and disadvantaged in the community."[450] As earlier acknowledged, these "hospitals" continued to also be settings for other charitable works such as the teaching of orphans and feeding of the poor and needy; eventually they began to admit "disadvantaged people as well as disabled and mentally infirm persons (and) many of these developed into standard hospitals."[451]

In the periods of the 6th and 7th Centuries, several great Christian hospitals were established, including the *Hotel Dieu* of Lyon (542 AD), the *Hotel Dieu* of Paris (650 AD) and *Santo Spirito* in Rome (689 AD). Historians Adelaide Nutting and Lavinia Dock noted that the *Hotel Dieu* of Lyon, France, "designed to care for pilgrims, orphans, the poor and the sick... was one of the first hospitals to separate those with contagious illnesses from those with more ordinary ills."[452] The French *Hotel Dieu*'s, or Houses of God, were primarily staffed by Augustinian Nuns who devoted their lives to the care of the sick.[453] The Sisters' entire world became the hospital where they both lived and worked with no thought of ever returning home."[454] As poignantly observed by historian Victor Robinson M.D., the Augustinian Nuns, ministering at the Hotel *Dieu*'s, lived "for twelve hundred years immured within these walls; alive yet not of this world; aloof from the human race, with the breath of God upon their faces. To and fro they walked the wards, back and forth throughout the days and years and centuries."[455]

Around the 11th, 12th and 13th Centuries, the period of the religious Crusades to the Holy Land, communities of Christian military men were founded to care for those injured in battle as well as for those returning home from a conflict. Three important religious/military nursing orders were: the "Knights Hospitallers of St. John of Jerusalem," founded by Peter Gerard around 1050 AD[456]; the German "Teutonic Knights," which originated in 1191[457]; and the "Knights of St. Lazarus" whose calling was especially to care for lepers.[458] Men suffering from leprosy were allowed to join the latter community; it was even rumored that the Master of the Order was himself a leper. Members of these early military orders wore a distinctive tunic emblazoned with the Cross of a Crusader and took vows of poverty, chastity and obedience, as well as a vow to care for the sick.[459]

The hospital of the early medieval era was, as noted, essentially an ecclesiastical facility with staggering mortality rates that encouraged a vision of cure only in the hereafter. For that reason, therapy focused more on the soul than on the body."[460] Physician and historian of medicine and nursing, Dr. James Walsh asserted that the patients "were not so fearful about death in the middle ages as we are apt to be" and added: "Who shall say that the contemplation of it did not often give that restful sense of submission to whatever would come that sometimes means so much in serious illness, and keeps the patient from still further exhausting vitality by worry as to the outcome?"[461]

From the period of the 11th to the 14th Century, the identity of the hospital, as a place "intended for sick persons only," emerged slowly; however, the management of the medieval hospital remained "in the hands of the Church."[462] The primary goal of the hospital continued to be "relief of the body when possible, but pre-eminently, the refreshment of the soul."[463] "Faith and love were more predominant features in hospital life than were skill and science."[464] Thus, the physical care provided by the hospital was elementary: "feeding, bathing, using herbals in a variety of vehicles, purging and the ever-available bloodletting by leech or phlebotomy."[465] It was to such religiously oriented healthcare and healthcare settings that Saint Catherine was introduced during her visits to the sick in the hospitals of 14th-century Siena.

We do not have a great deal of information about the specifics of daily care and treatment for the later medieval hospital patients in settings such as *Santa Maria della Scala*, *Casa della Miseracordia* and *San Lazzaro* where Catherine served. Some hints of the hospital milieu in the Middle Ages, however, may be gleaned from artwork describing the medical, spiritual and nursing care of the period. As explained in the previous chapter, the research method that guided this exploration of Saint Catherine of Siena's healthcare ministry was that of hermeneutic phenomenology as articulated by Max van Manen. To supplement verbal and/or written data, van Manen suggests that the investigator may also examine and analyze artistic materials related to the phenomenon under study.[466] Van Manen asserted that, "for the artist as well as the phenomenologist, the source of all work is the experiential lifeworld of all human beings. Just as the poet or the novelist attempts to grasp the essence of some experience in literary form, so the phenomenologist attempts to grasp the essence of some experience in a phenomenological description."[467] Some artistic sources which may be considered include visual art forms such as paintings and sculpture, as well as written portrayals of the phenomenon reflected in poetry and prose.

One of the most important windows into the daily life of the medieval Sienese hospital, where Saint Catherine ministered to the sick, is contained in the famous painting by narrative artist Domenico di Bartolo entltitled: "The Care and Healing of the Sick" (circa 1440); the work was commissioned as a fresco for the *"Pellegrinaio,"* or Pilgrim Hall, of Siena's great *Ospedale Santa Maria della Scala*. It is asserted that this fresco, together with several others, "show us that Domenico was truly the first renaissance painter of Siena."[468]

The group of frescos in the *Pellegrinaio* "depict events from the history of the hospital, as well as its charitable works, feeding the hungry, taking in pilgrims, bringing up orphans."[469] Bartolo's frescos take us back to life in a charity hospital as it was experienced in the 14th Century. In the paintings we see "the hospital Brothers distributing bread to the poor and to pilgrims... cripples limping away after receiving their share; an entirely naked man is clothed; a woman carrying a child on her arm and holding another by the hand receives provisions; a Brother returns home with foundling children in a basket on his back."[470] Domenico di Bartolo's work "The Care and Healing of the Sick" is described as "arguably his masterpiece."[471] Art historian Thomas Hyman observed that "Domenico created a series of extraordinarily moving encounters between the fortunate and the broken... expensively gowned patricians... and the naked and the dying."[472] The painting of the *Santa*

Maria della Scala frescos allowed di Bartolo to "fully deploy his considerable narrative and descriptive gifts. Some of the interiors of the scenes of charitable acts reproduce actual spaces of the hospital populated with contemporaries."[473]

In "The Care and Healing of the Sick," "there are details which win praise (such as) the anatomy of a figure... whose wounds are being washed," which is considered appropriate for the era.[474] As with each of the frescos painted by Domenico, this painting provides the observer with "a treasure trove of information about the Scala and its many charitable functions."[475] For example, critic Bruce Cole commented that "Care of the Sick" shows, with great accuracy, the interior of a hospital ward. The patients are looked after by doctors and lay superintendents of the *Scala*, who are carefully depicted doing their good deeds. An image of washing a patient's feet, in the painting's center foreground is "borrowed directly from the traditional image of Christ washing the feet of his disciples."[476] Cole noted that "everywhere in the 'Care of the Sick,' Domenico di Bartolo has emphasized the splendor of the costume and the complexities of the decorations... nowhere else in Siena is there such a profusion of objects and portraits."[477]

Catherinian scholar Johannes Jorgensen asserted that Domenico's frescoes take us "straight into life as it was lived... centuries ago."[478] Commenting on the fresco "The Care and Healing of the Sick," Jorgensen especially noted the image of a bedridden patient: "his head is bandaged, his face sallow and partly covered with a stubby growth of beard; the coverlet, striped red and yellow is drawn right up to the ears... he seems to have just received the last sacraments."[479] Ultimately, Jorgensen concluded: "The whole picture gives a rich and almost festive impression; one sees that no effort has been spared to make everything as comfortable as possible for the patients."[480]

In a 2007 article, *Irish Medical Times* reporter Brenda McCann commented that "The Care and Healing of the Sick" is the "most appealing" of the *Santa Maria della Scala* medieval frescos "because it so convincingly conveys the intensity of the atmosphere in a busy ward."[481] McCann notes: "an orderly helps a patient on a stretcher while two doctors confer over a urine sample. In the center a young man's thigh wound is being washed prior to surgery, and a monk listens to a patient's confession."[482] Di Bartolo's painting is described on the current website of the *Ospedale Santa Maria della Scala* museum as the most famous of all of the frescoes in the facilities' Pilgrim Hall.[483]

112

When one studies the painting carefully, the exquisitely rich detail in the fresco provides a breathtaking amount of information descriptive of the daily life and activities of the medieval hospital. The work portrays a multiplicity of scenarios reflecting various hospital ministries: diagnostic activity by physicians, physical care and psychological support of the sick by nursing Oblate Brothers, spiritual assessment and intervention carried out by a Dominican Friar, supervision of care by the Rector of the hospital, and the interest of visiting donors who supported the hospital's ministries to the sick and the poor. In essence, the artist presents a "clinical depiction" of life in the 14th-century hospital.[484]

Directly in the center of the painting is the image of a partially clothed young man, with an exposed bleeding thigh wound. The patient is seated on a chair with one foot immersed in a basin of water; the other foot is being gently dried with a towel held by a kneeling Oblate Brother. Directly behind the wounded man's chair is another Oblate Brother holding a blanket to shield the patient's nakedness from the eyes of others in the room. On the floor are pictured the patient's slippers, arranged carefully side-by side, and a pitcher, probably containing more water. The two nursing attendants may be understood to be "Oblates Brothers" of the confraternity serving the sick at *Santa Maria della Scala* as their manner of dress appears similar to that described for members of the nursing brotherhood: a tan tunic, black shoes and black head covers. There is a third identically dressed attendant, partially visible in the background, holding a folded towel in his hands.

Also, behind the scene of the Oblates caring for the wounded young man, are observed a number of differently attired gentlemen, whom the *Santa Maria della Scala* website identifies as: the "Rector" of the hospital, supervising the caregiving activity; a physician; a well-dressed donor and a group of Oblates of the religious confraternity serving in the hospital.

To the left of the fresco are two other important images; one pictures two physicians, identified by their distinctive robes and head coverings, one of whom is holding a clear glass vial containing yellow liquid. As well as McCann's commentary in the "Irish Medical Times," other critics of the work have suggested that this scenario depicts of the act of examining the patient's urine, a standard diagnostic modality in the Middle Ages. In front of the physicians, at the lower left corner of the painting, di Bartolo has pictured another Oblate Brother attendant bending tenderly over an anxious patient lying on a litter. The ill person is reaching out to grasp the Oblate's shoulder; the Brother has placed one hand under the patient's back and the other behind the neck to support him. Although we only view a portion of the attendant's robe and head covering, he appears to be similarly dressed to the earlier described Oblates.

A significant religious scenario is presented on the right side of the painting in di Bartolo's portrayal of a Friar attired in the white habit and black mantle of the Dominican Order. The kindly Friar is leaning over a bedridden patient, partially kneeling, with one hand close to his ear; he appears to be hearing the sick man's confession and praying with him. This image reflects the importance of spiritual care in the daily life of the medieval hospital. Behind the patient's bed is a shelf containing implements of healing: several flasks and bottles which might contain medicine and drinking water.

In the far right background of the fresco, the artist has included a partial view of two litter bearers possibly bringing a newly deceased patient to the hospital for post-mortem care and a funeral. A cloth covering the black casket is emblazoned with several "ladders," symbolic of *la Scala* hospital. Below that is pictured a large bathing basin, over which is draped a towel, in readiness for a newly-admitted patient.

In picturing the hospital environment, Domenico di Bartolo did not forget the importance, especially in that era, placed on the presence of fresh air for patient healing. In viewing the upper portion of the hall in which the healthcare activities are occurring, one finds four large windows with the shutters turned back to allow air and sunlight to stream into the room; there is also an open side window displayed. Along the painting's top boarder the artist has sketched several shields, each containing a coat of arms with a staircase indicative of the hospital name: *Santa Maria della Scala* (scala: Italian for staircase). The latter portion of the hospital's name was chosen to represent the facility's location opposite the steps of Siena's great Cathedral, or *Duomo*.

In the fresco's right lower foreground one finds the surprising presence of a small cat and a dog. These animals may have been viewed by the hospital staff as acceptable pets related to both sanitation (elimination of rodents) and protection against intruders.

Finally, in the center of the painting, situated behind the primary caregiving activity of the ward's main treatment room, di Bartolo has placed a lattice-work rood screen which appears to serve the purpose of separating the treatment area from the main hall containing hospital beds. Behind the screen, one catches a glimpse of an attendant holding a small round tray before a patient, while three Oblate Brothers look on. It appears, from the inclusion of this background image, that Domenico wanted to remind the observer that routine care continued in other locations of the hospital even while newly admitted patients, those requiring surgery, seriously ill individuals and the deceased were attended to in the treatment area.

Domenico di Bartolo's narrative fresco "The Care and Healing of the Sick" has left us a precious gift in his magnificently detailed portrait reflecting the daily life and healthcare ministry of the medieval hospital.

Spirituality and 14th-Century Illness and Disease: The "Black Death," Leprosy and Traumatic Injuries

At the time of her ministry to the sick in medieval Siena, Saint Catherine was faced with a variety of diseases, illnesses and bodily injuries about which little formal medical knowledge existed; dermatological and gastrointestinal diseases abounded among the poor living in inadequate sanitary environments and receiving less than adequate nutrition. Even if a disease condition was diagnosed, such as that of a cancerous growth, frequently there was no standardized treatment known. Patients would simply have to be made as comfortable as possible, and encouraged to pray, while waiting for the disease to end their lives. Thus great importance was placed upon spiritual support especially for patients' experiencing the onset of serious illness. Three of the most prevalent illness conditions with which Saint Catherine was faced were: the bubonic plague, or "Black Death"; leprosy; and traumatic injuries suffered as a result of deadly feuds initiated by local citizens. Each of these conditions contained within its etiology a religious or spiritual interpretation.

The "Black Death"

The "Black Death," more commonly referred to as the bubonic plague, or simply the "plague," represented the greatest disease scourge of Saint Catherine's lifetime in Siena and the surrounding countryside. The first appearance of the plague in Siena did not have a major impact on Catherine and her family; this outbreak occurred in 1348 while the saint was yet an infant. The second plague epidemic in the city, in 1374, however, did touch both Catherine and many of her friends and loved ones as described in later chapters.

The "Black Death," identified as "the worst pandemic ever known… killed at least 25 million Europeans, more than one third of the population, and changed the lives of those who survived."[485] The "Yersinia Pestis" bacterium is the causative agent of the plague and can be transmitted by fleas, bites, scratches, aerosols or contaminated food.[486] Clinically, patients infected with the plague display symptoms such as nausea, fever and fatigue often combined with respiratory difficulties such as shortness of breath. A telling sign, responsible for the label "bubonic" plague, is the emergence of a swelling, or "bubo," which can be "located in the groin, in the axilla, and more rarely on the neck or the head."[487] Once these symptoms appear, death usually occurs within 36 to 48 hours for most victims. Anecdotes abounded in Siena of physicians and priests falling over dead while in the midst of ministering to their patients dying of the plague; the disease was highly contagious.

Spiritual care of plague victims was considered critical in Saint Catherine's time not only because of the disease's high mortality rate but also related to the perceived etiology of the illness held by some. A Christian moralistic reaction to a plague outbreak might result from belief in "biblical references to plagues as punishment for man's sins."[488] As a consequence some plague victims and their families were ostracized as sinners, as well as from fear of contagion. Physician James Eastman suggests that with such symptoms as "boils, gangrene, vomiting blood, madness, it (the plague) must have seemed more like Divine retribution than a potentially curable disease."[489] Churches in infected areas provided "pits" where dead bodies could be buried anonymously.[490]

The deadly prognosis and course of the disease also resulted in a fairly widespread breakdown of morality among affected citizens, and even among some of the clergy who lost many of their own.[491] People who were deprived of former occupations or homes because of the illness and death of family members sought any means of survival even if these involved acts of burglary or violence against their neighbors, and the ranks of the clergy needed to minister to victims of the plague were now greatly thinned. Ultimately an ethical problem related to the issue of contagion emerged as well. Plague sufferers were considered so dangerous that some healthy family members fled their homes leaving a parent or sibling isolated and alone to die without the comforting presence of a loved one or the sacraments of the Church.

It is, therefore, not difficult to understand why Catherine's presence in Siena in 1374, just as the second outbreak of the plague was in full swing, was a great blessing in terms of both the physical and spiritual care of those she tended. Specific examples of the saint's selfless and compassionate attention to those victimized by the horrors of the Black Death are included in the following chapter within a discussion of her Community/Public Health Ministry. As well as the plague, however, Catherine was also called upon to care for those with another devastating contagious disease of her age, that of leprosy.

Leprosy

Courage

"When I think of courage now, I see
 A braver woman who has thrown away
 The joys that make life beautiful, to stay
 A servant in the house of leprosy...
 This was the courage of the Man who chose
   The path to Calvary
 Nor feared its close.
       Theodosia Garrison[492]

Currently, the disease identified in the past as "leprosy," now more commonly labeled "Hansen's disease," is somewhat less feared than in the Middle Ages. Hansen's disease is caused by a bacteria known as Mycobacterium Leprae; the infected person may not show any symptoms for some years after initial contact with the organism. When, however, symptoms begin to appear they can be severely disfiguring and may result in loss of sensation in the affected areas. Today, Hansen's disease patients can be medicated with a variety of drugs including antibiotics. Although the disease may be transmitted through some bodily secretions, once the illness has been treated, most patients are not highly infectious. While still a frightening diagnosis, the identification of Hansen's disease or leprosy is less terrifying than in the medieval period.

In the Middle Ages there were a number of theories about how "diseases came into existence and spread. Some of these theories blamed

117

supernatural causes such as God visiting His righteous wrath on sinful mankind."[493] Such thinking was often applied to the disease of leprosy, as to the bubonic plague as noted earlier. A confirmed diagnosis of leprosy carried with it a stigma that was for some more frightening than the fear of disfigurement, for it "separated a man from society because of the infection that he carried outwardly and the moral corruption that lay within him."[494] The perceived sinfulness of the victim of leprosy was supported by the biblical text in Leviticus chapter 13, which described the leper as "unclean." Leprosy sufferers were thus "considered ritually unfit and were separated from other members of the community."[495] During biblical times, lepers were forced to live in caves outside of the city limits and were mandated to ring a bell or clapper when walking about in order to warn passers-by of their disease.

Medieval victims of leprosy were prevented from worshipping in churches with healthy members of the congregation and most were relocated from their homes to specialized hospitals or leper houses. These "Leper houses (Lazar Houses or Leprosaria) originated during the 11th Century when Europe began experiencing an epidemic of leprosy."[496] A "marked feature of the countryside in a great many places in most European countries in the middle ages was the presence of a leper hospital."[497] The number of leper hospitals "appears to confirm the acute problem that leprosy presented to medieval society; a problem that necessitated the wide-scale foundation of institutions specializing in the provision for, and if we are to trust the traditional sources, the exclusion of, those affected with leprosy."[498] These institutions simply cemented the belief that lepers were "outcasts" who needed to be "excluded from society."[499]

The leper hospitals of the time were generally staffed by members of Christian religious communities, "men and women who renounced the world and lived according to a rule in leper houses or hospitals for the poor, ministering to the destitute and infirm devoutly and with humility."[500] The touching poem "Courage," penned in the early 20th Century by Theodosia Garrison, "has pictured very beautifully and very strikingly the quiet courage of the women who nurse lepers."[501] Garrison's poem begins by suggesting that the author initially pictured courage in the guise of a "crimson-clad" youth preparing for battle or a "glad" martyr "courting hurt and blame." As the poem progressed, however, the poet identified courage as contained within the vocation of the leper's nurse. As observed by historian James Walsh, "Surely most of us have the feeling that she (Garrison) has portrayed; we feel that the quiet courage of the woman who remained in humble obscurity beside the bedside of her lepers far transcends that of the young soldier."[502]

At the poem's close, after Theodosia Garrison has described the painful task of the caregiver who must, day after day, face the "white death which no human hand can stay," she reminds us not only of the bravery but of the spiritual commitment of the leprosy nurse with the words: "This was the courage of the Man who chose the path to Calvary, nor feared its close."[503]

Traumatic Injuries

One of the unique ministries attributed to Saint Catherine was the mediation of feuds among citizens of Siena; these local feuds were notorious in medieval towns. It may seem curious to identify this activity of the saint in relation to her care of the sick. Catherine's desire to intervene in these sometimes deadly feuds, however, derived directly from her nursing experiences in the community and in the hospitals. As Catherine traversed the streets of Siena and cared for patients in the hospitals, she frequently encountered men who had suffered traumatic, sometimes life threatening, injuries as a consequence of feuding. In Siena, there were reportedly "grave quarrels among the citizens, numerous revolts and ferocious hatred between certain families."[504] Catherine "soon came to realize that not a few of the men, particularly those who were treated at the hospitals, came there as a result of the wounds inflicted in connection with family feuds which were so common in the cities of Italy about this time."[505]

Nurse historian Sister Charles Marie Frank observed: "Catherine noted that many cases of stab wounds were admitted to the hospitals and her practical nature decided that prevention was better than cure so she went out into the streets to prevent quarrels, establish peace among dissenters and eliminate stabbings."[506] One of Saint Catherine's additional ministries related to the feuds was to "organize a group of young men who were willing, for her sake, to be stretcher bearers... to pick up the wounded from the street and carry them to the hospitals."[507] Without this band of courageous assistants who volunteered to transport the injured for treatment, many would have died where they had fallen.

Catherine soon "became famous as a peacemaker among warring Italian families."[508] She was, in the words of Augusta Theodosia Drane:

> A true Italian and a true Dominican also. She loved her country, and names it in her letters with unmistakable tenderness, and she inherited the traditions of an Order, one of whose chief works, in the early centuries of its existence had been the healing of party feuds. Everywhere throughout Italy the friars appeared as the apostles of peace. It was not long before Catherine acquired such a reputation for success in reconciliation of long-standing family feuds, that appeals were made for her arbitration from all quarters in the vicinity of Siena.[509]

In a book devoted entirely to the subject of "feuds and feuding" in the Middle Ages, Jette Netterstrom explained the concept of "feud" as: "a state of bitter and lasting mutual hostility; especially such a state existing between two families, tribes or individuals, marked by murderous assaults in revenge for some dreadful insult or wrong."[510] Netterstrom explains that the definition "emphasizes the long lasting character of the feud, the reciprocity between the feuding parties and the mutuality of their violent actions; it furthermore emphasizes the homicidal aspect and the revenge element."[511] Jette Netterstrom concludes, however, that "feud violence need not be 'murderous' and may consist of non-lethal physical harm."[512] He admits, ultimately, that "feuds may be very difficult to resolve, because the game tends to be one with a less-than-zero sum insofar as honor is concerned. Thus, feuds can be long-lasting or all but interminable unless some strong force militates for pacification."[513] Catherine of Siena was indeed such a "force."

Author Helgi Porlaksson supports Netterstrom's assertion that feuds did indeed take place in medieval Western Europe.[514] For Porlaksson, some distinctive features of a medieval feud included: two opposing groups being involved; the groups taking turns to carry out acts of violence against each other; a culture of honor as the motivating factor underlying the feud; and the establishment of "culturally accepted procedures for the resolution of feuds."[515] Several additional characteristics of medieval feuds were identified as: the feud starting "to avenge an act perceived as a wrong, generally violent injury or often a killing"; the feud signaling "a lasting enmity between those who inflicted it and the victim"; the level of response being "constrained by a notion of rough equivalence, requiring the keeping of a score"; the "quantum and nature" of the response being fueled by emotions; and "the response being open to public view and ritualized in ways that proclaim the acts to all as legitimate and honorable."[516] Thus, one can understand why Catherine's mediation needed to be carried out with wisdom, delicacy and cultural sensitivity to the emotions of the feuding parties.

Finally, there is discussion in the literature on the distinction between the concepts of "feud" and "vendetta." A "vendetta" is described as an act which is "clearly vengeance" and retaliation for a specific injury.[517] Trevor Dean identified a "culture of vengeance" in Italy from the "thirteenth to the fifteenth centuries."[518] This culture, Dean explained, had four major components: "a language of conflict… dominated by notions of friendship and enmity"; a "positive value" placed on vengeance; vengeance as part of "civic education"; and feuds considered "not just as expressions of personal hatred but as mechanisms to protect family honor."[519]

When medieval citizens became involved in either a feud or a vendetta there was the significant possibility of violent acts culminating in traumatic injuries or even death. It was because of her experiences of witnessing and caring for patients with such feud or vendetta related injuries that Saint Catherine sought to mediate the conflicts whenever possible. A specific example of Catherine's ministry among feuding Sienese citizens is included in the following chapter.[520]

Spiritual Ministry in the Siena Hospitals

As discussed earlier, factors such as antiquated medical education for attending physicians, as well as unsophisticated diagnostic tools and techniques, severely limited medical and nursing activities in the medieval hospitals, making them more suited to "care" of the sick rather than to "cure." Because of the high mortality rate among patients, hospitals of the era were often viewed as ecclesiastical facilities with a plan for cure to come only in the hereafter. Thus, the importance of spiritual ministry was paramount for hospitalized patients. The three primary Siena hospitals where Catherine cared for the sick were the great charity hospital *Santa Maria della Scala*, the more modest *Casa della Miseracordia* and the hospital for lepers outside the city walls, *San Lazzaro*.

Santa Maria della Scala

Legend suggests that the *Santa Maria della Scala* Hospital was founded in the late 9th Century as the vision of a poor cobbler, Sorore, described as "a man of humble position, who after the manner of the early Christians was wont to take pilgrims and needy persons into his own frugal home for hospitality."[521] The first documents describing the facility as a *Xenodocium et hospitalis* (hostel and hospital), however, were dated March 29, 1090.[522] *Santa Maria della Scala* closed its doors as a healthcare facility in 1990, making it one of the longest serving hospitals in the world; the former hospital site is now the "*Santa Maria della Scala* Museum." The hospital was named for both the Blessed Virgin and the steps, or *scala*, the latter referring to the facility's location directly across from the *scala* of the Sienese Cathedral. As well as caring for the sick, *Santa Maria della Scala* was noted for its charitable activities of educating orphans, feeding the poor and elderly and providing hospitality for pilgrims. The hospital's myriad ministries were supported by the gracious gifts of wealthy donors as well as by the Canons of the Cathedral of Siena.[523]

The hospital, sometimes called simply *La Scala*, was primarily staffed by lay Brothers or Oblates who were described as "God-fearing, honest and efficient."[524] The Order of nursing Brothers established at *La Scala* was "it was said, the earliest order of hospital brothers under a regular rule."[525] The head of the hospital "was the 'rector,' usually a rich merchant or banker, who on appointment bequeathed all his possessions to the hospital."[526] The lay Brothers or Oblates, known familiarly as the "Brothers of *Santa Maria della Scala*," also turned over their lands and possessions to the hospital when they entered the Order.

The formal name of *Santa Maria della Scala*'s lay brotherhood, or confraternity, was "The Company of the Discipline of the Virgin Mary."[527] Augusta Drane described the history of the community:

> This company was far more ancient than the hospital itself, and traced its origin to those first Christians of Siena who converted to the faith by the martyr St. Ansano, assembled in the catacombs for the secret exercise of their religion. When the great hospital was built at a later period the vaults were not destroyed... and still assigned to the use of the company. Here the Brethren had their own chapel and rooms in which they assembled and took the discipline... they carried on a great number of good works, attending the hospitals both in and out of the

city, and assisting the poor, the sick, orphans and pilgrims... this confraternity was the very life and center of the piety of Siena.[528]

Catherinian biographer Johannes Jorgensen characterized the nursing Brothers of *La Scala* as "a voluntary brotherhood, the members of which simply gave themselves and all that they possessed to serve the sick and the poor."[529] Jorgensen described the rules of the hospital which guided how "the Rector and the Brethren... should live their lives."[530] The Brother/Oblates were to rise early and attend morning Mass in the Chapel of the hospital:

> They were likewise under obligation to take part in evensong and compline... Beside the bell for prayers, there is another bell in the hospital and when it rings 'all the brethren shall wait upon the sick and bring them food... when the sick people have eaten, the brethren shall eat, the Rector presiding at their meals, and no one shall speak but a book shall be read aloud, and without a valid reason no one may eat elsewhere in the hospital, neither in the dormitory, nor in any cell, nor in the kitchen... no brother may receive gifts without the leave of the Rector, for there must be no distinction and in the refectory all shall eat and drink the same.[531]

As to care of the sick, the Brother's rule specified that there should be "an infirmarian whose task it is to procure and maintain all that is necessary 'to remove disease and regain health, and a pellegriniero, who receives the sick on their admission and supervises the good conduct of the servants so that the poor folk and sick are well served.'"[532] The strictness of the Oblates' rules is reflected in such mandates as "forbidding the brethren to eat or drink outside the hospital, nay they may not even sit down when they are 'in a layman's house' but must 'perform their errand standing,' nor may they leave the hospital without the permission of the Rector."[533]

Perhaps the most important dimension of patient care contained in the Brothers' rules, defines the appropriate spiritual care of the sick at *Santa Maria della Scala*:

> All the priests who are housed in the said hospital are requested in charity by the Rector and the Brethren to attend to the confession of the sick and to give them absolution and penance... And the said priests shall be bound to give the sick the Body of Our Lord Jesus Christ and all

the sacraments of Holy Church when asked to do so and it seemeth right to them. And in all these things the priests must use care and watchfulness. Likewise the nurses attending to the sick and the servants must have a care to tell the sick to confess their sins and to receive the sacraments of the Church.[534]

Being Siena's largest hospital, and situated directly across from the Cathedral, the *Spedale di Santa Maria della Scala* was a "crossroads of classes, ages, occupations, ranging from the neediest to those who had suffered misfortune while on pilgrimage."[535] The hospital provided a venue for volunteer ministry for lay citizens such as the Mantellate of which Catherine was a member.[536] It became one of the primary settings where the saint would serve her ailing neighbor.[537]

Casa della Miseracordia

There is not a great deal of information available about the less prestigious general hospital in Siena, the *Casa della Miseracordia*. It is, nevertheless, always referred to as one of the hospitals where Saint Catherine ministered to the ill and the infirm. Fra Raimondo indicated that the *Casa della Miseracordia*, or "House of Mercy" hospital, was "founded in about the middle of the 13th Century by Saint Andrea Gallerani and was situated in the road known as the Via della Sapiema."[538] In 1240, the pious Sienese nobleman Andrea Gallerani also established the Confraternity of *Miseracordia* Brothers and "laid upon the Brothers the twofold task of nursing the sick and burying the dead."[539] It was reported that "those who visited Siena at the time observed the 'black-hooded Brothers, who with a Crucifix and lighted torches, came at eventide to fetch the dead and carry them through the darkening streets to the *Miseracordia* cemetery outside Porta Tufi.'"[540]

Catherine cared for the sick at the *Casa della Miseracordia* as she had become a friend and mentor to the Rector Matteo di Cenni dei Fazio and was, in fact, called to the hospital when Matteo himself became a patient at the *Casa* while experiencing symptoms of the bubonic plague. There was significant spiritual support for the patients at the *Casa della Miseracordia* for we are told that Blessed Raymond of Capua, "in his zeal for souls which was the spirit of his Dominican Order, went very often to visit and minister to the sick at the *Casa della Miseracordia*."[541] Both Raymond and Catherine were "in the habit of calling at the *Miseracordia* every day to confer with Rector Matteo upon matters connected with the relief of the poor."[542]

During the plague epidemic, Catherine was called upon to minister to a Hermit named Fra Santi who was suffering from possible symptoms of the disease. When the saint recognized the seriousness of Fra Santi's condition, she "caused him to be taken out of his cell and brought to the *Miseracordia* where she came to him, with some of her Sisters, and nursed him, providing all such things as she thought necessary."[543] Fra Santi was comforted by the ministry of Catherine who not only cared for his body but looked especially to the "health of his soul."[544]

San Lazzaro

San Lazzaro was the "leper hospital" outside *Porta Romana*, which Catherine courageously used to visit; we are told that she walked, twice each day, the half-hour trek from her home to the leper house.[545] While, as with *Casa della Miseracordia*, we do not have specific details about the care at *San Lazzaro*, there are a number of descriptions of leper hospitals in the literature on healthcare in the medieval period. Nurse historians Gladys Sellew and Joseph Nuesse pointed out that, during the later Middle Ages, "while many Lazer Houses were built for lepers, limited medical knowledge made these houses chiefly custodial in character."[546] Despite the supervisory nature of the care in leper hospitals, James Walsh asserted that leper refuges were not all "as a rule, the ugly, forbidding-looking institutions we are likely to think... (some) were rather pretty enclosures... with a cultivated garden and... a chapel."[547] Walsh suggests further that those who served in the leper hospitals "saw that the lepers were properly cared for and that the institutions were carried on in such a way as to secure isolation, and yet at the same time, make the condition of the lepers as satisfactory as possible."[548]

Walsh does admit, however, that while "the lepers themselves were not absolutely confined within their hospitals (and) were allowed to go out on the highways, (this was only) provided they kept to the windward side of people who were passing, and on condition that, by means of a clapper or a bell, they warned the passerby of their presence, so as to avoid all personal contact."[549]

It was the "avoidance of personal contact" that was particularly traumatic for the victim of leprosy, especially for those whose disease progression forced them to be confined to the hospital. As several anecdotes from the period reveal, it was those patients whom Catherine cared for on her visits to San Lazarro. A case example of the saint's ministry to a San Lazarro patient with advanced leprosy is presented in Chapter Six.

As with other hospitals in the Middle Ages, the inclusion of spiritual care for the patients in leper hospitals was paramount. Religious caregivers reminded the leprosy patients that, although their physical diagnosis and prognosis were devastating, they were very close to God in their suffering. It was suggested that the text from scripture "Whom the Lord loves, He chastises" was for them "literally true."[550] Visitors to the leper houses asked the patients to be remembered in their prayers; it was felt that "these people who had to suffer so much and with little hope of ever being cured, though they were never entirely without hope, must be very close to heaven and their prayers must have special import."[551] "As a result of this," Walsh reported, "the lepers themselves often came to feel that they were intermediaries between heaven and earth and they offered up their sufferings for the benefit of mankind and particularly for those who had been kind to them, or who, for some special reason, had asked for their intercession."[552] In the end, Walsh asserted, "this gave (the lepers) a definite mission in life and made them feel that their sufferings were not in vain."[553]

This chapter, which has focused on the spiritual ministry of healthcare in the Middle Ages, describes the medical milieu which Catherine of Siena entered when she responded to Christ's call to minister to the sick. The limited diagnostic procedures, antiquated physician education and minimal hospital therapeutics of the era provided significant challenges for the young Mantellata nurse. Catherine, however, was not dismayed, for her call to serve the sick came from her Beloved Spouse to whom her heart belonged. Saint Catherine "made herself the nurse... of the abandoned poor."[554] The saint saw in the sick the image of God: "To all appearances one takes care of a leper, administers to a cancerous patient, in reality he is rendering honor to God. And it is always back to God that Catherine brings events and discussions, so that every day is a fabric or prayer."[555] In the following chapter examples of Catherine's tender and compassionate nursing care, carried out in the home, in the hospital, in the community and in the prisons, are described. As these anecdotes reveal, Catherine is an awe-inspiring role model for all who minister to the ill and the infirm.

Chapter 6. "Hands Made to Serve"
The Lady with the Lantern

*"Your hands were made to serve your neighbors when you see them
sick... your feet were given to you to serve by carrying your body to
places that are holy and useful to you and your neighbors for the
glory and praise of my Name"*
Catherine of Siena: Dialogue 144

A Servant's Hands
Hands which touched with tenderness
those who suffered illness or
injury.

Hands which touched with gentleness
those who were broken in body
or in spirit.

Hands which touched with compassion
those who were lonely or
afraid.

Hands blessed with Christ's own love
and mercy were those of His
servant Catherine.

Since the late 19th Century, Florence Nightingale, the founder of
professional nursing, has been known affectionately as "The Lady with
the Lamp." This honorific was derived from Miss Nightingale's dedicated
ministry to the English soldiers during the terrible siege of the Crimean
War. The title was adopted by her nursing colleagues and students
following publication of a letter written by a young soldier who had
experienced Florence's care. The soldier explained that at night, as Miss
Nightingale passed the long rows of wounded men carrying her small
lamp, grateful soldiers would kiss her shadow as she passed.[556] The
memory has also been preserved by one of the world's greatest poets,
Henry Wadsworth Longfellow, in the work "Santa Filomena" which

reads: "Lo, in that house of misery, a lady with a lamp I see, pass through the glittering gloom... and slow as in a dream of bliss, the speechless sufferer turns to kiss, her shadow as it falls, upon the darkening walls."[557]

While we have no letter or poem describing Saint Catherine as the "Lady with the Lantern," we do have numerous reports of her traveling the darkened streets of Siena on her way to night ministry at the great hospital of *Santa Maria della Scala*, carrying a small lantern. Catherine also traversed Siena at night during the second horrendous plague outbreak, armed only with lantern and scent bottle, as she sought to assist those who had collapsed in the streets. One finds many references to Catherine's lantern in nursing history; Dr. M. Patricia Donohue observed that Catherine is "frequently pictured carrying a lighted lamp, which she carried on her nightly visits to La Scala hospital," and added that "Her lamp was as famous as the Nightingale lamp of later years."[558]

In discussing Catherine's care for plague victims, historians Josephine Dolan, Louise Fitzpatrick and Eleanor Herrmann reported that throughout the epidemic, the saint "could be seen going about the streets of Siena at night. With a lighted lantern she would look for forsaken victims so that she might comfort them."[559] Adelaide Nutting and Lavinia Dock described a memorial to Catherine which identified "the little lamp which she carried on her nightly visits to the hospital, La Scala."[560]

As well as the nurse historians, biographer Augusta Drane supported the accounts of Catherine's lantern in reporting that "among the relics of *Fullonica* (the workshop in a dyer's home) is the *lanthorn* (British Lantern) she carried with her when called forth on some errand of charity during the night."[561] And Dominican Sister Suzanne Noffe revealed that in the saint's "cell" in her former home on the Vicolo del Triatoio Catherine's small lantern is displayed in a glass case.[562] Catherine's nighttime beacon is also mentioned in the writings of historians Victor Robinson[563] and Isabel Stewart and Anne Austin[564], as well as in works of biographers Alice Curtayne[565], Sr. Jean David Finley[566], Johannes Jorgensen[567], and Sigrid Undset.[568]

In Siena, at the time, "curfew rang out at nine in the winter and ten in the summer, ordering the city gates to be closed for the night and all citizens to retire to their houses. Anyone who went out after that bell had ceased was compelled by law to carry a light, because the narrow winding streets were not illuminated, save for a rare lamp burning before some shrine."[569] When Catherine served at *Santa Maria della*

Scala during the night she was not able to return home until daylight; Sister Catherine Meade explained: "Today a chapel beneath the hospital, the Cappella della Notte, commemorates the nights that Catherine was able to take a brief rest from her nursing duties 'when the curfew required her to remain out of the street until the morning bell.'"[570] The lower floor of the hospital provided space for the religious meetings and services of a lay confraternity.[571] It was here that Catherine was assigned a room when she would "work at the hospital beyond the ringing of the evening curfew."[572]

Catherine's small room at *La Scala* is described as being:

> Deep down in the wilderness of rooms, stairs, passages, cellars and crypts of the vast building, not far from the caves when San Sano had said Mass for the first Christians. Here she had her place of rest; visitors are still shown a little narrow room containing a recumbent statue of her. A sanctuary lamp burns before the statue, silver hearts gleam faintly in the niche above the image of the sleeping saint.[573]

Ultimately, through her nursing of the disadvantaged ill and infirm both in their homes and in the hospitals, Catherine became, Sister Mary Jean Dorcy asserted, "the 'lady with lamp' who would guide thousands of Dominican Sisters to the bedsides of Christ's poor."[574] Saint Catherine was "a teaching Sister, giving to others the fruits of her contemplation," enduring the sometimes less than grateful responses of her patients "with a prayer and a quiet smile."[575]

Together with her lantern, Saint Catherine is reported to have carried a small "scent bottle" on her visits to the sick in their homes and in the hospitals. In ministering to seriously ill patients Catherine would bring the scent bottle to the bedside to introduce "some refreshment into their hospital room."[576] The saint carried the bottle with her to the streets of Siena as well, especially during the 1374 outbreak of the *Bubonic plague.* One biographer pointed out that Catherine "did not shrink from a few bad smells" for she "walked untiringly from hospital to hospital and up the dirty stairs of the houses of the poor" armed only with her lantern and scent bottle.[577] The scent's aroma was "supposed to be a protection against infection from the pestilential air."[578] It also provided "alleviation to sufferers in that fetid atmosphere."[579] Catherine "toiled with the sick unremittingly" and also rallied those who helped her to not be fearful of bending "closer to the lived, swollen faces (of plague victims) choking down the nausea of that pestilential odor."[580]

Medieval scent bottles contained aromas of fruit, spices or herbs such as lemon or orange water, rosewater, rosemary, lavender, basil and sandalwood. Some medical practitioners believed that as well as comforting a patient with a pleasant odor, the scents had a therapeutic effect in actually clearing the air of foul smelling organisms. Adelaide Nutting and Lavinia Dock, in an historical discussion on the medieval use of scents such as lavender and rosewater, pointed out that in healthcare facilities of the Middle Ages "the causes of bad air were only too plainly shown in the absence of ventilation and in a primitive system of dealing with utensils."[581] In a small book on the history of "scent bottles," Alexandra Walker explained that scents or perfumes had, in the past, been "put to medicinal uses."[582] Walker reported that "Hippocrates wrote of the use of aromatic fumigation in preventing contagion, and later Arab doctors used perfumed substances to treat patients and also to scent their own garments... substances with strong scents were believed to be protective against contagious diseases."[583]

Saint Catherine was significantly ahead of her time in the use of "scents" for therapeutic purposes. In the past few years, the practice of "aromatherapy" has become an accepted remedy by a variety of physicians and nurse practitioners as revealed by the number of scholarly articles on the topic. The incorporation of scents, or "aromatherapy," as an intervention modality in contemporary healthcare is defined as "the therapeutic use of essential oil that is derived from plants, flowers, leaves, barks, seeds, roots, resins, stems, and fruits, and extracted commonly by a process of distillation with the intent to calm, balance, and rejuvenate mind, body and spirit."[584]

Some 21st-century medical practitioners even consider aromatherapy to be useful for the prevention and treatment of specific diseases and/or illness conditions. The use of "healing scents" is advised for the relief of emotional distress[585], for the reduction of anxiety[586], and to treat the overall anxiety/depression syndrome.[587] Experimental research on the use of Lavender aromatherapy with patients in an intermediate care unit resulted in lowered blood pressures and improved perceived quality of sleep among study participants.[588]

A review of data elicited in research exploring the use of aromatherapy to reduce nausea and vomiting suggested that "the inhaled vapor of peppermint or ginger essential oils not only decreased the incidence and severity of symptoms but also lessened antiemetic requirements and consequently improved patient satisfaction."[589] Several scholarly articles explored both the physiological and psychological effects of aromatherapy.[590] Researcher Sala Horowitz concluded that the study findings to date indicate that "the age-old practice of aromatherapy using essential oils is an effective alternative or adjunct to pharmacologic therapies for promoting general well-being and for treating many health problems."[591] And, a contemporary textbook on critical care nursing suggested the use of aromatherapy for seriously ill patients noting that "some scents have been associated with specific beneficial effects. For example, lavender oil and other floral scents are said to be relaxing, citrus oils to be positive mood enhancers, and peppermint oils to be promoters of mental stimulation."[592]

Saint Catherine's use of the medieval scent bottle may have had therapeutic effects far beyond those known or understood in the era of medieval medicine.

Catherine's Ministry of Holistic Healthcare: Body, Mind and Spirit

As with the use of the medieval "scent bottle," Catherine was blessed with foresight in her attention to the body, mind and spirit connection in caring for the sick. Saint Catherine was fully aware of the needs of the body for medical care when physical ailments or injuries presented themselves; she attended to these either herself, through referral to the care of a physician or by recommending hospitalization. Catherine also spent many hours listening to and counseling anxious patients in order to comfort their minds; this is reflected in the anecdotes included in the following pages, as well as in her many letters of support and consolation to fearful or depressed acquaintances and friends. And, most importantly, a sick or injured person's spiritual needs remained always foremost in Catherine's mind and her ministry; she prayed with and for patients and advised them to pray for themselves and to receive the sacraments of the Church whenever possible. She also encouraged the sick to confess their faults, placing hope and trust in God's loving forgiveness. Such spiritual guidance brought solace and peace especially to critically ill or dying patients.

Modern medicine's interest in holistic healthcare is relatively recent, having been initiated around the mid to later 20th Century. Early on, medical and nursing practitioners were primarily concerned with a patient's physical health; slowly the importance of the mind-body connection led the healthcare field to take the psychological and emotional state of an individual into consideration when diagnosing and treating. Healthcare professionals were, however, decidedly more reluctant to attempt to incorporate the spiritual concerns of their patients into therapeutic protocols. The spiritual and religious needs of an individual were believed to fall within the pastoral care purview of the Chaplain, be he priest, rabbi, minister or other spiritual practitioner. Nurses were:

> Allowed to pray for their patients; they were expected to assist at religious rituals such as the distribution of Holy Communion or anointing of the sick in a hospital setting. The nurse was not, however, to infringe on the territory of the pastoral care provider or on the patient's privacy; nursing's responsibility in regard to patients' spiritual needs was primarily considered to be a response to requests for spiritual care, which would then be referred to an appropriate pastoral caregiver.[593]

With the advent of the holistic healthcare movement, however, the spiritual and religious needs of those who were ill began to be considered by the healthcare team when diagnosing and planning treatment. The current support of the holistic healthcare movement is reflected in the publication of at least three U.S. journals devoted to the topic: *The Journal of Holistic Health Care,* the *Journal of Holistic Nursing* and *Holistic Nursing Practice.* An editorial in the *Journal of Holistic Nursing* cited a definition of holistic nursing from the American Holistic Nursing Association as follows: "holism involves studying and understanding the interrelationships of the bio-psycho-social-spiritual dimensions of the person, recognizing that the whole is greater than the sum of its parts."[594] A professional support for the inclusion of spiritual care within holistic healthcare was initiated with the mandate for assessment of patients' spiritual needs by JCAHO (The Joint Commission for Accreditation of Health Care Organizations) as promulgated in its "standards for spiritual assessment and spiritual care for those who are hospitalized."[595]

Nurturance has also been identified as a key concept related to holistic healthcare[596], as were spiritual care[597] and prayer.[598]

Contemporary holistic nursing is described as "a legitimate specialty practice and its ever increasing influence in the health/well-being of people and the healthcare system is dependent upon nurses who demonstrate courage and commitment."[599] It is evident from the above characteristics of holism, including nurturance, assessment of spiritual needs, spiritual care, prayer, courage and commitment, that Catherine of Siena was, in all of her ministries to the ill and the infirm, a dedicated practitioner of holistic healthcare.

A truly impressive dimension of Saint Catherine's embrace of holism was that she practiced it within so many of what we would today call "specialty areas" of nursing and healthcare. Catherine was a hospital nurse, as witnessed by the many nights she spent at *Santa Maria della Scala* caring for the sick during the long hours when other staff were sleeping. Catherine also spent daytime hours not only at *La Scala* but also ministering to the sick at *Casa della Miseracordia* and at the leper hospital *San Lazzaro*. The Mantellata Sister was a home health nurse as well; this dimension of her caregiving is described in the many accounts of her visits to the sick in their dwellings when called upon to relieve suffering. And, Catherine was a community /public health nurse when walking about Siena, especially during the plague epidemic, seeking out those who had fallen ill in the street with no one to help them.

Catherine practiced psych/mental health nursing as identified in her letters to those who were anxious or depressed over such concerns as age-related illness or loss of a loved one; and the saint became well known for her prison ministry, particularly to those who had been condemned to die. Finally, Catherine carried out spiritual assessment and provided spiritual care whenever appropriate in her ministry to the ill and the infirm. In terms of the latter ministry, Saint Catherine was, again, "light years" ahead of the practice of nursing the sick which only recently incorporated the concepts of assessment of patients' spiritual and religious needs and provision of spiritual care as "components" of the nurse's role.

Ministry of Hospital Care

Perhaps the most neglected dimension in published accounts of Saint Catherine's healthcare activities is that of her ministry to the sick in the hospital. Early Catherinian biographers tended to focus more on the saint's spiritual interventions among the ailing. Victor Robinson, in a history of nursing text, suggested in a somewhat pithy comment, that within the medieval art world the Italian masters "preferred to portray Catherine in a divine swoon rather than in the mundane act of rolling a bandage."[600] We read frequently of the saint's selfless care for plague victims in the community, of her visits to the ill and infirm in their homes, of her spiritual care of those incarcerated in the prisons and of her concern for citizens involved or injured in local feuds. However, as the following anecdotes reveal, the Mantellata Sister also spent many hours, both during the day and night, ministering to the sick in the hospital.

In Saint Catherine's era, "all the Dominican tertiaries who could helped voluntarily in the Sienese hospitals in fulfillment of their rule which bade them visit the sick."[601] Catherine, when emerging from her time of solitude to follow the Lord's call to serve her neighbor, "now did likewise" and "became familiar with all the charitable institutions of the city."[602] At *La Scala*, it is reported "there were periods when Catherine almost lived in the building."[603] Although not easily achieved, the saint had earlier won a hard fought victory over the need for sleep and was able to serve the sick throughout the night.

One biographer wrote that, when Catherine spent the night at the *La Scala* Hospital, "she would take over the watch in the small hours, the cold and comfortless hours before dawn, when the patient's life is at its lowest ebb and the nurses are worn out and without courage."[604] Catherine "gladly took on herself the charge of hopeless cases and the most difficult and ungrateful patients," and it was also reported that "the good Sisters of La Scala were more than willing to let her take them over as soon as they learned of her indefatigable patience and her unquenchable good humor and serenity."[605]

Fra Tommaso Caffarini wrote in his "*Supplemento*" to Fra Raymond's *Legenda* of the saint's "habit of attending the sick in the hospitals and specifically notes the fact of her serving them at night, which explains why she may have required the use of a little room in which to rest."[606] As Fra Caffarini observed of Catherine:

> Whenever there was a question of serving God or performing any works of charity, she readily quitted her cell to employ herself for the good of her neighbors, as our Lord commanded her after her three years of retirement. She was not afraid of serving the sick in the hospitals, even at the most fatiguing hours of the night; nor did she

shrink from those miserable creatures who were suffering from the most repulsive maladies.[607]

During the vicious 1374 outbreak of the "Black Death" in Siena, it was reported that "for more than a year" Catherine "rarely went home but spent her nights and days in the *La Scala* wards tending to the afflicted."[608] Nurse historian Patricia Donahue commented: "Although there was little that could be done for the victims of the plague, she (Catherine) exhibited her willingness to comfort them. She recruited many young men as stretcher bearers to transport the stricken from all over the city to wards of the hospital, which she supervised."[609]

It is striking to read repeatedly of Saint Catherine's commitment to caring for the hospitalized sick during the night. The night shift is often a time of trauma and stress in a hospital; it covers the staffing period when attending physicians, supervising nurses and other key medical team members are absent, attempting to refresh body and spirit for the next day's activities. This is, nevertheless, the time when some of the most challenging medical emergencies arise. Patients who are critically ill may come to a crisis point in their illness trajectory, either physically or emotionally, during the darkest hours of the night. To our knowledge, Catherine had no formal training in caring for the sick yet she took on the night nursing role as a young Mantellata Sister, courageously serving the anguished patients of the medieval hospital. The saint embraced this nursing ministry with tenderness, with compassion and with a deep love of neighbor which she had been taught by Christ, her Beloved Spouse.

In considering Saint Catherine's ministry in the 14th-century hospital setting, one cannot help but stand in awe of her competence and her willingness to care for the desperately ill patients admitted to such facilities as *Santa Maria della Scala.* For the 21st-century healthcare practitioner sources of support abound in the educational field. As well as myriad books and audio-visual materials explaining such topics as anatomy and physiology, pathophysiology, pharmacology and characteristics of the various medical and nursing specialty areas, newer works are continually emerging on such topics as "informatics,"[610] the use of "electronic health records,"[611] and the spiritual needs of the ill and infirm.[612] Catherine had not even rudimentary medical or nursing education materials to guide and support her caregiving, nor had she the kind of pastoral training that today's hospital chaplains and other spiritual care staff receive.

. In one of my earlier books on servant leadership in nursing, I suggested that the:

> Contemporary health care venue most in need of servant leadership is the modern American hospital. With its complex technology, incredible array of medical and social services, high powered administrative structure and demanding financial constraints, the modern hospital may seem, at times, like a vast and confusing wilderness to both patients and caregiving staff. Being able to negotiate a steady course through this often bewildering system can be greatly and gently facilitated by the presence of a cadre of servant leaders within the institution.[613]

Catherine of Siena was indeed such a servant leader, as pointed out in the previous chapter. We can only imagine how blessed her presence was to the hospital of the middle ages which, while lacking current technological sophistication, yet may also have seemed like a "vast and confusing wilderness" to both patients and caregivers of the era.

Saint Catherine's hospital ministry at the Sienese hospitals, especially those of *Santa Maria della Scala (La Scala), Casa della Miseracordia* and *San Lazzaro,* can best be understood through the description of case examples documented in the words of two of her closest companions, Fra Raimondo (Blessed Raymond) of Capua and Fra Tommaso d'Antonio Caffarini.

Santa Maria della Scala (La Scala)

Fr. Tommaso Caffarini asserted that Catherine did not shrink from caring for the most difficult hospital patients, and the nursing Brothers and Sisters were more than willing to let her take over the care of some of the most obstreperous individuals. Fra Caffarini related one such instance in his *"Supplementum"* to Blessed Raymond's *Legenda.* In Fra Tommaso's account Saint Catherine:

> once bestowed her whole care on an unhappy woman who for years had lived an abandoned life (as a prostitute), and who now lay dying on a wretched bed, where she complained that she could find no one to assist her, or give her the kind of food she liked. Catherine resolved to take care first of the body and then of the soul of this poor creature. She prepared her the necessary food, and waited on her day and night,

while at the same time she encouraged her to repent and have confidence in God's mercy.[614]

In commenting on this case of a "woman of the streets," Johannes Jorgensen pointed out that, "When spending the night at the hospital, Catherine did so in order to be at hand in case of need. She often took the dog-watch" during the stressful hours of the night and "had a predilection for the most trying patients, most of all for those whose characters were difficult."[615] Jorgensen expanded on Fra Tommaso Caffarini's description of the patient:

> For instance, there was a woman who for many years had led a gay and lawless life, and who now was an inmate of the hospital (*La Scala*). Of course nothing there was good enough for her; she would rage and complain by turns, weep out of pity for herself and her lot, or in a temper throw the food at the nurses' heads. It was not advisable to mention religion to her, she foamed with the infidelity of a sensual woman and with personal hatred of Jesus Christ. Catherine approached this soul, sunk in the depths of its nature. She began by cooking for this woman of the streets and succeeded in pleasing her. Then she tried slowly and cautiously to turn her mind. We do not know what the bride of Christ may have said to her unhappy sister in Eve in the hospital of Siena, but there is a letter, dating from a little later in Catherine's life, written to 'a public sinner in Perugia' and the tone in it would no doubt be the same.[616]

The letter to which Jorgensen referred is identified as Letter T 276 and entitled "To a Prostitute in Perugia, Written at the Request of One of the Woman's Brothers." Catherine begins the letter by expressing her deep sympathy and care for the woman with the words: "My daughter, I weep with sorrow that you who are created in God's image and likeness and redeemed by his precious blood have no concern for your dignity or for the great price that was paid for you."[617] The letter continues with the saint's concern regarding the woman's lifestyle and advice to change: "Leave, oh leave this dangerous servitude into which you have been led."[618] As the message proceeds Catherine begs the prostitute to seek recourse to Our Lady, "Mother of mercy and compassion who will lead you into Christ's presence."[619] She also identifies the woman with St. Mary Magdalene "reminding her of the sinner of Magdala, of the ointment poured over the feet of Jesus in house of the Pharisee, and of the blood of Jesus which was shed in return upon her when she knelt the next time at His feet, at Calvary."[620] Catherine advised: "Hide thyself, then in the wounds of the Son of God, plunge deep down in the fire of love which consumes all thy misery and all thy sin… be no longer a limb on the body of the devil… but love the Crucified… remain in the love of God."[621] "In her words," Johannes Jorgensen commented, "Catherine could make the darkest soul listen and hardest heart tremble with weeping."[622]

Saint Catherine concluded her counsel with the gentle advice: "Keep living in God's holy and tender love."[623] How consoling these compassionate words must have been for the letter's recipient, and for the patient at *La Scala* who we trust may have received a similar message from the saint's own lips.

In commenting on Catherine's treatment of the same *Santa Maria della Scala* patient, Catherinian biographer Arrigo Levasti also shared his perception of the spirituality of the saint's service. He began with the thought that in her nursing ministry Catherine "began to care assiduously for those in direct need, *les grands malheureux*."[624] Levasti went on to explain:

> She visited, fed and consoled a prostitute whom everyone else avoided, fearing to soil themselves by approaching her. No one would even toss her a piece of bread. Catherine saw the wretched woman's forsaken condition, understood the despair in her soul, and forced herself to care for her, and to kindle in her heart a fire of love very different from that which, mingled with pain and humiliation, she had known all her life.[625]

Levasti suggested that Catherine saw in this woman the ability to achieve a deep love of God and thus the "maiden of Fontebranda… spared no pains, perhaps to the scandal of some, in nursing and helping this abandoned prostitute. She was sure that she would find in her a light, dimmed but not quenched by sin, that the careless, scornful passers-by never suspected in the sick, famished outcast."[626]

In Catherine's tender care of the patient described above, if we accept Johannes Jorgensen's suggestion that she was most probably counseled with the same compassion and gentleness as reflected in the Virgin's "Letter to a Prostitute," the Mantellata nurse restored not only the woman's trust in the love of God but her dignity as well. In a letter to *America* magazine, an oncology nurse described the pain of one her patients who bemoaned the loss of dignity experienced as a recipient of chemotherapy treatment. The nurse explained that in such painful situations, "a patient's dignity is not lost; it is just entrusted to someone who cares."[627] In this case, it would indeed seem that the dignity of the suffering "woman of the streets" was, when she met Saint Catherine, truly "entrusted to someone who cared."

Casa della Miseracordia

As an example of St. Catherine's healthcare ministry carried out in the more modest Siena hospital, the *Casa della Miseracordia,* one need only consider the case of the Hermit Santi, a well-respected and holy solitary who had lived a life of poverty and prayer in the city of Siena for 30 years. Fra Santi was believed by those who knew him to be a saint; he only ventured forth from his hermitage after meeting Catherine. Augusta Drane commented that, for Catherine's sake, "he gave up the quiet of his cell and the manner of life he had been so long used to in order to labor for others; he constantly affirmed that he found more peace and profit to his soul in following and listening to her than he had ever found in solitude."[628] Fra Santi suffered from heart disease, but Saint Catherine "taught him to bear his continual sufferings not only with resignation, but even with joy."[629]

One day Fra Santi fell ill with the plague, which had been devastating so many of his neighbors. When Catherine learned of the illness, she immediately requested that Santi be moved from his hermitage to the *Casa della Miseracordia* hospital to be treated by the physicians. Catherine then went to the hospital to see him herself; she was accompanied by several of her Mantellata Sisters and they "nursed" Fra Santi, "providing for him all such things as they as they thought necessary."[630] Going to his bedside, Blessed Raymond tells us, "Catherine whispered softly into his ear, 'Have no fear; however ill you may be you won't die at this time.'"[631] Santi's friends were certain that he was about to die; they "felt united to Santi in his sufferings because of the friendship that bound (them) to him."[632]

Catherine returned to the hermit's bedside and again assured him "Don't be afraid, because you won't die." Although Fra Santi seemed to his friends "to have lost the use of his senses," he heard Catherine "perfectly and had more faith in what she said that in the death he felt to be so near. And, in fact, the virgin's words triumphed over nature, and the power of God, more certain than anything human and far beyond our human imagining, brought his well-nigh dead body back to life."[633] While his friends were waiting for Santi to breathe his last breath and were planning the funeral "the time at which people generally die of the plague came and went."[634]

Catherine returned a third time and whispered to the very sick hermit: "I command you, in the name of Our Lord Jesus Christ, not to die," and "It was no sooner said than done. The dying man revived, his strength returned, he sat up in bed and asked for something to eat; and in a short time he was completely recovered and lived for many years."[635]

After his recovery Fra Santi told his friends that, when Saint Catherine whispered her comforting words in his ear, "he had felt the strength of her power holding back his spirit when it was about to issue from his body. He told everyone that it was no natural power that had cured him but the Divine Power alone, and added that he regarded the miracle as a real, genuine resuscitation."[636] Santi asserted that "he was still alive only because Catherine had commanded him, in Jesus' name, to live."[637] Blessed Raymond pointed out that the "sanctity" of the hermit's life and his "natural prudence guaranteed that he was to be believed in everything he said."[638]

San Lazzaro

A significant example of Saint Catherine's ministry at the leper house of *San Lazzaro* is that carried out with the "poor, sick woman called Tecca who was obliged to go into hospital because she was too poor to get proper treatment for her illness at home."[639] Blessed Raymond of Capua explained that Tecca was:

> So short of money that she hardly had the bare necessities. The complaint she was suffering from was leprosy, and it increased to such an extent that it spread over her whole body. This made her more and more miserable, because everyone was so afraid of catching the infection that they would not go near her; they were more inclined to send her right away from the city, as was usually done with people suffering from the disease.[640]

As soon as Catherine heard of Tecca's plight she:

Immediately hurried to the hospital, full of burning charity, saw the poor woman, embraced her and offered to help her and look after her for as long as she liked. And she suited the action to the word, for every day morning and evening, she would go to see her all by herself, preparing the things she needed to keep her alive, feeding her, looking after her with care and diligence, looking upon this leper woman, in fact, as her Heavenly Bridegroom.[641]

We are reminded by biographer Augusta Drane that if some stories of Catherine's "service of the sick," such as this account of her ministry to Tecca:

Seem to pass the limit of what is possible to flesh and blood, let it never be forgotten that Catherine, who was possessed of that magnificent gift, the perfection of faith, beheld in each poor sufferer to whom she ministered nothing less than the person of her Lord. She sought... and found Him in the hospitals of the lepers, and wherever sickness had assumed its most terrible and repulsive forms.[642]

Tecca accepted Catherine's continued offer of daily care and from their first meeting, the saint came to visit her "morning and evening, dressing her wounds and doing all that was requisite for her with as much care and reverence as if she had been her own mother."[643] Catherine carried out her nursing ministry to the leper woman with her usual courage and compassion for, as Jorgensen commented, "That which had been the great conquest of self for the delicate, poetical mind of Francis of Assisi, and the victory leading to a new life in him, was an ordinary matter of course for the brave young girl of Fontebranda" who saw only her Divine Bridegroom in the leper.[644]

As, unfortunately sometimes happens however, the sick woman eventually began to resent Catherine's tender care and "became arrogantly demanding. Seeing the virgin continually engaged in serving her, (Tecca) began to demand, almost as by right, what was done for her out of generous charity, and would reprimand her helper with wicked words, heaping further abuse on her when she failed to bring her what she wanted."[645] Tecca would criticize Catherine, when she arrived to nurse her, for spending too much time in church instead of with her patient; she tried to arouse an angry response. Saint Catherine, however, reacted with kindness and calm assuring Tecca: "'I shall soon get on with what you want me to do for you.' And she would quickly get the fire going, put the cooking pot on it, get her food and all the other things ready, and wait upon her with such extraordinary care and diligence that even the bad-tempered patient marveled at it."[646] With infinite patience Catherine "went to and fro in the narrow, stuffy and ill-smelling sickroom, and prepared a bath, under a continual shower of mockeries" from the obstreperous woman.[647]

Catherine's mother, Mona Lapa, complained bitterly about her daughter's care of the leper woman and continually expressed fear that Catherine might become a leper because of the contagion.[648] Saint Catherine could not cease her care of Tecca, however, because she accepted this ministry as a gift from her Spouse and Savior, the Lord Jesus. As she affirmed to Mona Lapa: "Have no fear, dear mother, what I do for this poor woman, I do for God and he will not let me suffer for it."[649] Although for a period of time the virgin appeared to have some signs of leprosy on her hands she had no fear and never considered discontinuing her ministry to Tecca.

Blessed Raymond recounted that it was not too long "before the sick woman's life approached its end, and finally, in the presence of the holy virgin, who effectively consoled her, she died."[650] "Then," Raymond concluded, "despite the horrible appearance of the body, Catherine carefully washed it, clothed it, laid it decently in the coffin, and finally, the funeral rites having been performed, buried it with her own hands."[651]

Ministry of Home Healthcare

As well as caring for patients in the three hospitals of Siena, Saint Catherine ministered to many ailing citizens in their homes. As her reputation for healing, as well as that of her holiness, spread throughout the city, Catherine was frequently called upon to practice what today we would call "home health care." Contemporary home healthcare is defined as "The delivery of health services in the home setting for the purposes of restoring or maintaining the health of individuals and families. The purpose of home healthcare is to provide support, treatment and information that caregivers and patients need to successfully manage their healthcare needs at home."[652] Another definition of home healthcare adds the dimension of "minimizing the effects of illness and disability" for both the patient and family.[653] The home healthcare activities of support, treatment and counseling were all carried out in the 14th Century by Saint Catherine as numerous anecdotes attest.

Within the early Christian community there was a long and edifying history of home healthcare, from the Deacons of the early Church who visited ill members in their dwellings up to the Middle Ages; this was Catherine's inheritance. One of the first groups of women to care for the sick in their residences after Saint Catherine's era were the Daughters of Charity of Saint Vincent de Paul. Vincent once told his Sisters: "You are not religious in the strict sense, and can never be because of your service to the poor… you have no grating to set you off from the dangers of the world; you must erect one in your own inner self, which will be far better.[654] Vincent's teaching was echoed in a now famous quote from the Daughters of Charity's rule of life: "Your convent will be the house of the sick; your cell a hired room; your chapel, the parish church; your cloister, the streets of the city, or the wards of the hospital."[655]

Saint Catherine's practice of home healthcare was, in fact, a precursor to the spiritual ministry identified several centuries later by Saint Vincent de Paul. Catherine was not a cloistered religious, her convents were indeed the houses of the sick, the wards of the hospitals, and the streets of the city, and as Saint Vincent advised, she also taught the value of maintaining a "cell" within the "inner self" where one could dwell in solitude with the Lord.

Four case examples from the writings of Blessed Raymond of Capua and Fra Tommaso Caffarini exemplify the home healthcare ministry of Catherine of Siena. One of the first instances of Catherine's care of the sick in the home occurred, in fact, in her own household, when one of the Benincasa servants became ill. In discussing the beginning of Catherine's public life, Blessed Raymond recounted that once the young saint became convinced that it was God's will that she quit her solitary cell and serve the neighbor, the ministry was initiated in her own home: "She began to apply herself with the utmost humility to the lowest kinds of housework (such as) sweeping, kitchen work."[656]

It was during this period of household service that Catherine's concern for the ailing was revealed. While Raymond did not provide much detail about the Benincasa servant's illness, he commented that Catherine was "busiest when one of the servants fell ill"; he reported that "she redoubled her labors, looking after the invalid and doing the housework in her stead."[657] As biographer Claire Antony noted, Catherine did housework while the rest of the family slept and "when

Lapa's servant fell ill, Catherine not only supplied her place, but waited upon the sick woman, and nursed her tenderly."[658]

The fact that Catherine cared for the family servant during a time of illness and also assumed her household chores, suggests that the Mantellata Sister was concerned not only for the physical health of the Benincasa maidservant but also sought to promote her mental and spiritual well-being; the servant, trusting that her household responsibilities were being attended to, could rest in the knowledge that she would not lose her employment. That information must have been a great comfort to the young woman attempting to recover from an illness. Catherine's behavior again reveals the importance she placed on holistic care for the sick.

In another example, Fra Tommaso Caffarini described Catherine's home care of a woman who suffered from periodic blood loss; Caffarini recounted that:

> A woman of Siena, of the Order of Penance of St. Dominic, Called Francesca di Marco, who was suffering from frequent loss of blood and harbored toward Catherine an affection full of confidence and faith, told Catherine of her trouble. The Virgin looked at her and said: 'I do not want you to feel more oppressed by this evil illness. I order the disease not to harass you any longer'. So it happened, and when the natural illness would come back, Francesca could find a spiritual joy that could not be explained. The Virgin, with similar commands, healed many people of different gender and conditions.[659]

Catherine showed compassion toward this suffering women, who had placed her trust in the saint. She did not simply suggest that Francesca put up with the condition of blood loss but commented that she did not want her to be "oppressed" by the illness and restrained the bleeding with her words. From a comment in Fra Tomasso's account, we understand that some "natural illness" did return for Catherine's patient, but now, after experiencing the saint's caring response, Francesca was able to embrace the condition with a spiritual "joy that could not be explained."

A third example of Catherine's home care is that which occurred when her sister-in law, close to giving birth, was "in the throes" of great pain. An anecdote explains that the laboring mother very much wanted Catherine to be present, and according to tradition, wished her to assist

144

her at the birth. Fra Tommaso Caffarini reported that "The Virgin was present in her body but her mind was in heaven, where she always lived, in order to implore mercy for the suffering woman... she seemed to be in the presence of God and the Lord granted what she asked of him. Almost without pain, the sister-in-law gave birth to a male child who grew up to become a religious and died a holy death."[660]

In this case example described by Fra Tommaso, we understand Catherine as present physically to provide support and comfort for her laboring sister yet also deeply immersed in prayer. Catherine seemed to recognize that she could not alleviate her sister-in-law's pain and so, as always, she turned to her Lord and Spouse to provide relief from the suffering; she trusted implicitly in His ability to provide solace and her faith was rewarded.

A fourth example of a distressed woman cared for by Catherine in the patient's home is revealed in the tale of a poor mother who had "lost her milk" and was no longer able to feed her newborn son. The woman's infant son had "for the love of Jesus" been christened by the Virgin. The mother, "not knowing what to do asked the Virgin to intervene with God so that He would provide for the breastfeeding of the baby. The Virgin, moved by compassion and love, agreed and posed a prayer and with many tears, asked God to have pity on the creature. As soon as she finished with her prayer, God in his mercy, granted the woman such abundance of milk to feed her son to his liking."[661]

Here again Saint Catherine's compassion and faith were revealed in her response to the desperate need of a distraught mother to feed her infant. Fra Caffarini tells us that Catherine was moved not only by pity but also by love. This was a theme in the Virgin's caregiving, regardless of setting or of illness or disease; she truly loved those who sought her care and saw in each of them her beloved Bridegroom to whom her heart and ministry belonged.

Finally, an example of a spiritual occurrence during one of Catherine's home visits, worth mentioning, is found in another brief anecdote shared by Fra Caffarini, in his *Supplemento Alla Vita.* Caffarini reported that:

> One day Catherine went to see a sick person who she often used to visit. While she was in the room, an extraordinary light appeared in her eyes and filled the sick room. Catherine was not able to explain such a splendor and the memory of it often caused her to weep with happiness. This amazing sight did not escape the sick person, either,

because as she mentioned to other people, she had seen the Virgin transformed in that light.[662]

The concept of Saint Catherine, as described by her patient, being "transformed in light" reveals something of the spiritual joy and radiance which emanated from the saint's person when visiting one who was ill. The theme is reinforced in descriptions of Catherine's countenance when caring for plague victims to whom she ministered in the streets of Siena. Catherine's appearance reflected her inner spirituality, the presence of the "cell" within her soul where the Lord dwelt, providing the sustenance which only His divine presence could bring.

Ministry of Public Health/Community Healthcare

Dominican Sister Jean David Finley observed the once Saint Catherine followed the Lord's call to serve her neighbor, in serving Him, she "became a familiar sight on the streets of Siena, crossing and re-crossing the lovely Plaza del Campo often as the pale pink bricks glowed like pearls in the last moments of daylight."[663] Finley explained: "for everywhere on the narrow streets that dipped down into the public square there were the sick in need of care in the hovels of the poor or in the hospital of *La Scala* near the Duomo."[664] Sister Jean David's observation is supported by biographer Don Brophy who asserted that in the early months after emerging from her three years of solitary prayer, Catherine's "attitude toward the world was being re-shaped."[665] She was "beginning to visit the sick in their homes and in the hospitals as Mantellate were supposed to do. Sometimes she was accompanied by Alessa Saracini or another Mantellata... but at other times she went out by herself, making her way up and down the steep, narrow streets of the medieval city to enter the dim, fetid rooms of the bedridden."[666] As the medical care of the 14th Century included very few remedies for cure, "the main service Catherine and her Dominican Sisters could provide was to clean and re-bandage the suppurating wounds, wash and feed the patients, and pray for them."[667]

Despite the difficult social and environmental conditions surrounding her care of sick, Richard Cardinal Cushing, in a small biography of Saint Catherine, pointed out, movingly, the spiritual meaning of the Virgin's ministry within the community. The people of Siena saw Catherine he wrote:

Daily moving about their city, never idle, but working, reading, going on errands of charity for the souls and bodies of others. They felt the joy of her presence. They caught the gracious gladness of her countenance that ever wore a smile; for Catherine was not at all of the sour-faced type of sanctity. They caught the cheery word that graciously fell from her lips as she passed, or heard perchance the helpful whisper of consolation. As she went on her way men stayed their labor to taste the joy her passing diffused. Wistfully, and always with reverence, they gazed at her as she passed. They felt the stirring of something better within them, such as a man often feels as he thinks of a mother whom death snatched from him in childhood; and they turned again to their work sensing that throb of the heart-strings one feels when one's better self is appealed to.[668]

In contemporary parlance, community health nursing, such as done by Catherine in the medieval era, is sometimes referred to with a joint label, that of "Community/Public Health Nursing." This term includes "concern with populations at risk" as well as "focusing on health promotion and maintenance of individuals' health."[669] Community/Public Health nursing is described as "population-focused, community-oriented nursing."[670] Community-based nursing is "nursing care directed toward specific individuals and families within a community."[671] Care that is community based "often refers to nursing care provided outside of acute care settings."[672]

The particular Sienese population at risk, which so concerned Saint Catherine of Siena, was that of the sick poor who were living in the city's "hovels." Although, as described in the discussions of "hospital care" and "home health care," Catherine ministered to those suffering from a variety of diseases and illness conditions, when we consider the saint's ministry in the community, it must be recognized that a significant component of her caregiving was directed toward victims of the plague.

The Plague Epidemic

When in the spring of 1374 Catherine returned from Florence to her home in Siena she found the city locked in the grip of a second outbreak of the dreaded bubonic plague; this epidemic exceeded the horrors of the earlier epidemic of 1348. It was "so violent that death claimed a third of Siena's people, among them Catherine's brother Bartolomeo, and her sister Lisa, as well as eight of Lapa's grandchildren. Another brother, Stefano, died of the plague at Rome."[673] Saint Catherine buried her young nieces and nephews with her own hands. "Catherine could easily have fled from the horror," biographer Igino Giordini pointed out. "Instead she chose to remain, with all her followers, to take care of the stricken, who had been pretty much deserted by their own people, offering personal service and all the material things she could lay hands upon."[674]

This second onset of the Sienese plague:

> Appeared in May, and it ravaged Tuscany all though the summer until September, spreading thence through northern and central Italy even across the Alps. While attacking all ages and classes, the mortality was particularly terrible among the children. And the black shadow of famine dogged its footsteps. There was fearful scarcity of everything- bread, wine, meat and oil were at unheard of prices. In the great Tuscan cities, the government collected all the materials that could be made into bread, and doled it out by ticket; but, even so, there was not enough to go round.[675]

In the words of biographer Augusta Drane:

> Never before had the plague been known to rage with equal violence...and a single day often sufficed to begin and end its fatal course. A panic seized the population; and whilst the more wealthy sought safety by flight, the poorer sort were abandoned in their misery with none to help them....Terrible indeed are the accounts left by historians of this awful time. In some streets not a creature was left alive to answer the call when the dead-cart stopped at their door. Sometimes the priests and those who carried the bier to the grave, fell lifeless while performing this last act of charity and were buried in the yet open sepulcher.[676]

"At Siena," Edmund Gardner recounted "the *Spedale di S. Maria della Scala* acted up to its great traditions and devoted all its resources to succouring the poor; and it was heroically supported by *Casa della Miseracordia* and the *Disciplinati* of Our Lady" (the Lay Brothers).... Nevertheless the death-carts went from street to street, gathering up the dead; the priests who tended the dying and buried the victims, in many cases shared their fate."[677] Catherine "with her companions... passed through the streets of the city, seeking out the most infected districts, entering the houses and the hospitals, tending the stricken, comforting and converting the dying, laying out the dead, many of whom she is said to have buried with her own hands."[678]

Each day in Siena:

> The smell of death and the shrieks of the dying filled the city. Wagonloads of dead were buried in mass graves outside the city walls. City services were discontinued because there were not enough workers. Crops were abandoned in the fields. In the convents and monasteries too, the epidemic took its toll. Every quarter of the city, every family, every occupation was devastated by the plague in that summer of 1374.[679]

"Tirelessly," we are told, "Catherine went from hospital to hospital, in and out of homes where the sick lay, to nurse them, pray for them, console them, wash them and clothe the corpses for burial. Day and night she moved among the victims of the plague, armed with only a small lamp and a smelling-bottle, which was supposed to be a protection against infection from the pestilential air."[680] This image of Catherine's ministry to plague victims is supported by the 14th-century account of her disciple and friend Fra Tommaso Caffarini:

> Once more, therefore was Catherine to be seen in the hospitals and the most infected parts of the city, assisting all no less with her charitable services than with her prayers. Never did she appear more admirable than at this time. She was always with the plague stricken; she prepared them for death, she buried them with her own hands. I myself witnessed the joy with which she tended them, and the wonderful efficacy of her words, which effected many conversions. Not a few owed their lives to her self-devoted care, and she encouraged her companions to perform like services.[681]

Nurse historian Agnes Pavey imagined that Catherine and her Sisters, who had "entered without fear the most infected quarters" of the city, "sang hymns of joy while wrapping up the poor, discolored corpses in their winding sheets."[682] Pavey admitted that we do not know all of the nursing interventions which Catherine and her companions carried out but we are told that Catherine's ministry and prayers "brought health to many sick persons" suffering from the plague.[683]

This ministry of care also greatly comforted plague victims at the end of their lives. We learned, from the accounts of numerous witnesses, that Saint Catherine prayed with and for her patients at the time of their death, as well as afterword, when she buried many herself. We do not know what words the Mantellata Sister used but we might speculate that, being a daughter of St. Dominic, Catherine may well have prayed the beautiful Dominican Matins antiphon, entitled *"O Spem Miram"* ("O Wondrous Hope"):

"O wondrous hope which you gave to those who wept at the hour of your death! You promised that you would come to the aid of your brethren: fulfill your promise."[684]

The antiphon was composed in 1256, under the guidance of Humbert of Romans, the fifth Master of the Order of Preachers. The message of hope contained in the responsory was meant to recall Saint Dominic's deathbed promise to the members of his Order. As he lay dying, Friars gathered around their founder's bedside to hear the message of his last testament, which was simply: *"Have charity for one another; guard humility; make your treasure of voluntary poverty."*[685] When the assembled Friars began to grieve over the impending loss of their beloved Master, Dominic promised: *"Do not weep, my children, I shall be more useful to you where I am now going than I have ever been in this life."*[686]

The ancient antiphon, as well as an accompanying prayer for the sick, is prayed frequently in contemporary Dominican priories, convents and churches.

A case example of Saint Catherine's ministry to plague victims is provided in the care of her confessor Blessed Raymond of Capua who began to exhibit plague symptoms after many days of ministering to those suffering from the "Black Death." Blessed Raymond provided the details of his own illness in the *Legenda*. Raymond revealed that, "encouraged by the virgin," he had visited "as many of the sick as he could" to comfort and instruct them.[687] In carrying out this ministry to plague victims, however, Raymond admitted that he was "almost alone" in the city and that "many were the calls he had from the sick"; thus, he was "always leaving the monastery and hardly had time to eat and sleep or even breathe."[688] In this physical condition of exhaustion and poor nutrition, contemporary healthcare practitioners would assume that Raymond's immune system was significantly compromised, making him an ideal candidate to become a victim of the *Yersinia Pestis* bacteria.

Blessed Raymond recounted his personal plague experience and Catherine's care:

> One night, after I had my usual brief rest, I was about to get up to say Lauds, when I felt a great pain in my groin. Touching it with my hand, I found it was a swelling. I was so scared that I hadn't the courage to get up, and I began to think I was dying. I longed for the daylight to come, so that I could go and see the virgin before it got any worse. In the meantime the inevitable fever and headache came down upon me. Then I really did get worried, but I forced myself to finish saying Lauds.
>
> As soon as it was light I got hold of a fellow Friar and went as best I could to the virgin's home; but for the moment it was a fruitless journey as she was not there, having gone off to see someone else who was sick. I decided to wait for her but, being unable to stand up on my feet, was obliged to lie down on a bed that was there, urging the people in the house to send for her as quickly as they could; which they did.
>
> When she arrived, and saw the state I was in, realizing what the matter was she knelt down by the bed and, putting her hand on my forehead, began to pray silently... during this time I felt certain symptoms over my whole body which made me fear that I was going to die from suffocation by sickness, a thing that I had already seen happen to a number of people. But it did not happen; instead, it seemed as though something was being violently drawn out of me, through all my bodily extremities at once. Then I began to feel better, and bit by bit I recovered... I was quite better; I still, it is true, felt a bit weak, but that must have been a sign that the disease had not been cured, or else that my faith was not quite solid enough.
>
> The virgin of the Lord...ordered a convalescent's meal to be prepared for me. I took the food from her own holy hands, and then she advised me to take a little rest, which gratefully and obediently I did.
>
> When I got up, I found myself as well as if I had never been ill. Seeing that I was better Catherine said: 'Go and work for the good of souls, and give thanks to the Highest for freeing you from this danger'.[689]

Obviously, Blessed Raymond, in a state of exhaustion from his consistent ministry to the plague victims of Siena, was an ideal candidate to be felled by the incredibly contagious disease. This appears to have been the case and it was Saint Catherine's heartfelt prayer to her beloved Spouse that moved the Divine Physician to heal his faithful Friar. It is also possible that Blessed Raymond had, in his fatigued state, become so attuned to the sequellae of the plague that he integrated these physiological responses into his own psyche and began to manifest similar symptoms. Regardless of the etiology or pathophysiology of Raymond's illness, the Lord did, in fact, hear Catherine's prayer and restored the Friar to health.

It is important to remember, in considering Blessed Raymond's illness experience and care, that as well as employing prayer, Saint Catherine also incorporated basic nursing theory into the Friar's treatment by ordering a "convalescent meal" and advising him to "take a little rest." Clearly, Catherine, from her experience in caring for the sick, was sensitive to the physiological need for adequate nutrition and relaxation, as well as faith and hope, if one is to successfully recover from a serious illness. Catherine once more demonstrated her gift for the practice of holistic healthcare in her attention to the Friar's body, mind and spirit.

Although, thankfully, Blessed Raymond recovered completely from his fearful plague experience; many of those to whom Catherine ministered did not survive. While we have no accounts of specific prayers the Virgin may have used in comforting dying plague victims, we can assume from her personal spirituality that she encouraged her patients to hope in God's mercy and the promise of eternal life. Such a message is clearly reflected in Catherine's letter T 273, written to Blessed Raymond, describing her consolation for a young prisoner facing execution and in other letters to those experiencing bereavement from loss of a loved one. Extant literature on the care of the dying asserts that one of the most important concerns for an individual facing the end of life is "the need for hope," which "can be equated with transcendent hope (which incorporates) theological meanings."[690]

Prison Ministry

As well as caring for the physically sick and dying, Sister Jean David Finley noted that Catherine had embraced a ministry to those whose souls were suffering in the local prison of Siena: "Witnesses to her canonization testified that it was her habit to spend occasional nights at the prison, helping prisoners who were to be executed the next day."[691] Catherine was always aware of the needs of the condemned criminals because in the town of Siena: "Even in times of peace, there was no escaping the sight of violent death, for all too frequently, condemned prisoners passed through the *Porta della Guistizia* on their way to the gallows hill outside the city."[692]

It was reported that as well as hardened criminals there were many incarcerated in the Italian prisons "whose crimes were of no blacker dye than those of Agnolo d'Andrea, condemned to death for giving a banquet" to which certain political activists had not been invited.[693] Catherine "saw in them," Augusta Drane observed, "the likeness of her adorable Master as he passed Calvary loaded with chains to die between two malefactors. Hence she was no stranger to the *Guistizia* or place of public execution... She came thither not once, but often, for Caffarini tells us in his deposition that he could not number the occasions when she gave help to the dying."[694]

To this day, prison ministry is probably one of the most neglected fields in terms of nursing specialty areas. Young nurses, recently out of school and having passed the NCLEX Exam (nursing licensure exam), talk excitedly about potential professional fields, such as critical care nursing, emergency department nursing, or neonatal intensive care nursing; rarely, however, does one hear of a newly minted nurse identifying prison nursing as his or her chosen calling. This may be partly due to the concept raised in an article published in the *Journal of Christian Nursing* entitled: "Prison Nursing: Rising Above Fear to Care."[695] In the paper, a nurse employed in a medium-security prison posed the question: "What kind of nurse would choose to work behind bars, caring both physically and spiritually for convicts?"[696] The article's nurse author asserted that "because of the hopelessness of prisoners, there is an overwhelming need for someone to listen and to care. The cellblock setting magnifies the rejection, perhaps of a lifetime, and intensifies prisoners' needs to be accepted."[697] The nurse reported: "God has often used me in just being kind to an inmate... I find, generally, they just want someone to listen."[698]

Contemporary literature on "prison nursing," more recently identified as "correctional nursing," focuses on the concept of "caring" as central to ministry to prisoners.[699] As pointed out by author Ann Norman, "Prison nurses have to look after the needs of people with difficult, complex and challenging health problems/behaviors who are at a very vulnerable stage of their lives. Nurses are well placed to offer support, encouragement, and act as advocates for people, some of whom can see no real hope for their future."[700]

In attempting to understand the difficulties encountered by today's nurses engaged in correctional nursing, one might imagine the challenges faced by Saint Catherine as she entered the prison environment of medieval Siena. As historian James Walsh explained, "In order to prevent feuds as far as possible, the most stringent laws were enacted, and those who took part in street quarrels in which anyone was wounded, even though death did not follow, were condemned to death and a number of executions were ordered for the sake of the moral effect on others... executions were by the ax of the headsman..."[701] Walsh reported that "Catherine visited these young men in prison and endeavored to get them to repent of their hatred toward others."[702]

Friar Martin Gillet, who ultimately became Master of the Dominican Order, wrote poignantly of Saint Catherine's solace for prisoners:

> Although the poor and the sick absorbed the greater part of her time, Catherine also occupied herself with the prisoners of Siena. We have a beautiful letter, dated April 9, 1377, and addressed to the Sienese prisoners whom she greeted as 'My dear sons in Christ, the sweet Jesus'. The purpose of this letter is clear: to urge these unfortunate persons to be patient and to invite them to receive the sacraments at Easter. Catherine makes no direct reference to their sufferings in prison, nor to the reasons, just or unjust, of their imprisonment. That was a delicate subject and she would be in danger of injustice toward the prisoners or the authorities who had sentenced them. She takes up the most important problem, that of sin in general, whose prisoners we all are and from which Jesus delivered us by dying on the Cross for love of us.[703]

Friar Gillet quotes from Catherine's letter: "Christ bore pain, calumny, mistreatment and outrages; He was bound, scourged and nailed to the Cross; He was covered with insults and injuries and tormented by thirst. But He suffered everything with patience, forgiving and praying for those who crucified Him."[704]

Gillet continued:

> The lesson is clear, but how delicately it is presented. Jesus was innocent. It is for us, for our sins, that He endured all this pain with divine patience. After such an example, how can we complain, we who

are not free from sin? (Catherine's words) "He was a knight fighting on the battlefield... His crown of thorns was His helmet; His lacerated flesh... His armor; the nails in His hands, His gauntlets; the lance in His side, His sword; the nails in His feet, His spurs. See how well armed is our Knight. We ought to follow Him and look to Him for all consolation in our trials and tribulations."[705]

Friar Gillet concluded: "But Catherine was not content to write beautiful and consoling letters to the prisoners. When the time came for one of them to pay with his life for his crimes, or what was quite common in that day, for his political indiscretions, she would go to him and console him in his last moments, hoping at least to snatch his soul from eternal death."[706] Gillet cites the example of Catherine's care for the young prisoner Niccolo di Toldo, which is discussed in Chapter Seven as exemplifying Catherine's embrace of the ministry of presence.

A final note must be added regarding Saint Catherine's letter, T 260, which was entitled "To the Prisoners of Siena." In her introduction to the letter, Suzanne Noffke OP admits that, "Catherine's biographers and other commentators have traditionally assumed that this letter is addressed to all of the prisoners of Siena simply as prisoners." Noffke suggests, however, that the message was also meant for several Knights Hospitallers, taken prisoner after a battle because of the "knight imagery in the letter." Noffke does, nevertheless, point out that "Catherine seems to assume that the letter will be read to all of the prisoners, since she advises 'those who can' to prepare for their Easter confession and communion."[707]

Spiritual Assessment and Care

Until fairly recently, the topics of the assessment of patients' spiritual needs and the nurse's role in spiritual care were non-existent in the professional nursing lexicon. The arenas of spiritual needs and spiritual care fell under the heading of pastoral ministry and thus within the domain of the hospital chaplain. With the introduction of the holistic healthcare movement, however, and its newly described concern with the body, mind and spirit connection, the caregiving community began to explore and embrace the nurse's role in spiritual assessment and spiritual care. Although not every healthcare provider, with the exception of the chaplain, may feel comfortable providing spiritual care to a patient, it is the responsibility of all healthcare providers to be aware of and attentive to the spiritual and religious needs of his or her patient. If spiritual concerns of a patient are identified, one should suggest a consult with a pastoral care provider appropriate to the patient's faith tradition. An assessment of a patient's spiritual and religious needs can be conducted formally, by employing an instrument such as the "Spiritual Assessment Scale" or through informal conversation with the patient or a family member.[708] Spiritual Care, carried out by a nurse or other caregiver might include such activities as: praying with a patient, reading scripture or other spiritual materials, facilitating the patient's spiritual practices such as providing materials for religious devotions, seeking the intervention of a chaplain or simply listening to and discussing spiritual issues with the patient.

Saint Catherine of Siena can be said to have undertaken all the above identified activities, with the exception of reading prior to her own achievement of literacy. She is frequently described as having prayed with and for the sick, encouraged them to receive the sacraments, facilitated the intervention of a pastoral care provider, such as one of the Dominican Friars, and counseled the ill and the infirm at length about the love of God and His forgiveness and mercy.

While Catherine included assessment of an ill person's spiritual needs and the provision of spiritual care in all of her interactions with the sick, two examples particularly bear out the importance of this aspect of her caregiving ministry. Fra Tommasso Caffarini, in his *Supplento Alla Vita di S. Caterina da Siena* related the account of Saint Catherine's comfort for an ill woman who admitted to being concerned about the "health of her soul":

> A woman named Christophora, who was in the service of a certain noblewoman of Florence called Elizabetta, had a strong desire to speak with the virgin about the health of her soul, but her illness did not allow the trip to Siena. One day, while she was in bed and was awake, she had a vision of Catherine coming toward her, white and shining like the sun at sunset. Catherine sat down beside her, took all doubt from her mind, answering her questions as if she had been present in the body and then she left her consoled... The same thing happened to many spiritual sons and daughters; Catherine would appear during their sleep, answering them according to the needs of each.[709]

While Fra Tomasso does not explain how Catherine knew of Christophora's concern, the Virgin's letters attest to the fact that she became aware of the needs of ailing friends and acquaintances through her contacts in the community; she would then place the person in prayer, sometimes for many hours at a time.

A second, and more dramatic example of Catherine's provision of spiritual care, through prayer, is that described for a Sienese citizen, Andrea di Naddino dei Bellandi. This account of Catherine's spiritual intervention is provided in Blessed Raymond of Capua's *Legenda* as well as in a more recent Italian translation of Fra Caffarini's *Supplemento Alla Vita di Santa Caterina da Siena.*

As Fra Tommasso recounted the story:

> There was a man in Siena, much favored by fortune, called Andrea di Naddino dei Bellandi, rich in temporal goods but poor in spiritual things. He always dreamed of playing and eating well, and he never, or almost never, went to church. Confession, fasting, and any religious practices were unnecessary for him or non-existent. He never begged; he always cursed against God and all the saints, and it would take too long here to narrate all his pranks.
>
> On September of 1370, Andrea, who was already 40 years old, became sick with an incurable disease. Right away they found a priest willing to confess him, for the good of his soul, and later many other priests attempted the same thing, with no success. The feast of St. Lucia approached and still nobody could convince him to go to confession. Two days after this festivity, in the evening, the confessor of Catherine told her to pray to Jesus so that Andrea would go to confession... when Catherine arrived home... the virgin prayed for Andrea, humbly and devotedly until dawn. At around the same time, Andrea called all the women in the house and said to them: 'Go and look for a priest because I want to confess. Jesus appeared to me and he wants me to confess'. The women, very happy, and without wasting any time, called a priest. Andrea went to a general confession, and he also made his will, even though he never wanted to do it before. After all this, he died.[710]

Caffarini continued the story by relating that Catherine admitted to her confessor that:

> She had prayed and obtained for Andrea the remission of his sins, and lastly his freedom from the pain of hell. At the beginning, Andrea

rejected the divine inspiration, but God wanted to make justice. Finally, Jesus, because he wanted to be benignant, put a third person in the middle because both of them loved so much justice and mercy. This person, Catherine, told Jesus: 'Make justice on me, but have mercy on him. Send me to hell, but have mercy on him. I will insist on this until you will have granted me your mercy, because I know that it is You, the cause of this desire and of this pardon.'[711]

Caffarini concluded: "Our Lord then granted the mercy, and it was at that moment that Andrea called for confession."[712]

Soon thereafter, Augusta Drane recounted:

> The news ran through the city that Andrea di Bellandi had died penitent and fortified with the last sacraments. Men could not believe their ears, for he was known to everyone in Siena for his riches and his vices. They knew that all through his illness he had been vainly urged to by his friends both to confess and to make disposition of his worldly goods, which last matter he could not bear so much as to hear mentioned; but now they heard of the wise and excellent way in which he had drawn up his will and distributed his wealth, a thing no less astonishing to them than the fact that he had died a good Christian.[713]

The purpose of this chapter has been to identify and describe Saint Catherine of Siena's caregiving mission to the ill and the infirm through both theory and concrete examples of her ministry to the sick in the hospital, in the home and in the community, the latter focusing on Catherine's ministry during the plague epidemic and within Siena's prisons. Also described was the Virgin's ministry of spiritual intervention through intercessory prayer for those who were ailing. In all of her nursing activities the Mantellata Sister placed spiritual care as central to her mission but she also employed appropriate nursing theory and therapeutics to heal the body as well as the soul. Catherine practiced, in the 14th Century, what today we describe as holistic healthcare. She remained always concerned with the body, mind and spirit connection of her patients and remains a role model for all 21st-century caregivers involved in ministry to the ill and the infirm.

In the following chapter, Saint Catherine's medieval ministry to the ailing is analyzed in light of a contemporary framework, that of the "Sacred Covenant Model of Caring for the Sick."

Chapter 7. "The Measure of Your Love"
A Sacred Covenant of Caring for the Sick

"You are rewarded not according to your work or your time but according to the measure of your love"
Catherine of Siena: Dialogue 165

A Sacred Covenant
She was mystic and scholar,
this saint who embraced a
sacred covenant,

A sacred covenant of caring for the
sick and the poor,

A sacred covenant of encouraging the
anxious and the afraid,

A sacred covenant of comforting the
suffering and the sorrowful,

A sacred covenant of consoling the
dying and the bereaved.

Catherine of Siena,
A Sacred Covenant of love.

In the above quotation from Catherine of Siena's beautiful spiritual work, the *Dialogue*, the saint shares the Lord's message that we will be rewarded not because of any particular ministry in which we were engaged or for the time we spent accomplishing it, but rather for the love with which the service was embraced. Throughout the preceding chapters of this book anecdotes describing the saint's care of the sick poor reveal that, as the distinguishing characteristic of her ministry, each task was carried out with great love. Catherine joyfully welcomed her Divine Spouse's mandate to love her neighbors and to do for them what she could not, at the time, do for Him. While we are told that she did not learn to read for some years, Catherine clearly had internalized Jesus' teaching contained in Matthew 25: 35-36, 40: "I was hungry and you gave me food, I was thirsty and you gave me something to drink, I was a stranger and you welcomed me, I was naked and you gave me clothing, I was sick and you took care of me, I was in prison and you visited me... Truly, I tell you, just as you did it to one of the least of these who are members of my family, you did it to me."

Saint Catherine manifested her love of Jesus in caring for the sick and the poor in their homes, in the hospitals, in the community and in the prisons. The Mantellata Sister was gifted with the ability to care for individuals holistically; she was always aware of the body, mind and spirit connection when ministering to the ill. While the state of a person's soul was always foremost in her mind, Catherine nevertheless made provision for the physical care of the body, and spoke words of hope and comfort to console an anxious and fearful mind.

The purpose of this final chapter is to explore Saint Catherine's loving ministry to the ill and the infirm in light of a contemporary theoretical framework, that of a "Sacred Covenant Model of Caring for the Sick." The underlying aim is to demonstrate that examples of Catherine's ministry to the ill in 14th-century Siena remain relevant models for 21st-century ministers when contextualized in terms of a present day framework of caring for those who are ailing in body or in spirit.

A Sacred Covenant Model of Caring for the Sick

The "Sacred Covenant Model of Caring for the Sick" was first published in the 2014 edition of *Spirituality in Nursing: Standing on Holy Ground* in a chapter entitled: "The Spirituality of Caring."[714] Although several models of caring are extant in the nursing literature, this theory is unique in focusing on the spirituality of caring for the sick envisioned as a sacred covenant. The model builds on the author's previous research, the findings of which revealed both the sacredness and the covenantal nature of the caring relationship between those who minister to the ill and their patients. Data from these studies are included in: "A Sacred Covenant" in "The Nurse's Calling: A Christian Spirituality of Caring for the Sick"(O'Brien, 2001); "A Sacred Covenant: Prayer and the Nurse-Patient Relationship" in "Prayer in Nursing: The Spirituality of Compassionate Caregiving (O'Brien, 2003); "The Bible and the Nurse-Patient Covenant" in "The Nurse with An Alabaster Jar: A Biblical

Approach to Nursing" (O'Brien, 2006) and "The Sacred Covenant of Caring" in "A Sacred Covenant: The Spiritual Ministry of Nursing" (O'Brien, 2008).[715]

The Spirituality of Caring

The spirituality of caring for the sick, supportive of the sacred covenant model, is envisioned as comprised of three attributes: a calling of service, a blessed trust, and a commitment to reverence. These concepts were derived from the numerous explorations of the spiritual needs of persons suffering from both acute and chronic illnesses; data reflecting the themes were also generated in research on practicing nurses' perceptions of the spirituality of caring.

The "Sacred Covenant Model of Caring for the Sick" has been in the process of development for over 30 years through studying the healthcare needs of persons experiencing such diseases as chronic renal failure, hypertension, heart disease, cancer, and HIV/AIDS, as well as illness related experiences of migrant farmworkers and those of institutionalized and homebound elders. Repeatedly the concept of a sacred covenant emerged as the most frequently appreciated model of caring for the sick; this was affirmed by both patients and caregivers.

The model is philosophically:

> Grounded in the belief that covenantal caring is an essential concept undergirding ministry to the sick and, further, that professional caregivers embrace the concept both theoretically and operationally. It is believed that ministers to the ill and infirm experience in their caring activities a "sacredness" related to their call to be of service to those in need. Associated with this "calling of service" are the closely related concepts of "a blessed sense of trust" and "a commitment to reverence" governing nurse-patient relationships.[716]

The theology supporting the sacred covenant model of caring is derived from both Old and New Testament scriptures, for example, the Old Testament passage 'I have made a covenant with my chosen one' (Psalm 89, verse 3); and, in the New Testament, the parable of the "Good Samaritan" (Luke 10: 30-40).

The three attributes of the spirituality of caring for the sick, "a calling of service," "a blessed trust," and "a commitment to reverence" lead the healthcare minister to practice a covenantal model of caring. Five

161

behavioral themes which flow from the caregiver's perception of caring as a sacred covenant are "respecting life," "being present," "comforting with compassion," "creating bonds," and "becoming an advocate."[717]

Healthcare providers who perceive and practice their profession with the understanding that the vocation is one of service to others, given by God as a blessed trust, and encompassing a commitment to reverence, are thus moved to embrace a covenantal style of caring. For ministers to the sick who practice under the guidance of this model, key behavioral outcomes include: respecting the sanctity of human life, being fully present and listening caringly to patients and family members, comforting suffering patients with compassion, creating bonds of caring within the nurse-patient relationship and consistently advocating for the needs of patients and families.

A critical component of the caregiver-patient relationship is the degree of trust engendered between the interacting parties. This element of trust is lived out in caregiver-patient partnerships in terms of a covenant relationship:

> Although not always formally articulated as such, the presence of an understood covenant between a patient and a caregiver not only supports the confidence between the partners, but also sets up parameters for appropriate behaviors and attitudes. This covenant can be viewed as sacred given the nature of the intimacy, indeed the holiness, of the caregiver-patient relationship.[718]

The sacredness of the healthcare minister's caring relationship with a patient "derives directly from the sacredness of the vocation, the sacredness of the call to care for the most vulnerable members of our society, the ill and the infirm."[719]

A hospital charge nurse observed: "Caregiving has so much to do with the patients and families trusting you as a nurse. There is a plan to that, a blessed plan from God. It's like the trust becomes a holy covenant between the nurse and the patient; a covenant which the nurse is committed to in the carrying out of her profession"; and an ICU nurse mused:

> You have these really sick patients who are fragile and afraid, and you have families who are spacing out over what's happening to their family member; they trust you and you have to give them 100%. Your

head can't be someplace else when you're working in the unit; all of you, body, mind and soul, has to be there...every day you have a mission; sometimes it seems like a mission impossible, but with God's help you can make it through the shift and leave feeling that you really have accomplished a mission of healing.[720]

Catherine's Covenantal Ministry

In order to validate consideration of Saint Catherine's care for the ill as providing inspiration for today's healthcare ministers, the saint's caregiving activities are described within the context of the "Sacred Covenant Model of Caring for the Sick." Case examples of Catherine's service to the sick are presented for each of the model's three sacred covenant attributes: a calling of service, a blessed trust and a commitment to reverence, as well as the five behavioral themes flowing from the perception of caring as a "sacred covenant": respecting life, being present, comforting with compassion, establishing bonds and becoming an advocate.

Sacred Covenant Attributes

A Calling of Service

The concept of being called to serve was a key theme in a study of servant leadership among contemporary practicing nurses.[721] Nurse respondents welcomed the opportunity to discuss their professional roles in terms of a call to serve others: the idea of servanthood, of being of service to the sick, was not in any way perceived as placing the caregiver in a lower position. It was, in fact, considered a privilege to serve the ill. For a number of nurses the positive attribution placed on the concept of service was derived from the Christian scripture; that is from the example of Jesus, who as 'the Son of Man came not to be served but to serve' (Matthew 10:45").[722]

As one nursing leader commented: "Most nurses I know see nursing as a calling of service... I think there is a quiet, deep inside knowing that this is what I am supposed to do. This feels right and is nourishing to me and to others so this is the spiritual calling."[723] Several other practicing nurses also spoke of seeing nursing as a calling of service: "When I think of nursing as a vocation, I think of our lives being called by God to serve our neighbor and to live as Christ, loving and helping where we can as He loved and helped us"; "The nursing vocation brings to mind the chance to help others through difficult situations in their lives and to be of service in some way to help them grow through their suffering"; and "You have to see nursing as a vocation, as a calling to serve… I take this very seriously. I come here (to the hospital) in the morning and I really feel that it is what I was called to do."[724]

We are told by her biographers that, from an early, age Saint Catherine believed her life was to be lived as a calling of service. What it appears the saint did not understand, until near the end of three years of solitary prayer, was that the Lord was calling her to serve Him in ministry to the sick. Once Catherine heard clearly God's call to this ministry, however, she embraced the vocation unreservedly and joyfully. Providing voluntary service to the sick poor in their homes and in the local hospitals was a primary ministry of the Dominican Mantellate Community to which Catherine committed her life. As discussed in Chapter Six, the saint spent many hours in caring for the sick of Siena, in their homes, in a variety of hospitals and in the community; she ministered in the latter especially during the era of the 1374 Black Death epidemic.

A case example of Catherine's response to "a calling of service" is that represented by the tender and compassionate care that she lovingly and selflessly provided to a woman named Andrea suffering from advanced breast cancer. A biographer affirmed:

> In addition to the poor… Catherine was attracted to the sick. She who endured suffering so courageously, could not bear to see others suffer, especially when their suffering separated them from God instead of drawing them nearer to Him. Catherine, the patroness of nurses and of all those who care for the sick, hovered lovingly around the beds of the sick and in certain instances carried her devotion to the point of heroism. For example, one cannot read the account of the care and conversion of Andrea without trembling before a spectacle which surpasses the expectations of human nature and disconcerts the most intrepid wills and the most generous hearts.[725]

Blessed Raymond of Capua included the saint's ministry to Andrea as a primary example of Catherine's calling of service in his *Legenda* chapter entitled: "Charity Towards the Infirm."[726] According to biographer Arrigo Levasti we actually have three accounts of Catherine's care of Andrea: "that of Raimondo de Capua built up on witnesses remote memories, that of Bartolomeo Dominici written in his old age, and that of the Miracoli, written down shortly after events described, on October 10, 1374."[727]

As Blessed Raymond recalled, the cancerous growth which afflicted Andrea had progressed to such an advanced state that no one wanted to care for the poor woman or in fact to even go near her; nobody could bear to be in the same room with her. When, however, Saint Catherine heard of the sad case she immediately went to Andrea's home and "joyfully offered her services for as long as the illness lasted."[728] It appeared to Catherine that "heaven had reserved this unfortunate woman especially for herself."[729] As unpleasant as the tasks were, the saint cared for Andrea tenderly: "she was with the sick woman continuously... unbandaging the sore, wiping it, washing it, dressing it, showing no sign of repulsion, seemingly unwearied by the length of time it took her, and doing everything with such grace and cheerfulness that the sick woman herself was amazed to see such constancy of soul, such warmth of affection and charity."[730] "Day after day," biographer Augusta Drane recounted: "Catherine lavished on her patient the tenderest care; in spite of the repulsive nature of the services she has to perform, she never showed any sign of disgust or adopted any of those precautions which others had made use of in the tainted atmosphere of the sick room, lest by doing so she should give pain to Andrea's feelings."[731]

As time progressed, however, Andrea became annoyed over her dependency in the situation and began to criticize Catherine's caregiving to the other Sisters in the community. It was during this period when Catherine, deeply hurt by Andrea's cruel remarks and praying that her own distress might be relieved, was told by God that she had a choice between two crowns, one of jewels the other of thorns:

> Dearest daughter... it is necessary that at different times and different places you must be crowned with both these crowns. Choose then which you prefer: to be crowned during your life on earth with the crown of thorns, and I will keep the other for you for the life without end; or to receive the precious one now and to have the crown of thorns reserved for you after death? She answered: Oh, Lord, I have long renounced my own will and have chosen to follow yours; hence the choice is not mine. But since you wish me to reply, I will say at once that in this life I prefer to be always conformed to your most holy Passion and for love of you to embrace any pain as my refreshment.[732]

With these words the saint chose the crown of thorns and the acceptance of whatever suffering might be asked of her.

Catherine continued her faithful and loving ministry to Andrea despite the patient's hurtful gossip. Even Mona Lapa urged her daughter to not to continue to assist such a mean spirited old woman but Catherine replied: "Dearest mother... know in your charity that if I were to abandon this sick woman, there would be no one else to take my place and she would die at once... with these words she went back to the sick woman and looked after her quite happily as though she had never said a word against her."[733]

In the end, Andrea's heart was moved by the tenderness and compassion of Catherine's nursing and she recognized her own guilt in the unwarranted criticism; "she asked the virgin's pardon, confessing that she had sinned gravely in slandering her so unjustly... Then the virgin of the Lord threw herself into the arms of her calumniator, did everything she could to comfort her, and assured her that she would not leave her and did not feel in the slightest degree offended."[734]

As evidenced in the ministry to Andrea, Catherine was described as being selfless in her caring of those she was called to serve. The saint was filled with solicitude for the sick she nursed and for all those who sought her spiritual advice and guidance. She was sensitive and gentle when they were anxious and suffering. Even though Catherine, often personally adopted extreme penances in such areas as fasting from food and drink, she advised the sick for whom she cared "against all kinds of exaggerated self-discipline which might weaken their health; she told them to eat, drink and sleep moderately, but sufficiently to keep strong in body and soul, so they could carry on God's work in the way demanded of them by their positions in the world."[735]

Twenty-first-century ministers to the sick, such as nurses, physicians and chaplains, are also sometimes called to attend patients the sequellae of whose illnesses may make the caregiving challenging. While modern medicine provides for the alleviation of a number of vicious side effects of illness and disease, in some cases unpleasant symptoms remain. This is true for many chemotherapy patients, especially those with advanced disease. In her tender and committed ministry to the advanced cancer patient Andrea, despite the difficulty of some of the caregiving tasks, Catherine teaches the true meaning of caring for the sick when envisioned as a sacred calling of service. In serving Andrea, Catherine

166

was also serving her Blessed Lord; she modeled for us how we also can serve Him in today's ministries to the ill and the infirm.

A Blessed Trust

One cannot begin to consider the attribute of the spirituality of caring labeled "a blessed trust" without calling to mind one of Florence Nightingale's best loved quotes: "And remember every nurse should be one who is to be depended upon... she must have a respect for her own calling because God's precious gift of life is often literally placed in (his/her) hands."[736] What a blessed trust nurses and all who care for the sick have been assigned by Nightingale, a trust "essential to a ministry that may at times truly place 'God's precious gift of life' in the caregiver's hands."[737]

In the words of one nursing leader: "All of nursing is a sacred trust, whether it be involved in direct patient care, administration, education or research... nursing is a blessing to be held in trust as a gift from God"[738]; another nurse asserted:

> I see my nursing as sacred, a holy gift from God. It's a trust also; I think I could even call it a blessed trust or a holy trust. It's God trusting me to care for His poor and sick people and trusting that I will do it with love and care and compassion. It's me holding these people in trust. They trust me to take care of them to the best of my ability. Their families trust me as a nurse...and it is definitely sacred because what we do has to do with the sacredness of life, with life and death.[739]

As demonstrated in Catherine's many caregiving activities carried out in the homes of the sick poor, as well as in the hospitals, the saint considered her ministry to the ill and infirm to a blessed mission entrusted to her by the Lord Himself. When Mona Lapa begged her daughter to give up her visits to the leper Tecca at San Lazzaro and to Andrea suffering from advanced cancer, Catherine replied that she could not possibly abandon the work her Beloved Spouse has asked her to perform; these ministries were indeed undertaken as a "blessed trust" by the saint.

A particular reflection of Catherine's perception of her ministry to the sick as a "blessed trust" was the fact that she seemed to possess an innate knowledge of how to approach persons with a certain disease or illness and what remedies to provide. We do not know, from any written sources, how the saint was educated in nursing the sick. We do not know how she learned to cleanse and bandage Andrea's cancerous sore. Yet, she approached her caregiving activities with a sense that the Lord would provide whatever was needed to fulfill her ministry as a blessed trust to care for Him in the guise of the least of His brothers and sisters.

In the following example we are provided with a powerful reflection of Catherine's trust in her healthcare ministry evidenced by her apparent understanding of both human physiology and human psychology. The anecdote, not found in the *Legenda* of Blessed Raymond of Capua, is, however, related by Catherine's other early biographer, Fra Tommaso d'Antonio Caffarini in his supplement to the *Legenda*, the "Supplemento Alla Vita di Santa Caterina da Siena":

> A woman of Siena named Gemma, a Sister of Penance of St. Dominic, attached to the Virgin so much that no leaf moved without her advice, complained to Catherine because she did nothing but sleep, especially when she wanted to pray and practice things pleasing to the Lord. The Virgin said: 'My sister, you are deceived; take strength and rest awake, and you will find the consolation of God.
>
> Then Gemma started to stay awake, but the following night she realized that she had hurt her left eye; it was red and swollen and she could barely see. She told the Virgin: 'Well, as you see, I listened to you and I got sick in one eye.' The Virgin answered: 'Just take a leaf of 'Sow Thistle' and put it on the eye.
>
> Hearing this, Gemma looked for and took up the leaf but having more faith in the Virgin than in the virtue of the plant, she sought a way to make Catherine touch it. Catherine guessing the desire of her companion, took the leaf in her hand and then handed it back saying: 'Put it on the eye'. As soon as she (Gemma) had, her sight was regained.'[740]

What is particularly important about this therapeutic intervention is the fact that the term "*Cicerbita*," the Italian word used by the saint, which translates to "Sow Thistle" in English, is indeed the name of an herbal plant possessed of a variety of medicinal properties including anti-inflammatory and anti-febrile characteristics. Even more interesting is that one can find scholarly journal articles describing the contemporary medicinal use of the plant. One example is the 2013 publication "Validation of Medicinal Values of Traditionally Used Sonchus Asper (Prickly Sow Thistle) Leaves for the Treatment of Skin Ailments."[741] Catherine recognized, in her 14th-century care of a sick woman with a sore eye, the healing ability of a medicinal plant which continues to be accepted in 21st-century medicine.

Saint Catherine's ministry to Gemma, suffering from a sore eye, teaches today's caregivers several lessons. First, although we do not know how Catherine gained her knowledge of the use of this herbal remedy, she clearly supported the value of medicine as witnessed by her prescribing of the healing plant "*Cicerbita*" or "Sow Thistle." Secondly, although Catherine had already advised Gemma about her sleeping habits, she did not fail to follow up, visiting her again thus allowing the patient to verbalize the additional complaint of an irritated eye. And, finally, when Catherine perceived that Gemma wished the saint to touch the leaf herself, she willingly did so, validating the patient's confidence in the remedy's healing power. This case example of caregiving teaches us that Catherine considered her ministry to be a "blessed trust"; a trust which she held seriously and persistently when caring for those who were suffering. This is a trust given to all contemporary ministers to the sick.

A Commitment to Reverence

A third characteristic of the spirituality of caring for the sick is the caregiver's commitment to reverence. This attribute is critical to the spirituality of caring displayed by those ministering to the ill and infirm:

> Nurses, and others who care for the sick, often have to undertake difficult and/or unpleasant tasks, both physical and emotional, in caring for their patients. While such caregiving activities are necessary to enhance healing and promote health, they may be uncomfortable, embarrassing, and sometimes painful for both patient and healthcare provider. Thus, a posture of spiritual gentleness, a posture of reverence, in undertaking such nursing actions is essential to promoting and achieving a philosophy of compassionate ministry on the part of the caregiver.[742]

Another of Florence Nightingale's well-known quotes is supportive of the concept of reverence in caring for the sick. Nightingale wrote that ministry to the sick is an art, "and if it is to be made an art, it requires as exclusive a devotion, as hard a preparation, as any painter's or sculptor's work. For what is having to do with dead canvas or cold marble compared with having to do with the living body, the temple of God's spirit."[743]

In the words of one present day nursing leader: "Nursing is sacred... holding something sacred demands an awareness of the sacredness of what it is, and also a commitment to reverence and real care"[744]; and a palliative care unit administrator poignantly observed:

> The nursing vocation goes hand in hand with being servants. I think that nursing is a sacred trust. That caring for those God has given to us as truly gifts is really being a servant. I think that holding something sacred demands an awareness of the sacredness of what it is and also a commitment to reverence and respect for our patients. I think that for me, as a nurse, it is truly cradling in each of these patients the face of God. That is the sacred trust we have been given. It is our responsibility and also our call to continue to live out that legacy as faithful servants.[745]

A concomitant characteristic to Saint Catherine's sense of caring for the sick perceived as "a sacred calling" and "a blessed trust," was her understanding of the "commitment to reverence." Over and over, in her caregiving activities in the homes of the ailing, during her activities in the hospitals of *Santa Maria della Scala*, *Casa della Miseracordia* and *San Lazzaro*, and when encountering plague victims fallen in the Sienese streets, we see Catherine demonstrating reverence for those who are ill. Between such patients as the abandoned woman of the streets for whom the virgin cared at *La Scala*, and the holy Hermit Santi to whom she ministered at the *Miseracordia*, Catherine made no distinctions; whether sinner or saint, the virgin treated all with the reverence with which she would treat her Blessed Lord whose image she saw in the sick poor under her care. Regardless of how the ill person responded to her ministrations, Catherine never ceased reflecting a devoted commitment to reverence in her caregiving.

A clear example of this reverence lies in the account of Catherine's ministry to a woman named Palmarina who was suddenly struck down with a serious, life-threatening illness. Blessed Raymond also included Catherine's care of Palmarina as an example of the saint's healthcare ministry in his *Legenda* chapter "Charity Toward the Infirm." Raymond begins the anecdote by explaining that Palmarina "had dedicated herself and all that she possessed to the house of the *Miseracordia*" (the *Casa della Miseracordia*).[746]

Despite her own commitment to the sick and the poor, Raymond reported that Palmarina was intensely proud and envious of Saint Catherine; this antipathy manifested itself in Palmarina speaking evil of the saint whenever the opportunity arose either privately and in public. Augusta Drane affirmed that "the praise which Palmarina heard bestowed upon Catherine excited in her such an envy that at length she could not bear to see her, or to hear her name spoken."[747] Blessed Raymond recalled that "the virgin did all she could to placate her with acts of humility and kindness but the woman had nothing but contempt for them."[748]

After the sickness overtook her, unfortunately Palmarina "showed more unreasoning hatred of the holy virgin now that she was ill than when she had been well."[749] When Catherine learned of this, she tried to console Palmarina by acts of concern and tender caring. The saint "frequently went to see her, appeared before her submissively, and with kind words and charming ways, did all she could to comfort her by endeavoring to serve her as much as she could in every possible way."[750]

Ultimately, Palmarina's illness worsened and she was in danger of dying without having received the sacraments. For several days, Catherine begged the Lord to intercede for the woman that she would repent of the behavior for the salvation of her eternal soul. God heard his daughter's heartfelt prayer, and Palmarina finally recognized her fault and begged forgiveness. As soon as Catherine learned of this "she went with all speed to see Palmarina, who manifested her pleasure and respect for her from whom she had formerly shrunk, with what signs she could, and with words and gestures confessed her sin. And then, having received the sacraments, with great contrition of heart, she died."[751]

Catherine's commitment to reverence in her ministry to the sick is graphically reflected in the admirable kindness and understanding demonstrated in her attention to the needs of Palmarina in her illness. Although the woman had long been a cruel detractor of Catherine's vocation, the saint was able to put the abuse aside and rush to help, especially when Palmarina's illness became critical. Saint Catherine, in practicing the reverence demanded of her vocation, held Palmarina's physical and spiritual well-being so closely in her heart that she used all means possible to console her. This commitment to reverence that

Catherine modeled profoundly is also demanded of present-day caregivers who minister in our complex and sometimes broken world. Today's caregivers may also be called upon to minister to 21st-Century "Palmarinas"; may we be blessed with the loving reverence so willing demonstrated by Saint Catherine.

Sacred Covenant Behaviors
Respecting Life

The concept of respect for life is so ingrained in the practice of caring for the sick that there is little discussion on the topic in the professional literature. For those whose primary tasks are to promote health and facilitate healing, respect for the sanctity of human life in paramount in their vocation. Comments shared by nurses in the author's past research reflect the importance placed upon the attribute of respecting and supporting those for whom they care. One example of respect for life is embedded in the words of a community health nurse who worked with the poor and underserved: "Most of my patients are underprivileged and when I go talk to them or visit them at home, I see myself as being of service... I'm trying to find the right words to be respectful, being as a servant... I see nursing as a blessed call to serve, especially those who are not as fortunate as I"[752]; and the head nurse of a critical care unit shared her perception that:

> Seeing nursing as a vocation, makes respect in caring for the individual paramount. It helps to bring to the front of my mind how indeed the power of using myself in serving others, in being there to serve, makes the work that I do not only better but more joyful. In working with other human beings and seeing their worthiness, and literally seeing God in them, you can't help but expect from yourself the best job you could possibly do.[753]

As well as having a spirit of tenderness toward the sick for whom she cared, Saint Catherine had a deep respect for the dignity of all human life, even for the lives of those considered sinners or criminals; perhaps it was because she described herself as a "sinner who was loved" by the Lord. Catherine often visited prisoners at the local jail and sometimes spent the night counseling them and praying with them. A moving anecdote related by Blessed Raymond provides an example of the saint's respect for the lives of two men who had been condemned as vicious criminals.

Raymond tells us that in this tale we will see how God's mercy, obtained through Catherine's merit, was given to two men who he described as "sinners already well-nigh dammed"[754]:

> By order of the chief justice two malefactors were arrested in Siena, and for their heinous crimes condemned to a most cruel death; they were to be put in a cart, bound to a post, and tortured by the executioners in different parts of their bodies with hooks and red-hot pincers. Neither in prison nor on the point of being led out to die did they show any desire to repent of their misdeeds nor would they confess to the priest.[755]

Raymond explained that the criminals were led through the streets in the cart, while being tortured, as a warning to others in the city.

As it happened on the morning of the criminals' punishment, Catherine was visiting a companion, Alessia, who saw the cart approaching from her window and alerted the saint to the painful scenario taking place with the plea: "O, mother! If ever you will see a pitiful sight, come now."[756] "In the street surged and roared a great crowd round an open cart, in which sat two wretched men, notorious brigands, who having been caught, were expiating part of their sentence on the way to the scaffold. Tightly bound to the stakes, their flesh was being torn from their bodies by the executioners."[757] Catherine's heart was deeply moved by the plight of the criminals and she immediately began to pray to God to have pity on the men. She implored the Lord with the following words: "My most merciful Lord, why do you show such contempt for your creatures, made in your image and likeness and mercifully redeemed by your precious blood, and permit them to be tortured in the flesh, and tortured more cruelly still by the spirits of hell?... I, therefore beg you in the name of all your mercy to care for these two souls and succor them."[758]

When the men arrived at the city gate, our Lord appeared to them asked them to repent of their crimes and promised them forgiveness. "Full of sorrow He (Christ) looked into the eyes and hearts of the sinners, and suddenly their defiance broke."[759]

"A ray of the divine light penetrated their hearts; they asked repeatedly for the priest and confessed their sins to him with visible signs of grief. Then they turned their blasphemies into songs of praise and... proclaimed that they would arrive at glory through their very tortures, which were the proof of great mercy."[760]

Those present, witnessing the criminals change of heart, were amazed and even "the torturers themselves were moved by the sight of such devotion and did not dare continues their cruelties."[761]

Another scenario which reflects Saint Catherine's respect for the sanctity of life relates to her willingness, even though sometimes reluctant, to be available to minister to anyone in need of care in whatever situation she found herself. One day, while traveling, the saint was resting at an Inn; she wished to remain anonymous. The Innkeeper, nevertheless, gave out the news that Catherine was within and crowds of people began to seek her out. One of the women was carrying a little boy whose body was badly swollen, especially his stomach. At first Catherine refused to engage in a healing ministry "in order to avoid worldly praises."[762] But, touched by pity for the sick child and his mother's faith, she agreed to hold him with the result that "she had hardly taken the little boy in her arms when he began to expel wind, and his body was seen to go down and recover perfect health."[763]

In the above anecdotes, especially in Catherine's concern for the souls of the condemned criminals, we find telling examples of the saint's respect for human life. This is a respect for the dignity of human life to which all caregivers to the sick are called. Saint Catherine had no thought of condemning the criminals; she made no judgment. Instead, the Virgin who could not save the men's earthly lives immediately took to prayer, begging the Lord to grant them the gift of repentance and thus the blessing of eternal salvation. While we may see only sinfulness in the criminals' behavior, Catherine saw only the potential for goodness; she respected the men's humanity and the Lord responded to her prayerful intercession.

Being Present

Repeatedly those who minister to the sick describe the act of being present as a key component of the spirituality of caring. For an anxious or depressed person, fearful of the implications of an illness trajectory, the presence of a caring nurse, physician, chaplain or pastoral care team member can provide consolation and hope.

174

An understanding of the importance of presence in caring for the sick is contained in the comments of the supervisor of a medical clinic who observed: "There is a way of having a caring presence with your patients. This is the time that you spend with the patients, listening with your heart to what they reflect in their attitude, their tone of voice, their facial concern... there is a feeling of trust, a feeling of presence, of being there for them."

Another nurse linked the concept of "listening" to the meaning of being present to her patients: "I learned... that just listening to patients, really listening with the heart, was one of the greatest healers for many kinds of suffering. Listening and being present with a caring heart can heal loneliness, fear, anger, grief and so many painful emotions that a patient may be suffering from."[764]

One of the acts of ministry most frequently commented upon by Catherine's biographers was that of her counseling and being present to a young Perugian nobleman by the name of Niccolo di Toldo. We are told that the youth had been sentenced to execution for carelessly speaking ill of a city official. The punishment was, according to Dominican Friar Martin Gillet, "quite common in that day, for political indiscretion." Niccolo had, in fact, "been condemned to death for a trifling thing, a few thoughtless words spoken out of bravado when under the influence of wine at a banquet."[765]

Father Joseph-Marie Perrin observed that we know about the case of Niccolo "from the account which Catherine gave, without mentioning his name, in one of her letters to Friar Raymond of Capua."[766] Biographer Thomas Luongo agreed, but also pointed out that there are other sources of knowledge about Catherine's ministry to Niccolo di Toldo as well. Although Blessed Raymond does not mention the ministry in his *Legenda Major*, it is discussed by Fr. Tommaso d'Antonio Caffarini in two of his works the *"Processo Castellano,"* a collection of testimonies about Catherine's sanctity and the *Leggenda Minore*, a shorter version of Raymond's *Legenda*.[767] In the *Leggenda Minore* Fra Caffarini described the event briefly and mentioned Niccolo di Toldo by name.[768]

In the *Processo Castellano*, Fra Tommaso gave specific details of the case, of his personal witness and of Catherine's intervention:

> Indeed once I went to the communal prison with her (Catherine) to visit one condemned to death, a young nobleman from Perugia who name was Niccolo di Toldo. He had been employed in some function by

the then senator of Siena, and during some unrest had ill-famed the senator of something concerning the city-state. For this he found himself thus sentenced without remedy, and chose to throw himself into the abyss of desperation. The virgin heard of him and as she was entirely jealous for the health of souls, so it happened that he who had at first paced his cell like a ferocious and desperate lion, by means of the virgin's presence, was so restored that he went devout and willing, just like a gentle lamb born to the slaughter, to the place of beheading. And thus he accepted death while still at a young age, in the presence of the Virgin, and with her receiving his head into her hands, with such marvelous devotion that it was like the transitus of some devout martyr and not the death of one who was condemned for a human crime. And everyone watching, among whom I was one, was so moved internally and from the heart that I do not remember any previous burial accompanied with as much devotion as that one.[769]

Johannes Jorgensen also related that, when Fra Tomasso first visited Niccolo in his cell, "he found him in a state of wild despair. He walked up and down like a madman, and would not make his confession or listen either to a monk of a priest... let them believe in God and love him if they liked. God was good to them and let them live."[770] Augusta Drane explained that finally Niccolo, in his "utter misery," thought of Catherine whom he had heard of but never met, "so forsaken of every other hope, the unhappy youth dispatched a messenger, and implored her to come to him in prison."[771] It was pointed out that "Catherine had to act fast" as Sienese executions were generally carried out very shortly after a sentence was pronounced, so she quickly prepared herself, met Tommaso Caffarini and "together they visited Niccolo in his prison cell."[772]

Catherine's commitment to being present to those who were suffering and dying is lauded by Edmund Gardner who commented that the saint was not repulsed by "the blood that splashed the streets and palaces of the Italian cities in the fierce faction-fights, the blood that is poured out upon the scaffold at the Sienese place of execution," but that it rather "fires her imagination and seems shed by Love itself."[773] He added: "We find the fullest realization of this in one of the most beautiful and famous of her letters, that to Fra Raimondo, describing the end of the young noble, Niccolo di Toldo."[774] This document, identified as Letter T273 is described by translator and editor Suzanne Noffke OP as one of Catherine's most "remarkable and famous" letters.[775] "This letter," biographer Giuliana Cavallini declared, "has been deemed sufficient in itself to qualify its author as a great writer; the human appeal of its dramatic character has made it one of the most popular, and the mystery about the sentenced man has fostered research."[776]

In the letter to Blessed Raymond, Catherine herself narrated the ministry to Niccolo without using his name: "I went to visit the one you know and he was so comforted and consoled that he confessed his sins and prepared himself very well. He made me promise for the love of God that when the time came for the execution I would be with him. This I promised and did."[777]

Catherine described taking Niccolo to Mass and providing the opportunity for him to receive the Holy Eucharist. She then said to him:

> Courage my dear brother, for soon we shall reach the wedding feast. You will go forth to it bathed in the sweet blood of God's Son, with the sweet name of Jesus, which I don't want ever to leave your memory. I shall wait for you at the place of execution... And, he said: "I shall go all joyful and strong, and when I think that you will be waiting for me there, it will seem a thousand years until I get there."[778]

Catherine continued:

> I waited for him at the place of execution. I waited there in continual prayer... I prayed and pleaded with Mary that I wanted this grace, that at his last moment she would give him light and peace of heart and afterwards see him return to his destination... Then he arrived like a meek lamb, and when he saw me he began to laugh and wanted me to make the sign of the cross on him. When he had received the sign I said: "Down for the wedding, my dear brother, for soon you will be in everlasting life!" He knelt down very meekly; I placed his neck (on the block) and bent down and reminded him of the blood of the Lamb. His mouth said nothing but "Gesu!" and "Caterina" and as he said this, I received his head into my hands, saying "I will!" with my eyes fixed on divine Goodness.[779]

Fra Tommaso Caffarini added, in a personal comment, that "at the moment when the axe fell, Catherine received the head into her hands being in ecstasy. Her eyes were fixed on heaven, and her eyelids motionless, so she remained for a long space. The spectators were all in tears, and declared they were witness the death of a martyr rather than the execution of a criminal."[780]

Saint Catherine own words reflected a similar conclusion: "Now that he was hidden away where he belonged, my soul rested in peace and quiet."[781]

In a contemporary article entitled "St. Catherine of Siena and the Spectacle of Public Execution," author Molly Morrison interprets Catherine's presence at Niccolo di Toldo's decapitation as "an example of a successful comforting ritual." Such rituals, Morrison pointed out, were"

> Commonly carried out by members of medieval confraternities who aided criminals about to be publicly executed...the comforter's main function was to strengthen the condemned prisoner in the time remaining before his impending doom. Since the eternal salvation of the prisoner was paramount, the comforter was to prepare him to make his last confession and receive the Eucharist.[782]

Morrison concludes that Catherine's narrative, as presented in her letter to Blessed Raymond, "clearly shows her as a comforter"[783] and adds: "Essentially the comforter's goal was to transform the gruesome event of public execution into a type of reenactment of the death of Christ or one of the martyrs. The comforter stayed with the condemned right up until the last, distracting him from the horror about to occur. Even the most dreaded moments were turned into a means of consolation."[784]

Saint Catherine's gift of being a "comforter," of being present for young Niccolo, both in prison and at the execution, provides a powerful example of the importance a caregiver's presence can be to one who is suffering. Professional caregivers, whether physician, nurse, or chaplain, cannot always end or even alleviate a patient's suffering; this is especially true for those whose illness has progressed to the stage described as "end of life." Catherine could not prevent Niccolo's death; she could not completely take away his anxiety about the sentence, but she could and did promise and provide him with her loving presence as his execution was carried out.

How often have we not heard ill seniors share thoughts to the effect that they were not afraid of death, rather it was "getting there" that worried them? Elders, in particular, often fear being alone when death comes; will anyone be there to comfort and console them in their final moments? How blessed we are as caregivers to be able to provide that loving presence for a dying person; to, as is sometimes described by hospice nurses, "midwife" patients at their birth into eternal life. The remarks of two nurses who had worked with the terminally ill reflect the presence of "midwifing the dying." One, a masters prepared clinician with 21 years of nursing experience, a significant portion of which involved working with patients at the end of life observed: "I help patients cross-over in the last few days. Part of our job is like being midwives in assisting people in getting to that next state, to their new life in God." And a pediatric oncology nurse with extensive experience in working with dying children shared a poignant midwifing experience with a little boy of five: "I bonded with him and with the family. When he was dying we picked him up and we held him and prayed with him and sang to him, and I felt like a midwife; that was really a gift. Being a midwife to him; it was like helping him to be born into eternal life."[785]

Comforting with Compassion

An expanded definition of compassion that includes the concept of presence and which is particularly appropriate for ministry to those who are ill, is offered by theologian Michael Downey:

> Compassion is the capacity to be attracted and moved by the fragility, weakness and suffering of another. It is the ability to be vulnerable enough to undergo risk and loss for the good of another. Compassion involves a movement to be of assistance to the other, but it is ineluctably a movement of participation in the experience of the other in order to be present and available in solidarity and communion. Compassion requires sensitivity to what is weak and/or wounded, as well as the vulnerability to be affected by the other. It also demands action to alleviate pain and suffering.[786]

A head nurse described compassion as central to her calling: "Seeing nursing as a calling, I think makes me more compassionate as a nurse. I empathize with my patients. I can be more filled with compassionate care. I'm with them and it's not just the tasks I do for them but also being there for their emotional needs... these people are depending on me"[787]; and another added:

I was attracted to nursing out of a deep compassion for human beings and to be able to alleviate suffering in some way. If I can just give someone a hand because we all go through this-the suffering the patient is going through. And, nursing is a form of reconnecting with humanity because we're all part of the human family. They say that sorrow shared is divided and joy shared is multiplied. And that is what really happens in nursing.[788]

As previously demonstrated in Saint Catherine's ministry to the sick, a hallmark of her caring interactions was the saint's tender comfort; regardless of a person's position, beliefs or previous life situation, Catherine was unfailingly merciful and compassionate to those who were ill. She did not wish to see anyone suffer unnecessarily if she could provide care which might lead to either physical or spiritual healing. Dominican Mary Ann Fatula observed that it was by the experience of personal suffering that Catherine learned mercy and compassion; in light of Catherine's teaching, Fatula advised: "If we ourselves try to see with the eyes of God's love, we can learn to focus on others' goodness rather than on their failings, and in this way, turn our judgment into one of mercy and God's own compassion."[789]

A significant example of Saint Catherine's compassionate caregiving was that extended to the woman Bartolomea, who was seriously injured in an accident at her residence. One day a balcony of the woman's home, which was filled with heavy things, gave way suddenly while Bartolomea was standing on it; she fell some distance and had multiple cuts and bruises. Although a physician was called to treat her, Bartolomea still complained of severe pain. When Catherine heard about the injuries, she went immediately to Bartolomea to try and comfort her. "Seeing that she was suffering such agonies, Catherine touched the parts that were hurting her as though soothing them, and the victim allowed her to do so because she was sure that only good could come from contact with her."[790]

Raymond explained that "as the virgin's hand passed from one painful spot to another, the pain vanished. When, she realized this, the woman begged Catherine to put her hand on one particular spot, which the virgin willing did... and the pain vanished."[791] Bartolomea continued to beg Catherine to touch her injuries, "until the moment came when she who a little while before had been unable to make the slightest bodily movement began to turn this way and that, obviously quite

180

recovered."[792] Similar details of the event were also recorded by Fra Tommaso Caffarini in his *Supplemento Alla Vita di Santa Caterina da Siena*.[793] Augusta Drane reported that, "The woman kept silence whilst Catherine was present lest she might alarm her humility, but afterwards she said to the physicians and neighbors who surrounded her: 'Catherine, Lapa's daughter, has cured me by touching me.'"[794]

In two other occurrences, described as "healings" by Blessed Raymond, Saint Catherine's compassion was called upon; these cases involved individuals suffering from serious physical distress, one from a long-term fever and the other with a painful throat condition.

In the first instance, an acquaintance of Catherine, Gherardo dei Buonconti, introduced the Virgin to a young man of around 20 years, begging her to pray for his health. The youth "had been plagued almost continuously for eighteen months by quotidian fever (a form of intermittent but recurring fever); he had lost all his strength and there was no medicine that seemed to give it back to him. The young man's thin, pale face confirmed these words. The virgin, moved to compassion, at once asked the youth how long it was since he had been to confession."[795]

Gherardo's friend admitted that he had not confessed for many years. Catherine told him that she believed that this neglect of the sacrament was associated with his sickness and advised: "Go, therefore, and wash away the sins that affect your soul, for they are the real cause of your bodily infirmity."[796] After confessing to a priest, he returned to Saint Catherine "who put her arm round his shoulders and said: 'Go, son, with the peace of our Lord Jesus Christ, for I do not want you to suffer from the fever any more,'"[797] From that time on, the young man's fever ceased.

Another person, whose illness was brought to Saint Catherine's attention, was a Sister of Penance of St. Dominic, suffering from a throat condition, which the physicians had labeled "quinzy" (peritonseller abscess): "When the secretions began to descend from the head to the throat she failed to do anything about it and so aggravated the condition that treatment that had at first seemed to do it good became absolutely ineffective. The inside of her throat, which was already constricted to begin with, was growing more constricted every day and threatening to suffocate" her.[798]

When Saint Catherine, whose help the Sister of Penance sought, saw the seriousness of the condition, "she had compassion on the woman who could hardly breathe."[799] Catherine put her hand on the Sister's throat, made the sign of the cross, and the woman was soon cured.

Throughout the earlier chapters of this book myriad examples of Saint Catherine's compassion are described; compassion for those with stigmatizing diseases such as leprosy or plague; compassion for those who were looked down upon because of their lifestyle; compassion for prisoners; and compassion for all who were suffering from physical or emotional distress.

In those examples as well as in the three cases described above, Catherine's example challenges today's caregivers not to fail in compassionate ministry to those who are ill. With the injured Bartolomea, the feverish young man, and the Sister experiencing "quinsy," Catherine consistently used her gift of compassionate caring to alleviate the ill or injured person's suffering. While present day caregivers may not be possessed of Saint Catherine's gift of healing, we do have many tools in our therapeutic arsenals which may be used in compassionate care and comfort for a suffering patient.

Creating Bonds

The concept of healthcare ministers bonding with patients, creating bonds of caring and mutual respect, is central to the sanctity of the caregiver-patient relationship. When true concern is demonstrated on the part of a minister to the sick, mutual bonds of caring, reflecting the covenantal nature of the partnership may emerge.

In the words of a nursing supervisor: "I feel that nursing itself is a type of ministry to the sick. We have a special bond with patients that is unique... I feel that we are called to a higher calling as we are a spiritual profession in a way that we understand the whole person, as he or she is."[800] And a critical care nurse commented: "When you make a connection with people who are sick, as a nurse, it becomes personal. And you begin to realize that you have a real impact on their lives. You can't help but know that you are in a relationship that is something beyond the client and the person serving. You can say 'I helped that patient.'"[801]

One of Saint Catherine's gifts was her ability to establish bonds with those who became her companions and disciples and also with those to whom she ministered. Catherine had established bonds of friendship with numerous patients and staff members at the great *Santa Maria della Scala* hospital, the largest healthcare facility in Siena, as well as at the more modest institution: *Casa della Miseracordia*. She had created a special bond of friendship with the *Miseracordia*'s Rector, Matteo di Cenni dei Fazio.

Rector Matteo was described as having "a quality about charity which immediately appealed to Catherine. He directed his little world with an impassive kind of efficiency which spoke of the burning flame in his breast."[802] As a friendship grew between them, Rector Matteo confided to Catherine "that his youth had been dissolute and that his present life was an act of reparation."[803] The Rector or administrator of the 14th-century Sienese hospital such as the *Miseracordia*, committed his life and all of his possessions to the institution. Even though not a consecrated religious, he and his Brothers in the lay confraternity serving the hospital made promises of poverty, chastity and obedience; Matteo, as the hospital rector, was also the superior of the confraternity of Brothers.

In the *Legenda*, Blessed Raymond recounted a visit to *Casa della Miseracordia* in which he learned the distressing news that the rector, his friend Matteo, had been taken ill with symptoms of the plague. Matteo was a "greatly respected man who led a good and holy life; the whole of Siena was grieving at the prospect of losing him."[804] This occurred during the 1374 plague outbreak which overwhelmed the hospitals in Siena; Matteo, and his Brothers, had been working day and night to care for the ill who were brought to their door. The *Miseracordia* was considered a "focal point in the battle against the plague."[805] Raymond related that as he entered the *Miseracordia* hospital he "found Matteo being carried from the church to his own room by the brothers and clerks, like one dead. He had lost his usual color and all his strength and power of speech, for when I asked him how he felt he was unable to reply."[806]

When Blessed Raymond asked what had happened, he was told: "Last night, at about seven, while he was tending one of the sick, the plague attacked him in the groin and in a short time reduced him to the state in which you now see him."[807] Raymond then heard Matteo's confession, gave him absolution and asked again how he felt. At this point Matteo replied that he had severe pain in his groin and headache. Raymond felt his pulse and skin and discovered that Matteo was suffering from a fever; he requested that a physician be called. The doctor's message, after observing Matteo's urine, was grave: "This water shows that there is blood in the liver, a common feature of the pestilence; and I am therefore afraid that the *Miseracordia* will soon find itself without its worthy rector."[808] When Raymond asked if there was any kind of medicine that may be used to heal Matteo, the physician replied: "We will see tomorrow but to tell you truly, I have small hope of doing him any good, the disease is too far gone."[809] In the meantime Raymond reported:

> Catherine had heard that Matteo had been struck down by the plague. As she was very fond of him because of his virtues, she hastened to see him fired by charity and, as though angry with the plague itself, and even before she reached him she started shouting from a distance, "Get up, Messer Matteo, get up, this is no time for lying in a soft bed." At the words of this command, the fever and the swelling in the groin and all the pain immediately disappeared and Matteo felt as well as if he had never been ill at all. Nature had obeyed God through the mouth of the virgin, and at the sound of her voice, his body had been restored to perfect health.[810]

Because of the bonds of friendship which Saint Catherine developed with her followers, many others came to trust her caring and her unique ability to heal the ill with her prayers, her comfort and her encouraging words. Two of the saint's younger disciples also found themselves in grave need of Catherine's gift for healing of sickness; they were Neri di Landoccio dei Pagliaresi and his friend, Stefano di Corrado de Maconi.

Neri di Landoccio, who had been traveling with Catherine in Genoa, came down with acute and painful intestinal distress: "he was tormented continuously day and night by atrocious pains in his bowels; when the attacks came upon him he would howl piteously, and no bed could hold him. Being unable to stand upright, he would crawl round amongst all the beds in the room as though trying to escape from the pain."[811] When Blessed Raymond described Neri's suffering to Catherine, she "told him to call the doctors in and get him to have the usual medical treatment."[812] Raymond did as Catherine had requested: "I got hold of two doctors and we followed their instructions meticulously; but Neri, instead of getting better, got worse... the doctors, in fact, continued to treat him, but as there was no improvement in his condition, they... had lost all hope of saving him."[813]

Finally, Neri's comrade, Stefano, begged Catherine to pray for Neri that his life be saved, which she promised to do. Stefano rushed to Neri's bedside to encourage his friend with the promise of the virgin's prayers. The physicians returned again to discover that Neri had taken a turn for the better and ultimately was restored to health.

After Neri had recovered from his illness, however, Stefano took sick with symptoms of a high fever and vomiting, as well as a severe headache. His companions all felt it was a result of Stefano's long hours of care and worry over Neri's illness. Catherine went to visit Stefano, as soon as she heard of his condition. "When she realized that he had a violent fever, she said in a sudden fervor of spirit: 'I command you by the power of holy obedience not to suffer from this fever any longer'. Blessed Raymond commented that it seemed as if "nature obeyed the virgin's voice as though it had been the voice of the Creator Himself...the fever disappeared and Stefano was perfectly all right again."[814]

In the anecdotes describing the bonds which Catherine established with those for whom she cared, we are given examples of the value of such positive patient-caregiver bonding. Catherine had gotten to know Matteo di Cenni, the Rector of *Casa della Miseracordia* Hospital, during her service there; the two had a mutual respect and admiration for their respective ministries to the sick. While his friends and even a physician thought that Matteo was dying of the plague, Catherine believed otherwise. She knew her patient well. Thus, the saint, who was usually so gentle with those who were ailing, was confident in challenging Matteo with the message: "Get up, this is no time for lying in a soft bed." Catherine teaches us that knowing our patients and bonding with them will help us understand how to approach and assist them in their illness: when to use gentle kindness and compassion and when a firm hand is in order. The ability to distinguish when to use either of these approaches is a blessed gift for a caregiver.

Becoming an Advocate

Patient advocacy is another important component of caregiving for those who minister to the sick. Frequently, an ill person is either unable or unwilling to advocate for his or her own needs. It is the caregiver who must step in to assure that a patient's needs are being truly and completely met.

A medical-surgical nurse asserted: "You really have to become a patient advocate more than anything. Nursing was a vocation 23 years ago when I started and it is still a vocation now... I think the more you do it (nursing), the more you want to care for the patient because you know their needs, you know what needs to be done."[815] And a pediatric nurse gave a clinical example of being an advocate:

> I can give you a perfect example of patient advocacy in pediatrics. A child in a burn unit was going to be bathed after bandage removal so that she could be debrided; the child had had the treatment a couple of times and was obviously terrified because it caused a lot of pain. So, I said "Let's get her medicated before we start"; she only had Tylenol ordered... I said, "Let's call the doctor... I won't create that kind of pain in a child." So we called the doctor and got the appropriate dose of narcotic... He ordered Morphine, as we gave it and we waited for it to (take effect) get to her leg. The nurse concluded: "It was really a matter for me that I'm here to bring comfort, to be an advocate. I'm here to serve."[816]

As noted in Chapter Five, one group of persons for whom Catherine expressed great concern were those who suffered from traumatic injuries associated with feud-related violence. Catherine believed in prevention and promotion of health and thus engaged in counseling and advocacy for those involved in local feuds whenever possible; her goal was to prevent injuries before they occurred. One of the Sienese citizens who came to Catherine's attention was a man well known for his involvement in feuding named Nanni di Ser Vanni.

Blessed Raymond described Nanni as suffering from "one of the cities' worst characteristics; he was quite incapable of keeping the peace with anyone and was always starting private feuds; setting traps for people and then pretending to know nothing about it."[817] Nanni di Ser vanni was involved in a particularly dire feud in which one man had already been killed but he refused to settle the matter. When Catherine learned of this she tried to meet with him and "bring the unfortunate affair to an end but Nanni avoided her as a snake avoids a charmer."[818]

Raymond was finally able to broker a meeting between the man and Catherine and although Nanni had insisted that he "had no intention of mending his ways," the saint began to point out the "mortal peril he was in,"[819] In an attempt to soften a little, after meeting Catherine, Nanni admitted that he was currently enmeshed in four feuds, one of which he

186

would put in the saint's hands but the others he would continue to be involved with.[820] Catherine thus became Nanni's advocate through her intercessory prayer.

When the saint began to pray silently for Nanni di Ser Vanni, something touched his heart; he suddenly assented to the virgin's wish for an end to all the feuds, admitting: "My God, how contented I feel in my soul from having said I shall make peace!" And he went on; "Lord, God, what power is this that draws and holds me?... I own myself beaten... Most holy virgin, I will do as you say, not only as regards the enemy I told you about but with all the others too... Tell me how I can save my soul from the Devil's clutches."[821]

"Subsequently," Raymond reported, Nanni "was subjected to illnesses," but his devotion greatly increased, and "he gave many gifts to the church because of the transformation of his life."[822]

Catherine also assumed an advocacy role for one of her companions by the name of Giovanna di Capo. While Saint Catherine was traveling in Florence with some of her disciples, Giovanna, became ill unexpectedly. Although no reason could be found, one of her feet swelled up and she developed a fever: "handicapped as she was by these two complaints, she found it impossible to accompany the rest of the party."[823] Catherine did not want to leave Giovanna alone for fear that she might be treated badly by some of the criminals in the city, so she took to prayer begging the Lord to heal the woman so that she could accompany the group on their travels. Raymond described the outcome of Catherine's prayerful advocacy: "The woman fell into a sweet sleep while Catherine was praying and when she woke up she found herself perfectly well again. She got up out of bed and prepared for the journey, and that same morning she was travelling along the road with the virgin and the rest of the party, more hale and hearty than she had been in years."[824]

In many, perhaps most, caregiving situations the person ministering to one who is ill becomes an advocate. Patient advocacy is part of the calling of professionals in the healthcare system, whether nurse, physician, chaplain, or other member of the medical team. Sometimes creativity needs to be employed to gain acquiescence to our advocacy from the person being supported. Catherine displayed her personal faith and hope in communicating with Nanni di Ser Vanni. Even though Blessed Raymond tells us that Nanni avoided Catherine like "a snake avoids a charmer," the saint used her spiritual gift of trusting prayer to advocate for Nanni's soul as well as his body. Nanni di Ser Vanni's life was ultimately transformed by Saint Catherine's advocacy. Patient advocacy in the 21st Century also has the potential to bring about a transformation in an ill person's life and illness trajectory.

In this chapter Saint Catherine's ministry to the ailing has been explored as a sacred covenant of caring for the sick. Case examples are presented for the three attributes of the spirituality of caring: a calling of service, a blessed trust, and a commitment to reverence. Patient care scenarios are described for each of the behavioral themes identified in the model: respecting life, being present, comforting with compassion, creating bonds, and becoming an advocate. It is clear from the many illustrations of Catherine's attention to the ill and infirm that the saint did indeed practice a sacred covenant of caring. It is also clear that Saint Catherine of Siena truly deserves to be honored and revered as the "patroness" of all those who care for the sick.

Brief Chronology of Saint Catherine's Life

1347-Born in Siena on March 25th

1354-Vow of virginity at age seven

1363-Entered the Sisters of Penance of St. Dominic (the Mantellate) at age sixteen

1363-66-Lived for three years in contemplative solitude in the Benincasa home

1367-Began active ministry of caring for the sick and the poor in their homes, in the hospitals in the community and in the prisons

1374-Called to Florence for a general chapter of the Dominicans; returned to Siena in the summer and began caring for victims of the bubonic plague

1375-1380- Engaged in ministry to the clergy through visits and letter writing; dictated spiritual counsel later included in the *Dialogue and the Letters*

1380-Catherine's soul entered eternal life on April 29th

1461- Canonized a saint of the Church by Pope Pius II on January 29th

1970-Accorded the title "Doctor of the Church" by Pope Paul VI on October 4th

For a more detailed chronology of Saint Catherine's life and ministries see: Thomas McDermott OP, *Catherine of Siena: Spiritual Development in Her Life and Teaching*, Mahwah, N.J.: Paulist Press, 2008, pp. 7-10.

Epilogue. Catherine of Siena: Contemplative and Caregiver

The aim of the phenomenological research, upon which the book is based, was to identify, describe and analyze data reflective of the principles guiding Catherine of Siena's Mantellata vocation to care for the sick. The hope is that an understanding of the saint's 14th-century ministry to the ill, lived out as a sacred covenant of caring, can serve to inspire 21st-century healthcare providers seeking to embrace a similar calling.

While today's caregivers may not be able to mirror Saint Catherine's selfless commitment to caring for the sick, we can view her as the "ideal type" of healthcare minister; that is, as one whose spirituality of caring we may admire and prayerfully strive to imitate.

Catherine's image was that of a compassionate caregiver wholly dedicated to alleviating the suffering of the ill and the infirm; she was, also, a passionate contemplative continually seized by the wonder of God's presence and His love. The saint's spirituality of caring for the sick might well be reflected in the following prayer:

"The Prayer of a Contemplative Caregiver"

O God of magnificence and mystery, what must you be who gifted life with such beauty and such grace. Teach me to contemplate You, through tender care for the sacredness of all human life. Help me to revere the gifts of my ill brothers and sisters; to see in each person a reflection of Your face. Help me to love those I serve in their strengths and in their weaknesses; in caring for them, may I care for You, my Lord and my God. Let my caregiving become an unceasing hymn of praise to Your glory, that I may pray with the psalmist:

O Lord, our God, how awesome is your Name through all the earth. What are humans that You are mindful of them; mere mortals that You care for them? Yet you

191

have made them little less than a god; crowned them with glory and honor. You have given them rule over the works of Your hands, put all things under their feet...O Lord, our God, how awesome is Your Name through all the earth" (Psalm 8). Amen.[825]

St. Catherine of Siena pray for us!

Endnotes

Prologue

[1] Thomas M. Schwertner, "Preface" in *Saint Catherine of Siena: Her Life and Times* by Claire Mary Antony (St. Louis, Mo.: B. Herder, 1916), xvi-xvii.

Chapter 1. "A Heart Drawn by Love"

[2] See Dominican Thomas McDermott's website: *"Drawn by Love: The Mysticism of Catherine of Siena"*, http://www.drawnbylove.com/; also Thomas McDermott's books: *"Catherine of Siena: Spiritual Development in Her Life and Teaching"*, NY.: Paulist Press, 2008 and *"Filled with the Fullness of God: An Introduction to Catholic Spirituality"*, N.Y.: Bloomsbury, 2013.

[3] Augusta Theodosia Drane, *The History of St. Catherine of Siena and Her Companions* (London: Burns and Oates, 1880), 66.

[4] Ibid.

[5] Ibid., 45

[6] Edmund G. Gardner, *Saint Catherine of Siena: A Study in the Religion, Literature and History of the Fourteenth Century in Italy* (New York: E.P. Dutton & Co., 1907), 113.

[7] In this work the term "caregiver" is used as a generic descriptor for all those who minister to the sick including nurses, physicians, technicians, chaplains, pastoral care staff and other members of the healthcare team who attend to the needs of the ill and the infirm.

[8] Kenelm Foster and Mary John Ronayne, I, *Catherine: Selected Writings of St. Catherine of Siena* (London: Collins, 1980), 12.

[9] Suzanne Noffke, *Catherine of Siena: Vision Through a Distant Eye* (Collegeville, Minn: The Liturgical Press, 1996), 155.

[10] Martin S.Gillet, The Mission of St. Catherine, trans. Maria T. Lopez (St. Louis, Mo: B. Herder Book Co., 1946), 68-69.

[11] Alice Curtayne, *Saint Catherine of Siena* (Rockford, Ill: Tan Books and Publishers Inc., 1980), 10.

[12] Ibid.

[13] Claire Mary Antony, *Saint Catherine of Siena: Her life and Times* (St. Louis, Mo: B. Herder, 1916), 43.

[14] Raymond of Capua, *"The Life of St. Catherine of Siena"*, trans. George Lamb (Charlotte, NC: Tan Books, 2011), 3.

[15] Gillet, 14.

[16] Antony, 1.

[17] Arrigo Levasti, *My Servant Catherine*, trans. Dorothy M. White (Westminster, Md: The Newman Press, 1954), 2.

[18] Gillet, 17-18.

[19] Antony, 2.

[20] Raymond of Capua, 8.

[21] Antony, 8.

[22] Ibid., 8-9.

[23] Guiliana Cavallini, *Catherine of Siena* (New York: Wellington House, 1998), 100.

[24] Gillet, 77.

[25] Joseph Marie Perrin, *Catherine of Siena*, trans. Paul Barrett (Westminster, Md: The Newman Press, 1961), xiv.

[26] Catherine of Siena was officially canonized as a saint of the Roman Catholic Church in July of 1461 by Pope Pius II; she was accorded the title: "Doctor of the Church" by Pope Paul VI on October 4, 1970.

[27] Perrin, xvi.

[28] Ibid., xvi-xvii.

[29] Ibid., xiii.

[30] Ibid., xiv.

[31] Gillet, 72.

[32] Ibid., 72-73.

[33] Ibid., 73.

[34] Curtayne, xiii.

[35] Cavallini, 97.

[36] Maurice Powicke, *The Christian Life in the Middle Ages and Other Essays* (New York: Oxford University Press, 1966), p. 7.

[37] Bernard Guillemain, *The Later Middle Ages*, trans. S. Taylor (New York: Hawthorn Books, 1960), p. 82-89.

[38] John Adams, "Economic Change in Italy in the Fourteenth Century: The Case of Siena", *Journal of Economic Issues* 26:1 (1992): 125-134, 132.

[39] Gardner, 4.

[40] Ibid., 5.

[41] Cavallini, 109.

[42] William Caferro, "City and Countryside in Siena in the Second Half of the Fourteenth Century", *The Journal of Economic History* 54:1 (1994): 85-103.

[43] Gillet, 65.

[44] Igino Giordani, *Catherine of Siena: Fire and Blood*, trans. Thomas J Tobin (Milwaukee, WI: The Bruce Publishing Company, 1959), 3.

[45] Raymond of Capua, 9.

[46] Ibid.

[47] Gillet, 26.

[48] Raymond of Capua, 10.

[49] Antony, 7.

[50] Levasti, 9.

[51] Raymond of Capua, 11.

[52] Ibid., 10.

[53] Tom Grimwood, "The Body as a Lived Metaphor: Interpreting Catherine of Siena as an Ethical Agent", *Feminist Theology* 13:1 (2004): 62-76, 73.

[54] Patricia M. Vinje, *Praying with Catherine of Siena* (Winona, Minn.: Saint Mary's Press, 1990), 18.

[55] Ibid.

[56] Catherine of Siena, *The Dialogue*, translation and introduction by Suzanne Noffke O.P. (Mahwah, N.J.: Paulist Press, 1980), 158.

[57] Curtayne, 8.

[58] Raymond of Capua, 53.

[59] Sofia Cavalletti, *The Religious Potential of the Child*, trans. Patricia M. Coulter and Julie M. Coulter (Chicago: Liturgy Training Publications, 1992), 44.

[60] Ibid., 120.

[61] Margaret A. Burkhardt, "Spirituality and Children: Nursing Considerations", Journal of Holistic Nursing 9:2 (1991): 31-40, 34.

[62] George F. Handzo, "Talking About Faith with Children", *Journal of Christian Nursing* 7:4 (1990): 17-20, 17.

[63] Levasti, 11.

[64] Raymond of Capua, 15.

[65] Gillet, 29.

[66] Ibid., 30.

[67] Ibid.

[68] Giordani, 9.

[69] Judith Allen Shelly, "Jesus and the Children: A Mandate to Care", in *The Spiritual Needs of Children*, ed. Judith A. Shelly (Downer's Grove, Il.: Intervarsity Press, 1982), 11-16, 12.

[70] Perrin, xxxi.

[71] Shulamith Shahar, *Childhood in the Middle-Ages* (London: Routledge, 1990), 15.

[72] Ibid., 106.

[73] Ibid.

[74] Daniele Alexandre-Bidon and Didier Lett, Children in the Middle-Ages (Translation, Jody Gladding) (Notre Dame, Ind.: University of Notre Dame Press, 2000), 2.

[75] Ibid., 61.

[76] Ibid., 58.

[77] Raymond of Capua, 21

[78] Ibid., 24.

[79] Gardner, 11.

[80] Gardner, 11-12.

[81] Levasti, 15.

[82] Antony, 13.

[83] Ibid.

[84] Ibid.

[85] Gillet, 46.

[86] Raymond of Capua, 27.

[87] Antony, 15.

[88] Gillet, 49.

[89] Antony, 15.

[90] Raymond of Capua, 32.

[91] Ibid., 33.

[92] Ibid.

[93] Ibid.

[94] Giordani, 19.

Chapter 2. "On Two Wings You Must Fly"

[95] Raymond of Capua, *"The Life of St. Catherine of Siena"* (Translated by G. Lamb) (Charlotte, NC: Tan Books, 2011), 111.

[96] Ibid.

[97] Ibid., 91.

[98] Ibid., 91-92.

[99] Don Brophy, *Catherine of Siena: A Passionate Life* (New York: BlueBridge, 2010), 33.

[100] Ibid.

[101] Arrigo Levasti, *My Servant Catherine*, trans. Dorothy M. White (Westminster, Md: The Newman Press, 1954), 25.

[102] Martin S.Gillet, *The Mission of St. Catherine*, trans. Maria T. Lopez) (St. Louis, Mo: B. Herder Book Co., 1946), 53-54.

[103] Simon Tugwell, "Dominican Laity" in *Early Dominicans: Selected Writings*, ed. Simon Tugwell (Mahwah, N.J.: Paulist Press, 1982), 432-451, 432.

[104] Levasti, 26.

[105] Ibid., 27.

[106] Sigrid Undset, *Catherine of Siena*, trans. Kate Austin-Lund (San Francisco: Ignatius Press, 2009), 27.

[107] Claire Mary Antony, *Saint Catherine of Siena: Her life and Times* (St. Louis, Mo: B. Herder, 1916), 22.

[108] Raymond of Capua, 61.

[109] Augusta Theodosia Drane, *The History of St. Catherine of Siena and Her Companions* (London: Burns and Oates, 1880), 29.

[110] Ibid., 30.

[111] Raymond of Capua, 63.

[112] Drane, 31.

[113] Raymond of Capua, 64.

[114] Johannes Jorgensen, *Saint Catherine of Siena*, trans. Ingeborg Lund (London: Longmans, Green and Co., 1939), 33.

[115] Ibid.

[116] Drane, 27.

[117] Ibid.

[118] Ibid., 33.

[119] Raymond of Capua, 45.

[120] Undset, 34.

[121] Gillet, 56.

[122] Ibid.

[123] Raymond of Capua, 157.

[124] Drane, 35.

[125] Antony, 32.

[126] Ibid.

[127] Ibid., 25.

[128] Raymond of Capua, 83.

[129] Ibid., 81.

[130] Ibid.

[131] Ibid, 82.

[132] Igino Giordani, *Catherine of Siena: Fire and Blood*, trans. Thomas J. Tobin (Milwaukee, WI: The Bruce Publishing Company, 1959), 31.

[133] Ibid., 32.

[134] Ibid.

[135] Drane, 51.

[136] Ibid.

[137] Ibid.

[138] Antony, 26.

[139] Although Fra Tommaso della Fonte was Catherine's first confessor, the Saint had three other primary spiritual guides during her adult life. These were identified by Fr. Tommaso D'Antonio Caffarini in his deposition for the "Processo Castellano" (the document in support of Catherine's canonization), as Fra Bartolomeo Mantucci, Fra Bartolomeo Dominici and finally Fra Raimondo da Capua, who was to become Master of the Dominican Order after Catherine's death as noted by Martin Gillet, p. 38.

[140] Jorgensen, 36.

[141] Ibid., 52.

[142] Levasti, 40.

[143] Giordani, 22.

[144] Brophy, 41.

[145] Suzanne Noffke, "Catherine of Siena: Justly, Doctor of the Church?", *Theology Today* 60:1 (2003): 49-62, 61.

[146] Ibid.

[147] Ibid., 62.

[148] Karen Scott, "St. Catherine of Siena, 'Apostola'", *Church History* 61:1 (1992): 34-46, 36.

[149] Raymond of Capua, 88.

[150] Susan W. Rakoczy, "Transforming the Tradition of Discernment", *Journal of Theology for Southern Africa* 139 (2011): 91-109, 98.

[151] Raymond of Capua, 88.

[152] Ibid., 89.

[153] Ibid., 89-90.

[154] Ibid., 90.

[155] Ibid.

[156] Ibid.

[157] Antony, 42.

[158] Raymond of Capua, 87-88.

[159] Giordani, 36.

[160] Gillet, 164.

[161] Joseph Marie Perrin, *Catherine of Siena*, trans. Paul Barrett (Westminster, Md: The Newman Press, 1961), 95.

[162] Ibid.

[163] Ibid., 96.

[164] Antony, 34.

[165] Ibid.

[166] Jorgensen, 66.

[167] Drane, 61.

[168] Anne B. Baldwin, *Catherine of Siena: A Biography* (Huntington, In: Our Sunday Visitor Publishing Division, 1987), 38.

[169] Mary Ann Fatula, *Catherine of Siena's Way* (Wilmington, DE: Michael Glazier, 1989), 27.

[170] Ibid., 27-28.

[171] Gillet, 170.

[172] Giordani, 42.

[173] Thomas M. Schwertner, "Preface" in *Saint Catherine of Siena: Her Life and Times* by Claire M. Antony (St. Louis, Mo.: B. Herder, 1916), xvii.

[174] Gillet, 172.

[175] Ibid., 178.

Chapter 3. "Lose Yourself on the Cross"

[176] Thomas McDermott, *Catherine of Siena: Spiritual Development in Her Life and Teaching* (Mahwah, N.J.: Paulist Press, 2008), 101.

[177] Ibid.

[178] Algernon Charles Swinburne, *The Poems of Algernon Charles Swinburne*, Volume II (London: Chatto and Windus, 1911), 160-170.

[179] Ibid., 162.

[180] Ibid., 161.

[181] Raymond of Capua, *"The Life of St. Catherine of Siena"* (Translated by G. Lamb) (Charlotte, NC: Tan Books, 2011), 100.

[182] Catherine of Siena, *The Dialogue*, translation and introduction by Suzanne Noffke O.P. (Mahwah, N.J.: Paulist Press, 1980), 35; all citations from Saint Catherine's Dialogue contained in this work are taken from: Catherine of Siena, *"The Dialogue"*, translation and introduction by Suzanne Noffke OP, Mahwah, N.J.: Paulist Press, 1980.

[183] Ibid., 36.

[184] Ibid.

[185] Ibid., 37.

[186] Ibid., 37-38.

[187] Ibid., 38.

[188] Ibid.

[189] Ibid.

[190] Ibid., 39.

[191] Ibid., 121.

[192] Ibid.

[193] Mary Elizabeth O'Brien, *Servant Leadership in Nursing: Spirituality and Practice in Contemporary Health Care* (Burlington, MA: Jones & Bartlett Learning, 2011), 29.

[194] Ibid., 103.

[195] Ibid., 87.

[196] Ibid., 197.

[197] Ibid., 110.

[198] Raymond of Capua, 100.

[199] Ibid., 101.

[200] Augusta Theodosia Drane, *The History of St. Catherine of Siena and Her Companions* (London: Burns and Oates, 1880), 67.

[201] Ibid.

[202] Ibid., 68

[203] Ibid.

[204] Ibid., 71.

[205] Catherine of Siena, Letter T316, in Catherine of Siena, *The Letters of Catherine of Siena: Volume III*, translated with introduction and notes by Suzanne Noffke O.P. (Tempe, AZ: ACMRS Arizona Center for Medieval and Renaissance Studies, 2007), 328; in the present work the numbering of Saint Catherine's Letters is prefaced with the letter "T" which corresponds to the numbering of Italian linguist Niccolo Tommaseo as identified by Suzanne Noffke OP. For a complete history of prior translations and publications of the *Letters* see: "Introduction", in *The Letters of Catherine of Siena, Volume I*, translated with

introduction and notes by Suzanne Noffke OP, (Tempe, Arizona: Arizona Center for Medieval and Renaissance Studies, 2000), xvi-lvi.

[206] Letter T316, 328.

[207] Ibid., 331.

[208] Ibid.

[209] Raymond of Capua, 113.

[210] Mary Elizabeth O'Brien, *Spirituality in Nursing: Standing on Holy Ground*. (5th Edition). (Burlington, MA: Jones & Bartlett Learning, 2014), 343.

[211] Ibid., 343-364.

[212] Jeffrey A. Albaugh, "Resolving the Nursing Shortage: Finding Passion and Joy in Nursing", *Urologic Nursing* 25:1 (2005): 53-54, 54.

[213] Beverly Malone, "The Joy of Nursing", *Nursing Management* 9:1 (2002), 9-11, 11.

[214] Donna J. Middaugh, "Can There Really be Joy at Work?" *Medsurg Nursing* 23:2 (2014), 131-132, 132.

[215] Joseph Nassal, *The Conspiracy of Compassion: Breathing Together for a Wounded World* (Leavenworth, KS.: Forest of Peace Publishing, 1997), 49.

[216] Johannes Jorgensen, *Saint Catherine of Siena*, trans. Ingeborg Lund (London: Longmans, Green and Co., 1939), 13.

[217] Drane, 161.

[218] Ibid., 161-162.

[219] Timothy Radcliffe, "Preface" in *The New Wine of Dominican Spirituality* by Paul Murray (London: Bloomsbury, 2006), v-viii, vii.

[220] Paul Murray, *The New Wine of Dominican Spirituality* (New York: Bloomsbury, 2006), 169.

[221] Drane, 221-222.

[222] Richard Cardinal Cushing, *St. Catherine of Siena* (New York: St. Paul Editions, 1957), 26.

[223] Thomas McDermott, *Filled with the Fullness of God: An Introduction to Catholic Spirituality* (New York: Bloomsbury, 2013), 88.

[224] Ibid.

[225] McDermott, Catherine of Siena, 91.

[226] Edmund G. Gardner, *Saint Catherine of Siena: A Study in the Religion, Literature and History of the Fourteenth Century in Italy* (New York: E.P. Dutton & Co., 1907), 357.

[227] Joseph Marie Perrin, *Catherine of Siena*, trans. Paul Barrett (Westminster, Md: The Newman Press, 1961), 84-85.

[228] Giacinto D'Urso, *Catherine of Siena: Doctor of the Church, Notes on Her Life and Teaching*, translated with introduction and notes by Thomas McDermott OP (Chicago, Ill: New Priory Press, 2013), 57.

[229] Catherine of Siena, *Dialogue*, 64.

[230] Catherine of Siena, Letter T354, in *The Letters of Catherine of Siena: Volume IV*, translated with introduction and notes by Suzanne Noffke O.P. (Tempe, AZ: ACMRS Arizona Center for Medieval and Renaissance Studies, 2008), 244.

[231] Gardner, 357.

[232] Catherine of Siena, Letter T75, in *The Letters of Catherine of Siena: Volume II*, translated with introduction and notes by Suzanne Noffke O.P. (Tempe, AZ: ACMRS Arizona Center for Medieval and Renaissance Studies, 2001), 514-519, 517.

[233] McDermott, *Filled with the Fullness of God*, 90.

[234] Perrin, 85.

[235] McDermott, *Catherine of Siena*, 163.

[236] McDermott, *Filled with the Fullness of God*, 92.

[237] Perrin, 89.

[238] McDermott, *Catherine of Siena*, 169.

[239] McDermott, *Filled with the Fullness of God*, 92.

[240] McDermott, *Catherine of Siena*, 185.

[241] Perrin, 89.

[242] McDermott, *Catherine of Siena*, 93.

[243] Ibid., 192-193.

[244] D'Urso, 90-91.

[245] McDermott, *Catherine of Siena*, 192.

[246] Ibid., 193.

[247] Ibid.

[248] Elizabeth A. Dryer, *A Retreat with Catherine of Siena: Living the Truth in Love* (Cincinnati, OH: St. Anthony Messenger Press, 1999), 27.

[249] Ibid.

[250] Ibid.

[251] Ibid., 27-28.

[252] Thomas M. Schwertner, "Preface" in *Saint Catherine of Siena: Her Life and Times*, by Claire M. Antony (St. Louis, Mo.: B. Herder, 1916), xvi.

[253] Ibid.

[254] Robert K. Greenleaf, *Servant Leadership: A Journey Into the Nature of Legitimate Power and Greatness* (New York: Paulist Press, 1977).

[255] O'Brien, *Servant Leadership in Nursing*.

[256] Josephine A. Dolan, *Nursing in Society: A Historical Perspective* (Phila: W.B. Saunders, 1973), 47.

[257] Ben C. Johnson, *Pastoral Spirituality: A Focus for Ministry* (Phila: Westminster Press, 1988), 133.

[258] Ken Blanchard and Phil Hodges, *The Servant Leader: Transforming Your Heart, Head, Hands and Habits* (Nashville, TN: Countryman, 2003), 12.

[259] O'Brien, *Servant Leadership*, 41.

[260] Ibid., 210.

[261] Ibid.

[262] Laurie A. Feldman, "St. Catherine of Siena: An Exploration of the Feminine and the Mystic", *Anima* 4:2 (1978): 57-63, 60.

[263] Ibid.

[264] Gary Evans, "Spiritual Deviations: Late Medieval Mysticism", *Affirmation & Critique* 4 (1999): 56-58, 56.

[265] Bernard McGinn, "The Changing Shape of Late Medieval Mysticism", *Church History* 65:2 (1996): 197-219, 200.

[266] Ibid.

[267] Raymond of Capua, 316-325.

[268] Ibid., 316.

[269] Ibid., 316-324.

[270] Ibid., 324.

[271] McDermott, *Catherine of Siena*, 13.

[272] Ibid.

[273] Axel Ruth, "Representing Women in Medieval Miracle Narratives*" MLN (Modern Language Notes)* 126:4 (2011), 590-595, 591-592.

[274] Ibid., 593.

[275] Steven Justice, "Did the Middle Ages Believe in Their Miracles?, *Representations* 103:1 (2008): 1-29, 1.

[276] Thomas Gilby, "Introduction" in *"The Life of St. Catherine of Siena"*, trans. George Lamb, by Raymond of Capua (Charlotte, NC: Tan Books, 2011)ix-xiii, xiii.

[277] Raymond of Capua, 35.

[278] Ibid.

[279] Fernando E. Forcen, "Anorexia Mirabilis: The Practice of Fasting by Saint Catherine of Siena in the Late Middle Ages", *American Journal of Psychiatry* 170:4 (2013): 370-371, 371.

[280] Mario Reda and Giuseppe Sacco, "Anorexia and the Holiness of Saint Catherine of Siena", *Journal of Criminal Justice and Popular Culture* 8:1 (2001): 37-47, 37.

[281] Raymond of Capua, 27.

[282] Catherine of Siena, Letter T41 in *The Letters of Catherine of Siena: Volume I*, translated with introduction and notes by Suzanne Noffke O.P. (Tempe, AZ: ACMRS Arizona Center for Medieval and Renaissance Studies, 2000), 6-10.

[283] Suzanne Noffke, "Introduction to Letter T41, in The Letters of Catherine of Siena: Volume I, translated with introduction and notes by Suzanne Noffke O.P. (Tempe, AZ: ACMRS Arizona Center for Medieval and Renaissance Studies, 2000), 6.

[284] Catherine of Siena, Letter T41, p. 7.

[285] Ibid., 7-8.

[286] Ibid., 8.

[287] Suzanne Noffke, "Catherine of Siena: Justly, Doctor of the Church?", *Theology Today* 60:1 (2003): 49-62, 51.

[288] Karen Scott, "St. Catherine of Siena, 'Apostola'", *Church History* 61:1 (1992): 34-46, 37.

Chapter 4. "Ablaze with Loving Fire"

[289] Maiju Lehmijoki-Gardner, Daniel Bornstein, Ann Matter and Gabriella Zarri, *Dominican Penitent Women* (Mahwah, N.J.: Paulist Press, 2005), 178.

[290] Max van Manen, *Researching Lived Experience: Human Science for an Action Sensitive Pedagogy* (Albany, N.Y.: SUNY Press, 1990).

[291] Ibid., 9.

[292] Ibid., 10.

[293] Ibid., 29.

[294] Ibid., 175.

[295] Suzanne Noffke, *Catherine of Siena: Vision Through a Distant Eye* (Collegeville, Minn: The Liturgical Press, 1996), 125-152.

[296] Ibid., 125.

[297] Ibid., 126.

[298] Ibid., 128.

[299] Ibid., 126-129.

[300] Raymond of Capua, *"The Life of St. Catherine of Siena"* (Translated by G. Lamb) (Charlotte, NC: Tan Books, 2011), 48.

[301] Ibid., 129.

[302] Ibid., 142.

[303] Tommaso di Antonio Caffarini, *Supplemento Alla Vita di S. Caterina da Siena (Libellus de Supplementum Legende Prolixe Virginis Beate Catherine de Senis)*, A Cura di Angelo Belloni e Tito Centi (Firenze, Italy: Edizioni Nerbini, 2010), back cover.

[304] Ibid.; I translated quoted passages from the Italian editions of Fra Tommaso Caffarini's books: the *"Supplemento Alla Vita di Santa Caterina da Siena (Libellus de Supplementum Legende Prolixe Virginis Beate Catherine de Senis)"*, a cura di Angelo Belloni e Tito Centi, Firenze, Italy: Edizioni Nerbini, 2010, and the *"Leggenda Minore Di Santa Caterina Da Siena E Lettere Dei Suoi Discepoli"*, Scritture Inedite Pubblicate, Da F. Grottanelli, Bologna, Italy: Presso Gaetano Romagnoli, 1868. My English translations, together with Italian versions of the anecdotes cited from Caffarini's works, were reviewed for accuracy courtesy of Deacon Camillo Pasquariello.

[305] Lehmijoki-Gardner, 87.

[306] Augusta Theodosia Drane, *The History of St. Catherine of Siena and Her Companions* (London: Burns and Oates, 1880), xi.

[307] Ibid., xix.

[308] Edmund G. Gardner, *Saint Catherine of Siena: A Study in the Religion, Literature and History of the Fourteenth Century in Italy* (New York: E.P. Dutton & Co., 1907), viii.

[309] Johannes Jorgensen, *Saint Catherine of Siena.* (Translated by I. Lund) (London: Longmans, Green and Co., 1939), 401-412.

[310] Mary Elizabeth O'Brien, *Servant Leadership in Nursing: Spirituality and Practice in Contemporary Health Care* (Burlington, MA: Jones & Bartlett Learning, 2011); Mary Elizabeth O'Brien, *Spirituality in Nursing: Standing on Holy Ground.* (5th Edition). (Burlington, MA: Jones & Bartlett Learning, 2014).

[311] Alice Curtayne, *Saint Catherine of Siena* (Rockford, Ill: Tan Books and Publishers Inc., 1980), 219.

[312] Thomas McDermott, *Catherine of Siena: Spiritual Development in Her Life and Teaching* (Mahwah, N.J.: Paulist Press, 2008), 15.

[313] Guiliana Cavallini, *Catherine of Siena* (New York: Wellington House, 1998), 20.

[314] McDermott, 15.

[315] Pierre Madonnet, "Sainte Catherine de Sienne et La Critique Historique", extract from *L'Annee Dominicaine*, Janvier-Fevrier, 1923, pp. 6-7, cited in Thomas McDermott, *Catherine of Siena: Spiritual Development in Her Life and Teaching* (Mahwah, N.J.: Paulist Press, 2008), p. 16.

[316] Noffke, 137.

[317] Ibid., 140.

[318] Ibid.

[319] Ibid., 147.

[320] Ibid.

[321] Ibid.

[322] O'Brien, *Spirituality in Nursing.*

[323] Thomas J. Heffernan, *Sacred Biography: Saints and Their Biographers in the Middle Ages* (New York: Oxford University Press, 1988).

[324] Noffke, 54.

[325] Ibid.

[326] Edmund G.Gardner, *The Road to Siena: The Essential Biography of St. Catherine*, edited with forward and annotations by Jon M. Sweeney (Brewster, MA.: Paraclete Press, 2009), 7.

[327] Noffke, "Forward" in Catherine of Siena, *The Dialogue*, translation and introduction by Suzanne Noffke O.P. (Mahwah, N.J.: Paulist Press, 1980), xi.

[328] Ibid.

[329] Noffke, "Introduction" in Catherine of Siena, *The Dialogue*, translation and introduction by Suzanne Noffke O.P. (Mahwah, N.J.: Paulist Press, 1980), 11.

[330] Cavallini, 3.

[331] Catherine M. Meade, *My Nature is Fire: Saint Catherine of Siena* (New York: Alba House, 1991), 80.

[332] Mary O'Driscoll, *Catherine of Siena: Passion for the Truth and Compassion for Humanity* (New York: New City Press, 1993), 86.

[333] Ibid.

[334] Ibid., 86-87.

[335] Catherine of Siena, *The Dialogue*, translation and introduction by Suzanne Noffke O.P. (Mahwah, N.J.: Paulist Press, 1980), 300.

[336] Mary Elizabeth O'Brien, *The Nurse's Calling: A Christian Spirituality of Caring for the Sick* (Mahwah, N.J.: Paulist Press, 2001), x.

[337] Catherine of Siena, *The Dialogue*, 33-34.

[338] Anthony Maher, "A Night Nurse's Prayer", *The Catholic Nurse* 2:4 (1954), 30-31, 30.

[339] Catherine of Siena, *The Dialogue,* 36.

[340] Mary Elizabeth O'Brien, *Prayer in Nursing: The Spirituality of Compassionate Caregiving* (Sudbury, MA.: Jones and Bartlett Publishers, 2003), 97-98.

[341] Catherine of Siena, *The Dialogue,* 37.

[342] Ibid., 37-38.

[343] Ibid., 38.

[344] Ibid., 121.

[345] Ibid.

[346] Ibid., 130.

[347] Ibid., 131.

[348] Ibid., 136.

[349] Ibid., 142.

[350] Ibid., 158.

[351] Ibid., 159.

[352] Ibid., 190.

[353] Ibid.

[354] Ibid., 197.

[355] Ibid., 311-312.

[356] Edmund G. Gardner, *The Road to Siena: The Essential Biography of St. Catherine,* edited with forward and annotations by Jon M. Sweeney, (Brewster, MA.: Paraclete Press, 2009), 4.

[357] Ibid., 5.

[358] Martin S.Gillet, *The Mission of St. Catherine,* trans. Maria T. Lopez (St. Louis, Mo: B. Herder Book Co., 1946), 186.

[359] Ibid., 187.

[360] Suzanne Noffke, "Introduction to Letters", in Catherine of Siena, *The Letters of Catherine of Siena: Volume I,* translated with introduction and notes by Suzanne Noffke O.P. (Tempe, AZ: ACMRS Arizona Center for Medieval and Renaissance Studies, 2000), xv.

[361] Ibid.

[362] Ibid.

363 Cavallini, 8.

364 O'Driscoll, 19.

365 Ibid.

366 Ibid., 20.

367 Meade, 75.

368 Elizabeth A. Dryer, *A Retreat with Catherine of Siena: Living the Truth in Love* (Cincinnati, OH: St. Anthony Messenger Press, 1999), 22.

369 For a detailed explanation of the numbering of Saint Catherine's *Letters* see Annotation 204 in Chapter Three of this work.

370 Letter T40 in Catherine of Siena, *The Letters of Catherine of Siena: Volume II*, translated with introduction and notes by Suzanne Noffke O.P. (Tempe, AZ: ACMRS Arizona Center for Medieval and Renaissance Studies, 2001), 408-409, 409.

371 Letter T50 in Catherine of Siena, *The Letters of Catherine of Siena: Volume II*, translated with introduction and notes by Suzanne Noffke O.P. (Tempe, AZ: ACMRS Arizona Center for Medieval and Renaissance Studies, 2001), 593-596, 593.

372 Ibid.

373 Ibid., 596.

374 Letter T53 in Catherine of Siena, *The Letters of Catherine of Siena: Volume II*, translated with introduction and notes by Suzanne Noffke O.P. (Tempe, AZ: ACMRS Arizona Center for Medieval and Renaissance Studies, 2001), 576-577, 577.

375 Letter T132 in Catherine of Siena, *The Letters of Catherine of Siena: Volume I*, translated with introduction and notes by Suzanne Noffke O.P. (Tempe, AZ: ACMRS Arizona Center for Medieval and Renaissance Studies, 2000), 200-202, 202.

376 Ibid.

377 Letter T213 in Catherine of Siena, *The Letters of Catherine of Siena: Volume III,* translated with introduction and notes by Suzanne Noffke O.P. (Tempe, AZ: ACMRS Arizona Center for Medieval and Renaissance Studies, 2007), 295-304, 295.

378 Ibid., 296.

379 Letter T184 in Catherine of Siena, *The Letters of Catherine of Siena: Volume II*, translated with introduction and notes by Suzanne Noffke O.P. (Tempe, AZ: ACMRS Arizona Center for Medieval and Renaissance Studies, 2001), 308-315, 308.

380 Ibid.

381 Ibid., 311.

382 Ibid., 311-312.

383 Letter T69 in Catherine of Siena, *The Letters of Catherine of Siena: Volume I*, translated with introduction and notes by Suzanne Noffke O.P. (Tempe, AZ:

ACMRS Arizona Center for Medieval and Renaissance Studies, 2000), 64-67. 65;67.

[384] Letter T122 in Letter T184 in Catherine of Siena, *The Letters of Catherine of Siena: Volume II,* translated with introduction and notes by Suzanne Noffke O.P. (Tempe, AZ: ACMRS Arizona Center for Medieval and Renaissance Studies, 2001), 391-396, 391.

[385] Ibid., 394.

[386] Letter T72, in Catherine of Siena, *The Letters of Catherine of Siena: Volume II,* 330-332, 330.

[387] Ibid., 331.

[388] Letter T137, in Catherine of Siena, *The Letters of Catherine of Siena: Volume I,* 181-183, 181.

[389] Ibid.

[390] Ibid., T182.

[391] Letter T210, in Catherine of Siena, *The Letters of Catherine of Siena: Volume II,* 236-238, 236.

[392] Ibid., T237.

[393] Ibid.

[394] Letter T256, in Catherine of Siena, *The Letters of Catherine of Siena: Volume II,* 320-325, 321.

[395] Letter T68, in Catherine of Siena, *The Letters of Catherine of Siena: Volume III,* 84-88, 84.

[396] Ibid., 87.

[397] Letter T264, in Catherine of Siena, *The Letters of Catherine of Siena: Volume II, 477-483, 479-480.*

[398] Letter T63, in Catherine of Siena, *The Letters of Catherine of Siena: Volume III,* 44-45, 44.

[399] Ibid., 45.

[400] Letter T335, in Catherine of Siena, *The Letters of Catherine of Siena: Volume II,* 582-590, 584.

[401] Ibid., 588.

[402] Letter T81, in Catherine of Siena, *The Letters of Catherine of Siena: Volume III,* 37-40, 40.

[403] Letter T158, in Catherine of Siena, *The Letters of Catherine of Siena: Volume II,* 306-307, 307.

[404] Letter 221, in Catherine of Siena, *The Letters of Catherine of Siena: Volume II,* 179-184, 180.

[405] Ibid., 184.

[406] Catherine of Siena, *The Prayers of Catherine of Siena,* translator and editor Suzanne Noffke OP (San Jose: Authors Choice Press, 2001), xi.

[407] Ibid.

[408] Ibid., x.

[409] Cavallini, 15.

[410] Ibid., 15.

[411] O'Driscoll, 50.

[412] Ibid.

[413] Meade, 76.

[414] Catherine of Siena, *The Prayers of Catherine of Siena*, 72-74.

[415] Ibid., 116.

[416] Ibid., 149, 150-151, 155.

[417] Mary Elizabeth O'Brien, *A Sacred Covenant: The Spiritual Ministry of Nursing* (Sudbury, MA.: Jones and Bartlett Publishers, 2008), 41-42.

Chapter 5. "Make Yourself a Channel"

[418] Igino Giordani, *Catherine of Siena: Fire and Blood*, trans. Thomas J. Tobin) (Milwaukee, WI: The Bruce Publishing Company, 1959), 47.

[419] Augusta Theodosia Drane, *The History of St. Catherine of Siena and Her Companions* (London: Burns and Oates, 1880), 191.

[420] Sigrid Undset, *Catherine of Siena*, trans. Kate Austin-Lund (San Francisco: Ignatius Press, 2009), 67.

[421] Ibid.

[422] Paul B. Newman, *Daily Life in the Middle Ages* (Jefferson, North Carolina: McFarland & Company, 2001), 253.

[423] Undset, 68.

[424] Newman, 263.

[425] Charles H. Talbot, "Medicine" in *Science in the Middle Ages*, ed. David C. Lindberg (Chicago: The University of Chicago Press, 1978), 400-415, 400.

[426] Gladys Sellew and C.Joseph Nuesse, *A history of Nursing* (St. Louis: C.V. Mosby, 1946), 117.

[427] Undset, 67.

[428] Ibid., 67-68.

[429] Ibid., 68.

[430] Joseph Ziegler, "Religion and Medicine in the Middle Ages" in *Religion and Medicine in the Middle Ages*, eds. Peter Biller and Joseph Ziegler (Rochester, N.Y.: York Medieval Press, 2001), pp. 3-14, 4-5.

[431] Ibid. 5.

[432] Sara Nelson, "The Influence of Christianity on the Care of the Sick Up to the End of the Middle Ages", *South African Nursing Journal* 40:8 (1973): 18-19, 34, 19.

[433] Ibid., 19.

[434] James J. Walsh, *Old-Time Makers of Medicine: The Story of the Students and Teachers of the Sciences Related to Medicine During the Middle Ages* (New York: Fordham University Press, 1911), 160.

[435] Newman, 268.

[436] Ibid., 269.

[437] Mary Elizabeth O'Brien, *Spirituality in Nursing: Standing on Holy Ground.* (5th Edition). (Burlington, MA: Jones & Bartlett Learning, 2014), 29.

[438] M. Adelaide Nutting and Lavinia L. Dock, *A History of Nursing.* Volume 1 (New York: G. P. Putnam's Sons, 1935), 118.

[439] Charles Marie Frank, *Foundations of Nursing* (Phila.: W.B. Saunders, 1959), 35.

[440] Josephine A. Dolan, *Nursing in Society: A Historical Perspective* (Phila: W.B. Saunders, 1973), 56.

[441] O'Brien, 31.

[442] Dolan, 56.

[443] Frank, 38.

[444] Agnes E. Pavey, *The Story of the Growth of Nursing as an Art, a Vocation and a Profession* (London: Faber and Faber Limited, 1938), 102.

[445] Barbara M.Wall and Sioban Nelson, "Our Heels are Praying Very Hard All Day", *Holistic Nursing Practice* 17:6 (2003): 320-328, 321.

[446] M. Patricia Donahue, *Nursing, the Finest Art: An Illustrated History* (St. Louis: C.V. Mosby, 1985), 127.

[447] Ibid., 129-130.

[448] Jessica Mellinger, "Fourteenth-century England: Medical Ethics and the Plague" *Virtual Mentor* 8:4 (2006): 256-260, 257.

[449] Louise Cilliers, "The Evolution of the Hospital from Antiquity to the End of the Middle Ages", *Curationis* 25:4 (2002), 60-66, 63.

[450] Ibid., 65.

[451] Ibid., 63.

[452] Nutting and Dock.

[453] Lena Dietz and Aurelia R. Lehozky, *History and Modern nursing.* 2nd edition. (Phila: F. A. Davis, 1967), 25.

[454] O'Brien, *Spirituality in Nursing,* 34.

[455] Victor Robinson, *White caps: The Story of Nursing* (Phila: J.B. Lippincott Company, 1946), 50.

[456] Deborah M. Jensen, John F. Spaulding and Elwyn L. Cady, *History and Trends of Professional Nursing* (St. Louis, MO: C.V. Mosby, 1959).

[457] Donahue, 155.

[458] Lucy R. Seymer, *A General History of Nursing* (New York: Macmillan, 1949), 38.

[459] Ibid.

[460] Minkowski, William L."Women Healers of the Middle Ages: Selected Aspects of Their History", *American Journal of Public Health* 82:2 (1992): 288-295, 289.

[461] James J. Walsh, *The History of Nursing* (New York: P.J. Putnam's Sons, 1929), 71.

[462] Seymer, 38.

463 Ibid.

464 Robinson, 27.

465 Minkowski, 289.

466 Max van Manen, *Researching Lived Experience: Human Science for an Action Sensitive Pedagogy* (Albany, N.Y.: SUNY Press, 1990), 96.

467 Ibid. 96-97.

468 George H. Edgell, *A History of Sienese Painting* (New York: The Dial Press, Inc., 1931), 203.

469 Timothy Hyman, *Sienese Painting: The Art of a City-Republic* (New York: Thames & Hudson, 2003), 164.

470 Johannes Jorgensen, *Saint Catherine of Siena,* trans. Ingeborg Lund (London: Longmans, Green and Co., 1939), 77.

471 Hyman, 194.

472 Ibid., 195.

473 Keith Christiansen, Laurence B. Kanter and Carl B. Strehlke, *Painting in Renaissance Siena, 1420-1500* (New York: The Metropolitan Museum of Art, New York, 1988), 249.

474 Edgell, 204.

475 Bruce Cole, *Sienese Painting in the Age of the Renaissance* (Bloomington, IN.: Indiana University Press, 1985), 28.

476 Ibid., 29.

477 Ibid.

478 Jorgensen, 77.

479 Ibid.

480 Ibid., 78.

481 Brenda M. McCann, "Hospital of Santa Maria della Scala Links Art and History of Medicine", *Irish Medical Times* 41:12 (2007), 40.

482 Ibid.

483 "Domenico di Bartolo, The Care and Healing of the Sick (1440-1441)" *SMS Complesso Museale Santa Maria della Scala website:* www.santamariadellascala.com/w2d3/v3/view/sms2/percorsi/luoghi/l_edific i/piani/s, 6/23/2014, p. 2.

484 Hyman, 195.

485 Richard Walker, *Epidemics & Plagues* (Boston: Kingfisher, 2006), 26.

486 Didier Raoult, Nadjet Mouffok, Idir Bitam, Renaud Piarroux and Michel Drancourt, "Plague: History and Contemporary Analysis", *Journal of Infection,* 66 (2013): 18-26, 19.

487 Ibid., 24.

488 Jane Wright, "Looking at Pandemics: From Black Death to Swine Flu", *British Journal of School Nursing* 6:4 (2011): 200-201, 201.

489 James T. Eastman, "The Making of a Pandemic: The Bubonic Plague in the 14th Century", *The Journal of Lancaster General Hospital* 4:1 (2009): 10-17, 10.

210

[490] Ole J. Benedictow, "The Black Death: The Greatest Catastrophe Ever", *History Today* 55:3 (2005): 1-5, 1.

[491] Jerrold Atlas, "The Black Death: An Essay on Traumatic Change", *The Journal of Psychohistory* 36: 3 (2009): 250-259, 251.

[492] Theodosia Garrison, "Courage" in *The History of Nursing* by James J. Walsh (New York: P.J. Putnam's Sons, 1929), 45-46.

[493] Newman, 244.

[494] Herbert C. Covey, "People with Leprosy (Hansen's Disease) During the Middle Ages", *The Social Science Journal,* 38:1 (2001): 315-321, 316.

[495] David L.Kaplan, "Biblical Leprosy: An Anachronism Whose time has Come", *Journal of the American Academy of Dermatology* 28:3 (1993): 507-510, 507.

[496] Cilliers, 64.

[497] Walsh, *The History of Nursing,* 37.

[498] Simon Roffey and Katie Tucker, "A Contextual Study of the Medieval Hospital and Cemetery of St. Mary Magdalen, Winchester, England", *International Journal of Paleopathology,* 2 (2012), 170-180, 170.

[499] Ibid.

[500] Jessalynn Bird, "Texts on Hospitals, Translation of Jacques de Vitry, Historia Occidentalis 29, and Edition of Jacques de Vitry's Sermons on Hospitallers", in *Religion and Medicine in the Middle Ages,* eds. Peter Biller and Joseph Ziegler (Rochester, N.Y.: York Medieval Press, 2001), 109-134, 109.

[501] Walsh, *The History of Nursing,* 45.

[502] Ibid.

[503] Ibid., 46.

[504] Arrigo Levasti, *My Servant Catherine,* trans. Dorothy M. White (Westminster, Md: The Newman Press, 1954), 86.

[505] Walsh, *The History of Nursing,* 115.

[506] Charles Marie Frank, *The Historical Development of Nursing* (Phila.: W.B. Saunders, 1953), 115.

[507] Walsh, *The History of Nursing,* 117.

[508] Alice Curtayne, *Saint Catherine of Siena* (Rockford, Ill: Tan Books and Publishers Inc., 1980), viii.

[509] Drane, 223.

[510] Jeppe B. Netterstrom, "Introduction: The Study of Feud in Medieval and Modern History", in *Feud in Medieval and Early Modern Europe,* eds. Jeppe B. Netterstrom and Bjorn Poulsen (Oakville, CT.: Aarhus University Press, 2007), pp. 9-67, 41.

[511] Ibid.

[512] Ibid.

[513] Ibid., 56.

[514] Helgi Porlaksson, "Feud and Feuding in the Early and High Middle Ages" in *Feud in Medieval and Early Modern Europe,* eds. Jeppe B. Netterstrom and Bjorn Poulsen (Oakville, CT.: Aarhus University Press, 2007), pp. 69-94, 69.

[515] Ibid., 70-71.

[516] Hyams, 159-160.

[517] Trevor Dean, "Italian Medieval Vendetta", in *Feud in Medieval and Early Modern Europe,* eds. Jeppe Buchert Netterstrom and Bjorn Poulsen (Oakville, CT.: Aarhus University Press, 2007), pp. 135-145, 137.

[518] Ibid., 135.

[519] Ibid.

[520] Tommaso di Antonio Caffarini, *Supplemento Alla Vita di Santa Caterina da Siena (Libellus de Supplementum Legende Prolixe Virginis Beate Catherine de Senis,* A Cura di Angelo Belloni e Tito Centi (Firenze, Italy: Edizioni Nerbini, 2010).

[521] Nutting and Dock, 244.

[522] J.H. Baron, "The Hospital of Santa Maria della Scala, Siena, 1090-1990", *British Medical Journal,* 301 (1990); 1449-1451, 1449.

[523] Annabel Thomas, *Garrisoning the Boarderlands of Medieval Siena* (Burlington, VT: Ashgate Publishing, 2011), 16.

[524] Baron, 1449.

[525] Nutting and Dock, 244.

[526] Baron, 1449.

[527] Drane, 126.

[528] Ibid.

[529] Jorgensen, 73.

[530] Ibid., 74.

[531] Ibid.

[532] Ibid.

[533] Ibid., 76.

[534] Ibid.

[535] Jane Tylus, *Reclaiming Catherine of Siena: Literacy, Literature and the Signs of Others* (Chicago: The University of Chicago Press, 2009), 68.

[536] Ibid.

[537] Catherine M. Meade, *My Nature is Fire: Saint Catherine of Siena* (New York: Alba House, 1991), 9.

[538] Raymond of Capua, *"The Life of St. Catherine of Siena"* (Translated by George Lamb) (Charlotte, NC: Tan Books, 2011), 115.

[539] Jorgensen, 360.

[540] Ibid.

[541] Drane, 195.

[542] Ibid.

[543] Ibid., 197.

[544] Ibid.

[545] Walsh, *The History of Nursing*, 35.

[546] Sellew and Nuesse, 128.

[547] Walsh, *The History of Nursing*, 36.

[548] Ibid., 38.

[549] Ibid., 37.

[550] Ibid., 39.

[551] Ibid.

[552] Ibid.

[553] Ibid.

[554] Igino Giordani, *Catherine of Siena: Fire and Blood,* trans. Thomas J. Tobin) (Milwaukee, WI: The Bruce Publishing Company, 1959), 47.

[555] Ibid., 52.

Chapter 6. "Hands Made to Serve"

[556] Minnie Goodnow, *Outlines of nursing history.* (5th edition) (Phila: W.B. Saunders, 1934), 92.

[557] William Longfellow, "Santa Filomena", *Atlantic Monthly* 1: 22-23 (1857), p. 23.

[558] M. Patricia Donahue, *Nursing, the Finest Art: An Illustrated History* (St. Louis: C.V. Mosby, 1996), 136.

[559] Josephine A. Dolan, M. Louise Fitzpatrick and Eleanor K.Herrmann, *Nursing in Society: A Historical Perspective* (Phila; W.B. Saunders, 1983), 72.

[560] M. Adelaide Nutting and Lavinia L. Dock, *A History of Nursing.* Volume 1 (New York: G. P. Putnam's Sons, 1935), 230.

[561] Augusta Theodosia Drane, *The History of St. Catherine of Siena and Her Companions* (London: Burns and Oates, 1880), 125.

[562] Suzanne Noffke, *Catherine of Siena: Vision Through a Distant Eye* (Collegeville, Minn: The Liturgical Press, 1996), 161.

[563] Victor Robinson, *White caps: The Story of Nursing* (Phila: J.B. Lippincott Company, 1946), 47.

[564] Isabel M. Stewart and Anne L. Austin, *A History of Nursing: From Ancient to Modern Times* (New York: G.P. Putnam's Sons, 1962), 69.

[565] Alice Curtayne, *Saint Catherine of Siena* (Rockford, Ill: Tan Books and Publishers Inc., 1980), 75.

[566] Jean David Finley, *Catherine of Siena: Woman of Faith* (State College, Pa.: Jostens, 1980), 3.

[567] Johannes Jorgensen, *Saint Catherine of Siena,* trans. Ingebort Lund) (London: Longmans, Green and Co., 1939), 181.

[568] Sigrid Undset, *Catherine of Siena,* trans. Kate Austin-Lund (San Francisco: Ignatius Press, 2009), 165.

[569] Curtayne, 23.

[570] Catherine M. Meade, *My Nature is Fire: Saint Catherine of Siena* (New York: Alba House, 1991), 9.

[571] Noffke, 171.

[572] Ibid.

[573] Jorgensen, 80.

[574] Mary Jean Dorcy, *Saint Dominic's Family: Lives and Legends* (Dubuque, Iowa: The Priory Press, 1964), 178.

[575] Ibid.

[576] Josephine A. Dolan, *Nursing in Society: A Historical Perspective* (Phila: W.B. Saunders, 1978), 72.

[577] Jorgensen, 181.

[578] Undset, 165.

[579] Curtayne, 75.

[580] Ibid.

[581] Nutting and Dock, 252.

[582] Alexandra Walker, *Scent Bottles* (Buckinghamshire, UK: Shire Publications Ltd., 1987), 3.

[583] Ibid.

[584] Tzu-I Chiu, "Aromatherapy: the Challenge for Community Nurses", *Journal of Community Nursing* 24:1(2010): 18-20, 18.

[585] Andrea Butje, Elizabeth Repede, and Mona Shattell, "Healing Scents: An Overview of Clinical Aromatherapy for Emotional Distress", *Journal of Psychosocial Nursing* 46:10 (2008): 46-52.

[586] Jenni Moore, "Aromatherapy for Anxiety", *The Kansas Nurse* 88:3 (2013), 11-14.

[587] Gillian Van der Watt and Aleksander Janca, "Aromatherapy in Nursing and Mental Health Care", *Contemporary Nurse* 30 (2008): 69-75.

[588] Jamie Lytle, Catherine Mwatha and Karen K. Davis, "Effect of Lavender Aromatherapy of Vital Signs and Perceived Quality of Sleep in the Intermediate Care Unit: A Pilot Study", *American Journal of Critical Care* 23:1 (2014): 24-29, 24.

[589] Pei L. Lua and Noor S. Zakaria, "A Brief Review of Current Scientific Evidence Involving Aromatherapy Use for Nausea and Vomiting", *The Journal of Alternative and Complementary Medicine* 18:6 (2012): 534-540, 534.

[590] Hitomi Takeda, Junzo Tsujita, Mitsuharu Kaya, Masanori Takemura and Yoshitaka Oku, "Differences Between the Physiologic and Psychologic Effects of Aromatherapy Body Treatment", *The Journal of Alternative and Complementary Medicine* 14:6 (2008): 655-661; Deborah V. Thomas, "Aromatherapy: Mythical, Magical or Medicinal?" *Holistic Nursing Practice* 17:1 (2002): 8-16; Sala Horowitz, Áromatherapy: Current and Emerging Applications", *Alternative and Complementary Therapies,* 17:1 (2011): 26-31.

[591] Horowitz, 31.

592 Kathryn Bizek and Dorrie K. Fontaine, "The Patient's Experience with Critical Illness", in *Critical Care Nursing: A Holistic Approach,* eds. Patricia G. Morton and Dorrie K. Fontaine (Lippincott, Williams & Wilkins, 2009), 18-32, 27.

593 Mary Elizabeth O'Brien, *Parish Nursing: Healthcare Ministry Within the Church* (Sudbury, MA.: Jones and Bartlett Publishers, 2003), 42.

594 Victoria Slater, "Holistic Nursing Practice", *Journal of Holistic Nursing* 23:3 (2005):261-263, 261.

595 Standard R1.1.3.5., Joint Commission, *Comprehensive Accreditation Annual for Hospitals: The Official Handbook* (Oakbrook Terrace, Il.: The Joint Commission, 2003).

596 Julie Y. Sappington, "Nurturance: The Spirit of Holistic Nursing", *Journal of Holistic Nursing* 21:1 (2003): 8-19, 8.

597 Tony Bush and Nina Bruni, "Spiritual Care as a Dimension of Holistic Care: A Relational Interpretation", *International Journal of Palliative Nursing* 14:11 (2008):539-545.

598 Ann Ameling, "Prayer: An Ancient Healing Practice Becomes New Again", *Holistic Nursing Practice* 14:3 (2000): 40-48.

599 Bernadette Lange, Rothlyn P. Zahourek and Carla Mariano, "A Legacy Building Model for Holistic Nursing", *Journal of Holistic Nursing* 32:2 (2013):116-126, 116.

600 Robinson, 47.

601 Curtayne, 31.

602 Ibid.

603 Curtayne, 31-32.

604 Undset, 71.

605 Ibid.

606 Drane, 125.

607 Caffarini, *Supplementum*, Part 2, Tractus 3, Para.6, as cited in Drane,125.

608 Donahue, 136.

609 Ibid.

610 Marion J. Ball, Kathryn J. Hannah, Ulla G. Jelger and Hans Peterson, *Nursing Informatics: Where Caring and Technology Meet* (New York: Springer-Verlag, 1988).

611 Richard Gartee and Sharyl Beal, *Electronic Health Records and Nursing* (Boston: Pearson Education, Inc., 2012).

612 Mary Elizabeth O'Brien, *Spirituality in Nursing: Standing on Holy Ground.* (5th Edition). (Burlington, MA: Jones & Bartlett Learning, 2014).

613 Mary Elizabeth O'Brien, *Servant Leadership in Nursing: Spirituality and Practice in Contemporary Healthcare* (Burlington, MA: Jones & Bartlett Learning, 2011).

614 Caffarini, *Supplementum*, cited in Drane, 125.

615 Jorgensen, 80.

[616] Ibid, 81.

[617] Letter T272, in Catherine of Siena, *The Letters of Catherine of Siena:*Volume I, translated with introduction and notes by Suzanne Noffke O.P. (Tempe, AZ: ACMRS Arizona Center for Medieval and Renaissance Studies, 2000), 290-294, 290-291.

[618] Ibid., 291.

[619] Ibid., 292.

[620] Jorgensen, 81.

[621] Ibid.

[622] Ibid.

[623] Letter T276, in Catherine of Siena, *The Letters of Catherine of Siena:* Volume I, *294.*

[624] Arrigo Levasti, *My Servant Catherine,* trans. Dorothy M. White) (Westminster, Md: The Newman Press, 1954), 69.

[625] Ibid.

[626] Ibid.

[627] Sandy Focht, "Dignity Entrusted", *America* 179:20 (1998): 26.

[628] Drane, 145.

[629] Ibid.

[630] Ibid., 228.

[631] Raymond of Capua, "*The Life of St. Catherine of Siena*", trans. George Lamb (Charlotte, NC: Tan Books, 2011), 204.

[632] Ibid.

[633] Ibid.

[634] Ibid.

[635] Ibid., 205.

[636] Ibid.

[637] Undset, 167.

[638] Raymond of Capua, 205.

[639] Ibid., 111-112.

[640] Ibid. 112.

[641] Ibid.

[642] Drane, 73.

[643] Ibid.

[644] Jorgensen, 82.

[645] Raymond of Capua, 112.

[646] Ibid., 113.

[647] Jorgensen, 82.

[648] Ibid., 83.

[649] Drane, 74.

[650] Raymond of Capua, 113.

[651] Ibid.

[652] Karen S. Lundy, Karen B. Utterback, Debra K. Lance and Ilene P. Bloxson, "Home Health and Hospice Nursing", in in *Community Health Nursing: Caring for the Public's Health,* 2nd edition, editors Karen S. Lundy and Sharyn Janes (Sudbury, MA.: Jones and Bartlett Publishers, 2009), 970-995, 972.

[653] Elizabeth McNamara, "Hospitals Discover Comprehensive Home Care", *Hospital,* 56:1 (1982): 60-66, 61.

[654] M. Adelaide Nutting and Lavinia L. Dock, *A History of Nursing.* Volume 1 (New York: G. P. Putnam's Sons, 1935), 423.

[655] 1993, Daughters of Charity Vocation Program (video). Emmitsburg, Md.: Author.

[656] Raymond of Capua, 94.

[657] Ibid.

[658] Claire Mary Antony, *Saint Catherine of Siena: Her life and Times* (St. Louis, Mo: B. Herder, 1916), 45.

[659] Tommaso di Antonio Caffarini, *Supplemento Alla Vita di Santa Caterina da Siena (Libellus de Supplementum Legende Prolixe Virginis Beate Catherine de Senis)* A Cura di Angelo Belloni e Tito Centi (Firenze, Italy: Edizioni Nerbini, 2010), 58, paragraph 17.

[660] Ibid., 57, paragraph 12.

[661] Ibid.,57, paragraph 13.

[662] Ibid., 38, paragraph 5.

[663] Jean David Finley, *Catherine of Siena: Woman of Faith* (State College, Pa.: Jostens, 1980), 2.

[664] Ibid., 2-3.

[665] Don Brophy, *Catherine of Siena: A Passionate Life* (New York: BlueBridge, 2010), 57.

[666] Ibid.

[667] Ibid.

[668] Richard Cardinal Cushing, *St. Catherine of Siena* (New York: St. Paul Editions, 1957), 26.

[669] Melanie McEwen and Mary A. Nies, "Health: A Community View", in *Community/Public Health Nursing: Promoting the Health of Populations,* 4th edition, eds. Mary A. Nies and Melanie McEwen (St. Louis, MO.: Saunders, 2007),2-17, 3.

[670] Claudia M. Smith, "Responsibilities for Care in Community/Public Health Nursing" in *Community/Public Health Nursing Practice* , eds. Frances A. Maurer and Claudia M. Smith (St. Louis, Mo.: Saunders, 2005), 2-22, 3.

[671] Richard Hunt, *Introduction to Community Based Nursing,* 3rd edition (Phila.: Lippincott, Williams and Wilkins, 2005), 15.

[672] Karen S. Lundy, Sharyn Janes and Sherry Hartman, "Opening the Door to Health Care in the Community", in *Community Health Nursing: Caring for the*

Public's Health, 2nd edition, eds. Karen S. Lundy and Sharyn Janes (Sudbury, MA.: Jones and Bartlett Publishers, 2009), 4-29, 6.

673 Igino Giordani, *Catherine of Siena: Fire and Blood,* trans. Thomas J.Tobin (Milwaukee, WI: The Bruce Publishing Company, 1959), 83.

674 Ibid.

675 Edmund G. Gardner, *Saint Catherine of Siena: A Study in the Religion, Literature and History of the Fourteenth Century in Italy* (New York: E.P. Dutton & Co., 1907), 121.

676 Drane, 191-192.

677 Gardner, 121.

678 Ibid., 122.

679 Anne B. Baldwin, *Catherine of Siena: A Biography* (Huntington, In: Our Sunday Visitor Publishing Division, 1987), 64.

680 Undset, 165.

681 Caffarini, as cited in Drane, 221-222.

682 Agnes E. Pavey, *The Story of the Growth of Nursing as an Art, a Vocation and a Profession* (London: Faber and Faber Limited, 1938), 139.

683 Ibid.

684 Guy Bedouelle, *Saint Dominic: The Grace of the Word* (San Francisco: Ignatius Press, 1987), 260.

685 Theodoric of Apolda OP, *Vita Beatissimi Patris Dominici, In Suris, Historiae seu Vitae Sanctorum,* Vol. VIII, Turin, 1877, Book 5, Chapter 2, cited in Mary Jean Dorcy, *Saint Dominic* (Charlotte, North Carolina: TAN Books and Publishers, 1982), p. 135.

686 Augusta Theodosia Drane, *The Life of St. Dominic,* sixth edition (Charlotte, North Carolina: TAN Books, 2011), 225.

687 Raymond of Capua, 206.

688 Ibid.

689 Ibid., 206-207.

690 Nancy L. Conrad, "Spiritual Support for the Dying", *Nursing Clinics of North America,* 20:2 (1985): 415-426, 418.

691 Finley, 3.

692 Ibid.

693 Ibid.,4.

694 Drane, 227-228.

695 John B. Calsin, "Prison Nursing: Rising Above Fear to Care", *Journal of Christian Nursing* 9:2 (1992): 22-26.

696 Ibid., 22.

697 Ibid., 24.

698 Ibid.

699 Ann Norman, "Prison Health Care: What is it that Makes Prison Nursing Unique? *British Journal of Nursing,* 8:8 (1999): 1-2.; Ann Norman and Alan

Parrish, "Prison Health Care: Work Environment and the Nursing Role", *British Journal of Nursing,* 8:10 (1999): 12-15.; Constance S. Weiskopf, "Nurses' Experience of Caring for Inmate Patients", *Journal of Advanced Nursing,* 49:4 (2005): 336-343.; Jamie S. Brodie, "Caring: The Essence of Correctional Nursing", *Tennessee Nurse* 64:2 (2001): 10-12.; Nellie S. Droes, "Correctional Nursing Practice", *Journal of Community Health Nursing* 11:4 (1994): 201-210.; Tommy Williams and Elizabeth Heavey, "How to Meet the Challenges of Correctional Nursing", *Nursing 2014,* 44:1 (2014): 51-54.

[700] Norman, 1.

[701] Walsh, 118.

[702] Ibid.

[703] Martin S.Gillet, *The Mission of St. Catherine,* trans. Maria T. Lopez) (St. Louis, Mo: B. Herder Book Co., 1946) 174.

[704] Ibid.

[705] Ibid., 175.

[706] Ibid.

[707] Suzanne Noffke, "Introduction" to Letter T260 in Catherine of Siena, *The Letters of Catherine of Siena:* Volume II, translated with introduction and notes by Suzanne Noffke O.P. (Tempe, AZ: ACMRS Arizona Center for Medieval and Renaissance Studies, 2001), 316.

[708] O'Brien, *Spirituality in Nursing,* 58-66.

[709] Caffarini, *Supplemento Alla Vita,* 62, paragraph 5.

[710] Ibid., 42, paragraph 12.

[711] Ibid.

[712] Ibid.

[713] Drane, 113.

Chapter 7. "The Measure of Your Love"

[714] Mary Elizabeth O'Brien, *Spirituality in Nursing: Standing on Holy Ground.* (5th Edition). (Burlington, MA: Jones & Bartlett Learning, 2014), 415-450.

[715] Mary Elizabeth O'Brien, *The Nurse's Calling: A Christian Spirituality of Caring for the Sick* (Mahwah, N.J.: Paulist Press, 2001); Mary Elizabeth O'Brien, *Prayer in Nursing: The Spirituality of Compassionate Caregiving* (Sudbury, MA.: Jones and Bartlett Publishers, 2003); Mary Elizabeth O'Brien, *The Nurse with an Alabaster Jar: A Biblical Approach to Nursing* (Madison, Wi.: NCF Press, 2006); Mary Elizabeth O'Brien, *A Sacred Covenant: The Spiritual Ministry of Nursing* (Sudbury, MA.: Jones and Bartlett Publishers, 2008).

[716] O'Brien, *Spirituality in Nursing,* 436.

[717] Ibid., 428-432.

[718] Ibid., 421.

[719] Ibid., 424.

[720] Mary Elizabeth O'Brien, *A Sacred Covenant: The Spiritual Ministry of Nursing* (Sudbury, MA.: Jones and Bartlett Publishers, 2008), 48.

[721] Mary Elizabeth O'Brien, *Servant Leadership in Nursing: Spirituality and Practice in Contemporary Health Care* (Burlington, MA: Jones & Bartlett Learning, 2011), 192-199.

[722] O'Brien, *Spirituality in Nursing,* 417-418.

[723] O'Brien, *Servant Leadership in Nursing,* 103.

[724] Ibid., 106-107, 121.

[725] Martin S.Gillet, *The Mission of St. Catherine,* trans. Maria T. Lopez) (St. Louis, Mo: B. Herder Book Co., 1946), 172.

[726] Raymond of Capua, *"The Life of St. Catherine of Siena"* (Translated by G. Lamb) (Charlotte, NC: Tan Books, 2011), 121-126.

[727] Arrigo Levasti, *My Servant Catherine,* trans. Dorothy M. White (Westminster, Md: The Newman Press, 1954), 74.

[728] Raymond of Capua, 121.

[729] Ibid.

[730] Ibid.

[731] Augusta Theodosia Drane, *The History of St. Catherine of Siena and Her Companions* (London: Burns and Oates, 1880), 181.

[732] Raymond of Capua, 124.

[733] Ibid., 125.

[734] Ibid., 126.

[735] Sigrid Undset, *Catherine of Siena,* trans. Kate Austin-Lund (San Francisco: Ignatius Press, 2009), 78.

[736] Florence Nightingale, *Notes on Nursing: What it is and What it is Not* (London, U.K.: Harrison, Bookseller to the Queen, 1859), 71.

[737] O'Brien, *Spirituality in Nursing,* 419.

[738] O'Brien, *Servant Leadership in Nursing,* 159.

[739] Ibid.

[740] Tommaso di Antonio Caffarini, *Supplemento Alla Vita di S. Caterina da Siena (Libellus de Supplementum Legende Prolixe Virginis Beate Catherine de Senis,* A Cura di Angelo Belloni e Tito Centi (Firenze, Italy: Edizioni Nerbini, 2010), 58-59, paragraph 19.

[741] Haemendra Upadhyay, Amit Kumar, M.K. Gupta, Arvind Sharma and Anu Rahal, "Validation of Medicinal Values of Traditionally Used Sonchus Asper (Prickly Sow Thistle) Leaves for the Treatment of Skin Ailments", *Advancement in Medicinal Plant Research,* 1:1 (2013): 29-35.

[742] O'Brien, *Spirituality in Nursing,* 420.

[743] Monica E. Baly, *As Miss Nightingale said...Florence Nightingale Through Her Sayings: A Victorian Perspective* (London, U.K.: Scutari Press, 1991), 68.

[744] O'Brien, *Servant Leadership in Nursing,* 158.

[745] Ibid.

[746] Raymond of Capua, 115.

[747] Drane, 75.

[748] Raymond of Capua, 115.

[749] Ibid. 116.

[750] Ibid.

[751] Ibid., 117.

[752] O'Brien, *Spirituality in Nursing,* 438-439.

[753] O'Brien, *Servant Leadership in Nursing, 198-199.*

[754] Raymond of Capua, 181.

[755] Ibid.

[756] Drane, 115.

[757] Claire Mary Antony, *Saint Catherine of Siena: Her life and Times* (St. Louis, Mo: B. Herder, 1916), 71.

[758] Raymond of Capua, 182-183.

[759] Undset, 120.

[760] Raymond of Capua, 183.

[761] Ibid.

[762] Ibid., 214.

[763] Ibid., 214-215.

[764] O'Brien, *Servant Leadership in Nursing,* 133.

[765] Martin S.Gillet, *The Mission of St. Catherine,* trans. Maria T. Lopez (St. Louis, Mo: B. Herder Book Co., 1946), 175.

[766] Joseph Marie Perrin, *Catherine of Siena,* trans. Paul Barrett). (Westminster, Md: The Newman Press, 1961), 14.

[767] F. Thomas Luongo, *The Saintly Politics of Catherine of Siena* (Ithica, NY: Cornell University Press, 2006), 91-92.

[768] Tommaso di Antonio Caffarini, *Leggenda Minore di Santa Caterina da Siena e Lettere dei Suoi Discipoli;* Scritture Inedite Pubblicate, Da F. Grottanelli (Bologna, Italy: Presso Gaetano Romagnoli, 1868), 93-94.

[769] Caffarini, *Processo Castellano* 42, as cited in Luongo, 92.

[770] Johannes Jorgensen, *Saint Catherine of Siena,* trans. Ingeborg Lund (London: Longmans, Green and Co., 1939), 258.

[771] Drane, 228.

[772] Don Brophy, *Catherine of Siena: A Passionate Life* (New York: BlueBridge, 2010), 130.

[773] Edmund G. Gardner, *Saint Catherine of Siena: A Study in the Religion, Literature and History of the Fourteenth Century in Italy* (New York: E.P. Dutton & Co., 1907), 379.

[774] Ibid.

[775] Letter T276 in Catherine of Siena, *The Letters of Catherine of Siena:* Volume I, translated with introduction and notes by Suzanne Noffke O.P. (Tempe, AZ: ACMRS Arizona Center for Medieval and Renaissance Studies, 2000), 84.

[776] Guiliana Cavallini, *Catherine of Siena* (New York: Wellington House, 1998), 21.

777 Letter T273 in Catherine of Siena, *The Letters of Catherine of Siena,* Volume I, 86.

778 Ibid., 87.

779 Ibid., 88.

780 Drane, 230.

781 Letter T273, 89.

782 Molly Morrison, "St.Catherine of Siena and the Spectacle of Public Execution", *Logos, A Journal of Catholic Thought and Culture* 16:3 (2013): 43-55, 44.

783 Ibid.

784 Ibid., 45.

785 O'Brien, *Spirituality in Nursing,* 111.

786 Michael Downey, "Compassion", in *The New Dictionary of Catholic Spirituality* , ed. Michael Downey (Collegeville, Minn.: The Liturgical Press, 1993), 192-193, 192.

787 O'Brien, *Spirituality in Nursing,* 441.

788 O'Brien, *Servant Leadership in Nursing, 147.*

789 Mary Ann Fatula, *Catherine of Siena's Way* (Wilmington, DE: Michael Glazier, 1989), 53.

790 Raymond of Capua, 203.

791 Ibid.

792 Ibid.

793 Caffarini, *Supplimento Alla Vita,* 88, paragraph 55.

794 Drane, 199.

795 Raymond of Capua, 208.

796 Drane, 252.

797 Raymond of Capua, 209.

798 Ibid., 210.

799 Ibid.

800 O'Brien, *Spirituality in Nursing,* 441.

801 O'Brien, *Servant Leadership in Nursing,* 152.

802 Alice Curtayne, *Saint Catherine of Siena* (Rockford, Ill: Tan Books and Publishers Inc., 1980), 32.

803 Ibid.

804 "The Miracoli of St. Catherine of Siena" in *Dominican Penitent Women* eds. Maiju Lehmijoki-Gardner, Daniel Bornstein, Ann Matter and Gabriella Zarri, (Mahwah, N.J.: Paulist Press, 2005): pp. 87-104, 101.

805 Don Brophy, *Catherine of Siena: A Passionate Life* (New York: BlueBridge, 2010), 101.

806 Raymond of Capua. 199.

807 Ibid.

808 Ibid., 200.

809 Drane, 196.

810 Raymond of Capua, 200.

[811] Ibid., 211.
[812] Ibid.
[813] Ibid.
[814] Ibid., 212-213.
[815] O'Brien, *Spirituality in Nursing,* 442.
[816] O'Brien, *Servant Leadership in Nursing,* 174.
[817] Raymond of Capua, 188.
[818] Ibid., 189.
[819] Ibid., 190.
[820] Drane, 221.
[821] Raymond of Capua, 190.
[822] Ibid., 191-192.
[823] Ibid., 214.
[824] Ibid.

Epilogue

[825] Mary Elizabeth O'Brien, *Prayer in Nursing: The Spirituality of Compassionate Caregiving* (Sudbury, MA.: Jones and Bartlett Publishers, 2003), 97-98.

47802053R00135

Made in the USA
Middletown, DE
02 September 2017